Unity UI Cookbook

Over 60 recipes to help you create professional and exquisite UIs to make your games more immersive

Francesco Sapio

PUBLISHING

BIRMINGHAM - MUMBAI

Unity UI Cookbook

Copyright © 2015 Packt Publishing

First published: December 2015

Production reference: 1181215

Published by Packt Publishing Ltd.
Livery Place
35 Livery Street
Birmingham B3 2PB, UK.

ISBN 978-1-78588-582-2

www.packtpub.com

Cover image by Francesco Sapio and Lauren S. Ferro

Credits

Author
Francesco Sapio

Reviewers
Jack Donovan
Lauren S. Ferro

Commissioning Editor
Neil Alexander

Acquisition Editor
Nadeem Bagban

Content Development Editor
Mayur Pawanikar

Technical Editor
Deepti Tuscano

Copy Editor
Vikrant Phadke

Project Coordinator
Nidhi Joshi

Proofreader
Safis Editing

Indexer
Rekha Nair

Graphics
Jason Monteiro

Production Coordinator
Aparna Bhagat

Cover Work
Aparna Bhagat

About the Author

Francesco Sapio obtained his computer science and control engineering degree from the Sapienza University of Rome, Italy, with a couple of semesters in advance, scoring summa cum laude. Now he is studying a master's of science and engineering in artificial intelligence and robotics.

Besides this, he is a Unity3D expert and skilled game designer, as well as an experienced user of the major graphics programs.

Recently, he has been a reviewer of the book *Unity Game Development Scripting, Packt Publishing*.

Francesco is also a musician and composer, especially of soundtracks for short films and video games. For several years, he worked as an actor and dancer. He was a guest of honor at the theatre Brancaccio in Rome.

In addition, he is a very active person, having volunteered as a children's entertainer at the Associazione Culturale Torraccia in Rome. Also, he gives private lessons in mathematics and music to high-school and university students.

Finally, Francesco loves math, philosophy, logic, and puzzle solving, but most of all, creating video games — thanks to his passion for game designing and programming.

You can find him at `https://linkedin.com/pub/francesco-sapio/b8/5b/365.`

I'm deeply thankful to my parents for their infinite patience, enthusiasm and support for me throughout my life. Moreover, I'm thankful to the rest of my family, in particular to my grandparents, since they always encouraged me to do better in my life with the Latin expressions "Ad Maiora" and "Per aspera ad astra".

Besides this, I would like to thank my old Acquisition Editor for introducing me into this world and my current Content Developer for his kindness and patience.

Finally, a huge thanks to all the special people are around me who I love, in particular to my girlfriend; I'm grateful for all your help in everything.

About the Reviewers

Jack Donovan is a game developer and software engineer who has been working with the Unity3D engine since its third major release. He studied at Champlain College in Burlington, Vermont, USA, where he received a bachelor of science in game programming. Jack currently works at IrisVR, a virtual reality start-up in New York City, where he is developing software that allows architects to generate virtual reality experiences from their CAD models or blueprints. Before IrisVR, he worked on a small independent game team with fellow students. At that time, he also wrote the book *OUYA Game Development By Example* by Packt Publishing.

Lauren S. Ferro is a gamification consultant and designer with 10 years of experience designing interactive game and game-like applications across a variety of contexts. She has worked on, designed, and implemented strategies for a range of different purposes, from professional development to recommendation systems and educational games. She is an active researcher in the area of gamification, player profiling, and user-centred game design. Lauren runs workshops for both the general public and companies that focus on designing user-centered games and game-like applications. She is also the developer of the game design resource Gamicards (which will soon be available for purchase).

You can contact her on Twitter at @R3nza. Her website is www.laurensferro.com and her e-mail ID is contact@laurensferro.com.

www.PacktPub.com

Support files, eBooks, discount offers, and more

For support files and downloads related to your book, please visit www.PacktPub.com.

Did you know that Packt offers eBook versions of every book published, with PDF and ePub files available? You can upgrade to the eBook version at www.PacktPub.com and as a print book customer, you are entitled to a discount on the eBook copy. Get in touch with us at service@packtpub.com for more details.

At www.PacktPub.com, you can also read a collection of free technical articles, sign up for a range of free newsletters and receive exclusive discounts and offers on Packt books and eBooks.

https://www2.packtpub.com/books/subscription/packtlib

Do you need instant solutions to your IT questions? PacktLib is Packt's online digital book library. Here, you can search, access, and read Packt's entire library of books.

Why Subscribe?

- ▸ Fully searchable across every book published by Packt
- ▸ Copy and paste, print, and bookmark content
- ▸ On demand and accessible via a web browser

Free Access for Packt account holders

If you have an account with Packt at www.PacktPub.com, you can use this to access PacktLib today and view 9 entirely free books. Simply use your login credentials for immediate access.

Table of Contents

Preface

Unity is a very flexible and high-performance game engine. It allows you to build small – to large-scale enterprise video games. It is designed to promote rapid development and clean, pragmatic design and lets you build high-performing, elegant games quickly. The main aim of this book is to teach you how to implement complete user interface systems that can interact with all other parts of your game. The book is structured in recipes, so the expert user can read them in any order that they like. But for those who are still learning, it can be read in order, as it guides you from the basic topics to advanced features that can be developed within the UI. Furthermore, the book often refers to the relation between the player and the UI. In fact, this is a very important factor to take into consideration in order to design and implement a UI that feels suitable and ultimately create a successful game.

What this book covers

Chapter 1, UI Essentials, gives us the basic tools needed to deal with the UI. These will be used throughout this book. Once learned, these tools provide the foundations for creating even more complex interfaces.

Chapter 2, Implementing Counters and Health Bars, provides different ways to implement the most often used UI systems: counters and health bars. They serve many purposes, such as keeping track of virtual currency and the number of lives that a player has.

Chapter 3, Implementing Timers, deals with the way time is used and represented in our game. Timers are a good way for players to experience flow throughout the game, and countdowns can indicate how much time is remaining to complete a task. Furthermore, they can change over time. Both timers and countdowns are effective methods of altering the dynamics of gameplay.

Chapter 4, Creating Panels for Menus, teaches you how to make different kinds of panel to create interactive menus. These menus contain elements such as sliders and draggable and resizable features.

Chapter 5, *Decorating the UI*, explains how it is possible to implement dynamic elements to decorate our UIs. In fact, these are a great way to give the player a feeling that the UI is dynamic and alive.

Chapter 6, *Animating the UI*, extends the concept of giving life to a UI from the previous chapter. In addition, this chapter provides methodologies that allow players to switch between different menus.

Chapter 7, *Applying Runtime Customizations*, examines the different levels of customization for the player that can be achieved during runtime, such as text filtering and slider lockers.

Chapter 8, *Implementing Advance HUDs*, helps you develop skills for taking information from the 3D world and then implementing it within your HUD elements. Such elements may include displaying the distance to an object, radar for detecting objects, as well as a subtitle shower system.

Chapter 9, *Diving into 3D UIs*, focuses on teaching some advanced features for placing UI elements within a 3D space by taking advantage of the z axis. Furthermore, it covers various scripts that enable our UI to interact with the 3D world in order to exchange inputs/outputs.

Chapter 10, *Creating Minimaps*, explores the many purposes that minimaps can serve, such as identifying locations of interest, objects, and even characters, such as locations of enemies and other players, which can be shown as icons on the minimap.

What you need for this book

The only software you need is Unity 5.x, which can be downloaded from the official website:

`http://unity3d.com/`

However, it could be useful if you have some graphics programs for use throughout the recipes in this book for — rapid mock-ups and custom graphics.

Furthermore, Unity 5.x Pro is required to follow the last chapter of this book, since we will use render textures, which are available only with Unity Pro.

Who this book is for

If you are a game developer with some experience with Unity and C# and want to create the best interactive experience fast and intuitively, then this book is for you. If you are an intermediate game developer or an expert, these recipes will help you bring out the power of the new UI Unity system.

Sections

In this book, you will find several headings that appear frequently (Getting ready, How to do it, How it works, There's more, and See also).

To give clear instructions on how to complete a recipe, we use these sections as follows:

Getting ready

This section tells you what to expect in the recipe, and describes how to set up any software or any preliminary settings required for the recipe.

How to do it...

This section contains the steps required to follow the recipe.

How it works...

This section usually consists of a detailed explanation of what happened in the previous section.

There's more...

This section consists of additional information about the recipe in order to make the reader more knowledgeable about the recipe.

See also

This section provides helpful links to other useful information for the recipe.

Conventions

In this book, you will find a number of text styles that distinguish between different kinds of information. Here are some examples of these styles and an explanation of their meaning.

Code words in text, database table names, folder names, filenames, file extensions, pathnames, dummy URLs, user input, and Twitter handles are shown as follows: "Since we don't need to set the initial variables, we can erase the `Start()` function."

A block of code is set as follows:

```
public void Update()
 if (Input.GetKeyDown (key))
 {
 EventSystem.current.SetSelectedGameObject(
this.gameObject);
 }}
```

When we wish to draw your attention to a particular part of a code block, the relevant lines or items are set in bold:

```
using UnityEngine.UI;
using UnityEngine.EventSystems;
using UnityEngine;
using System.Collections;
```

Any command-line input or output is written as follows:

```
C:\Program Files\Unity\Editor\Unity.exe
```

New terms and **important words** are shown in bold. Words that you see on the screen, for example, in menus or dialog boxes, appear in the text like this: "Clicking on the **Next** button moves you to the next screen."

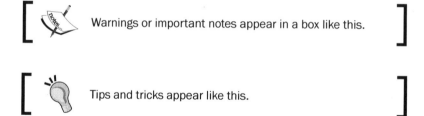

> Warnings or important notes appear in a box like this.

> Tips and tricks appear like this.

Reader feedback

Feedback from our readers is always welcome. Let us know what you think about this book — what you liked or disliked. Reader feedback is important for us as it helps us develop titles that you will really get the most out of.

To send us general feedback, simply e-mail feedback@packtpub.com, and mention the book's title in the subject of your message.

If there is a topic that you have expertise in and you are interested in either writing or contributing to a book, see our author guide at www.packtpub.com/authors.

Customer support

Now that you are the proud owner of a Packt book, we have a number of things to help you to get the most from your purchase.

Downloading the example code

You can download the example code files from your account at `http://www.packtpub.com` for all the Packt Publishing books you have purchased. If you purchased this book elsewhere, you can visit `http://www.packtpub.com/support` and register to have the files e-mailed directly to you.

Downloading the color images of this book

We also provide you with a PDF file that has color images of the screenshots/diagrams used in this book. The color images will help you better understand the changes in the output. You can download this file from `http://www.packtpub.com/sites/default/files/downloads/UnityUICookbook_ColorImages.pdf`.

Errata

Although we have taken every care to ensure the accuracy of our content, mistakes do happen. If you find a mistake in one of our books — maybe a mistake in the text or the code — we would be grateful if you could report this to us. By doing so, you can save other readers from frustration and help us improve subsequent versions of this book. If you find any errata, please report them by visiting `http://www.packtpub.com/submit-errata`, selecting your book, clicking on the **Errata Submission Form** link, and entering the details of your errata. Once your errata are verified, your submission will be accepted and the errata will be uploaded to our website or added to any list of existing errata under the Errata section of that title.

To view the previously submitted errata, go to `https://www.packtpub.com/books/content/support` and enter the name of the book in the search field. The required information will appear under the **Errata** section.

Piracy

Piracy of copyrighted material on the Internet is an ongoing problem across all media. At Packt, we take the protection of our copyright and licenses very seriously. If you come across any illegal copies of our works in any form on the Internet, please provide us with the location address or website name immediately so that we can pursue a remedy.

Please contact us at `copyright@packtpub.com` with a link to the suspected pirated material.

We appreciate your help in protecting our authors and our ability to bring you valuable content.

Questions

If you have a problem with any aspect of this book, you can contact us at `questions@packtpub.com`, and we will do our best to address the problem.

1

UI Essentials

In this chapter, we will cover the following recipes:

- ▶ Setting up a 2D texture to be a bordered sprite
- ▶ Resizing the UI according to screen size and resolution
- ▶ Adding and placing an image in the UI
- ▶ Adding a circular mask to an image
- ▶ Making an image scrollable
- ▶ Making text scrollable with a vertical slider
- ▶ Selecting buttons through the keyboard
- ▶ Using UI layout components

Introduction

This chapter explains how to use the essential tools for creating more complex interfaces. These tools include placing and scaling UI elements, using masks to shape figures, and making images and text scrollable along with sliders.

We start by creating a sprite with a border. It can be scaled up or down without distorting. Then, we will proceed with explaining how to make our UI resizable according to the resolution of our screen.

Later, we will introduce the most used UI component — the **Image (Script)**. Then, you will learn how to implement more complex transformations, such as masking it or making it scrollable.

We will also see how to select buttons using the input from the keyboard by introducing how we can develop scripts that are able to interact with our UI.

Finally, we will look at the UI layout components that allow us to easily create and structure a very wide UI.

Getting ready

To get started with this chapter, we will need to have Unity 5 running, and we must create a new project. The project can be set in 3D or 2D, depending on which one better suits the game that we wish to make. However, if it is set in 2D, Unity will automatically import our images as sprites. Lastly, ensure that you have some nice images of your choice for use in the examples, such an ancient map.

Setting up a 2D texture to be a bordered sprite

To properly scale a 2D texture to the screen size, we may need to make it bordered. This allows us to force the resolution, but not scale all the parts of our image, in order to maintain the original appearance of the image. Buttons are often bordered because their appearance depends strongly on how corners are scaled, and we don't generally want them to scale.

How to do it...

1. To begin, we need to import our image. We can do this by right-clicking on the **Project** panel and then selecting **Import new asset...**.

2. Using the navigation menu on your computer, locate an image and import it. As a result, the image will be in our project and it can be used everywhere within the current project.

> Another way to add images to the project is by dragging and dropping them into the **Project** panel.

3. Next, we need to select our image in the **Project** panel. In fact, this allows us to display all the import settings in the **Inspector** window, which we can then tweak.

4. In order to use images as part of the UI, **Texture Type** must to be set in **Sprite (2D and UI)**. This can be changed through the **Inspector** window after we have selected them. However, if our project is set as a 2D project, the image in the project will have already been imported with **Texture Type** set correctly.

5. Once we have done this, we click on the **Sprite Editor** button.

6. In each side of the figure, we can find four green points. By dragging them, it is possible to divide the image into sections. By doing this, we create the borders of our image. Therefore, let's drag them a bit inside the picture so that we can see the borders. We have to pay attention when we have curved corners, which can be the case if we are working on a button. In fact, we need to ensure that all the green lines that belong to the border are beyond the curvatures of the corners. Otherwise, they will not be scaled as they should.

7. Finally, we can click on the **Apply** button in the top-right corner of the **Sprite Editor** to save all our changes. After this, we can close the **Sprite Editor**, since we don't need it anymore.

8. As a result, the image has borders, and therefore can be scaled as it should. How to properly place this inside our UI, since it requires us to set the **Image (Script)** component to **Sliced**.

How it works...

Sometimes, some components of our UI need to be scaled. However, not all of them can be scaled freely. Otherwise, it could look different from what we thought it should be. Therefore, bordered images are used to scale everything as it should be. Borders tell Unity how it has to scale the picture. When we drag the green points in the **Sprite Editor,** we are dividing the image into nine sections. Each of these sections is scaled differently. The central sections are scaled in both *x* and *y* directions (vertically and horizontally). The side sections are scaled in only one direction: vertically for the right/left sections and horizontally for the upper/lower sections). Finally, the corners do not scale at all. You can see these nine sections and the scales in the following image:

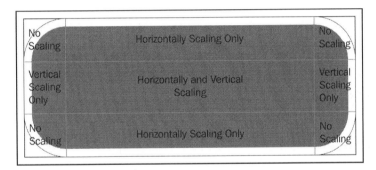

Let's consider an example to understand why a bordered sprite is important for the UI. Imagine that we have a button like the one in the preceding image and we have placed it on the screen. When the game runs on different devices, the resolutions will be different and Unity will scale our UI accordingly (see the next recipe for more information). Ideally, we want the button to look like the original one that we have designed as much as possible. This means, for instance, that we want to preserve the original curvatures of the corners, and therefore, we need to force them not to scale. This can be communicated to Unity using borders. In this way, the rest of the button can scale along with the screen size in order to fit it, but as a result, the button will look like the original one.

There's more...

The next subtopic will show us how to slice the sprite without using all of the nine sections.

Slicing with less than nine sections

As you have learned so far, we can use the nine sections of the border to define the scaling setting of an image properly. But we are not constrained to use all of them. In fact, it is possible to segment the image into fewer sections. This is useful when we have some UI elements that are attached to the border of the screen. In fact, in this case, the image will scale differently according to only those sections that have been defined. To do this, we need to drag only some of the green points from the corners, instead of what we did in steps 5 and 6, where we dragged all them. By tweaking these, we can achieve different ways of scaling our UI, and the right one depends on how we want our game to look in different resolutions. For instance, we can create something similar to this:

See also

> ▶ Since having a bordered image is very important when the UI is scaled on different resolutions and platforms, maybe it could be worthwhile taking a deeper look at resolution scaling. The following recipe, *Resizing the UI according to the screen size and resolution*, will explain how to resize the UI according to the screen resolution.

> ▶ Moreover, it is possible to learn more about how to place an image in the UI in the *Adding and placing an image in the UI* recipe.

Resizing the UI according to the screen size and resolution

One of the most difficult things to do in the older versions of Unity was scaling the UI (or GUI, the old Unity user interface system). In fact, the system was hard to learn, and most of the features had to be implemented by scripts, including scaling. However, in Unity 5, scaling the UI is much easier with the **Canvas Scaler (Script)** component. This component will take care of the scale of all UI elements that are contained in **Canvas**.

How to do it...

1. If we check the previous recipe, we can see in the **Hierarchy** panel that **Canvas** is already present in our scene. This is because whenever we create a UI element and **Canvas** is not present in the scene, Unity will create it for us. Of course, we can also create it on our own, and this can be done by right-clicking on the **Hierarchy** panel and then navigating to **UI | Canvas**.

2. Now that we have created **Canvas**, we can select it. In the **Inspector**, we can see all its properties and parameters, including all the components attached to it. By default, when a **Canvas** is created, the **Canvas Scaler (Script)** component is attached on it. Since this component can be removed, it may happen that it is not present anymore. In such cases, we can add it again by clicking inside the **Inspector** window on **Add Component** and then going to **Layout | Canvas Scaler**.

3. Next, we have to change the **Ui Scale Mode** property to **Scale With Screen Size** and ensure that **Screen Match Mode** is set to **Match Width Or Height**. Furthermore, we can adjust the **Match** variable; for example, we can move the slider to the middle by changing the value to **0.5**. We should now see this:

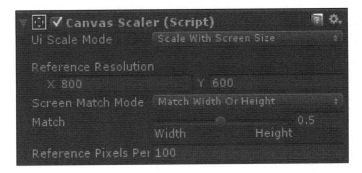

4. As a result, every UI element inside **Canvas** will be scaled according to our project's screen resolution, and they will all adapt to the device on which the game is running.

How it works...

In the Unity UI system, **Canvas** is a special game object. This is because all the UI elements must be contained inside it. In fact, elements that are not in it will not be rendered. By default, **Canvas** comes with three components attached to it. One of these three is **Canvas Scaler (Script)**. This component controls how all the UI elements that are contained in that specific **Canvas** will be scaled. By tweaking some of its properties, it is possible to achieve a scale setting that best suits our needs. In particular, we have set the **Match** slider, which allows us to proportionally crop the width and height of the view in order to adapt it to the resolution of the platform on which the game is running.

See also

▶ There are many other ways of scaling UI elements according to screen size to suit our requirements. To explore these methods, you can refer to the book *Unity 3D UI Essentials* by *Simon Jackson, Packt Publishing*, ISBN 139781783553617 (`https://www.packtpub.com/game-development/unity-3d-gui-essentials`).

▶ Furthermore, you can refer to the official documentation of Unity about this component at `http://docs.unity3d.com/Manual/script-CanvasScaler.html`.

Adding and placing an image in the UI

Since our UIs mostly consist of images, it's very important to learn how to handle them with the **Image (Script)** components in Unity. In fact, we will use them a lot in all the recipes of this book. In particular, here you can understand how to create a new image and properly place it in your UI.

How to do it...

1. Let's start by importing the image into our project, as we did in the first recipe of this chapter. We can do this by right-clicking on the **Project** panel and selecting **Import new asset**. Of course, it is also possible to drag the asset into the same panel and skip the next step.

2. We can navigate through our files to select the image that we want to import.

3. If we select our image in the **Project** panel, it is possible to see all its properties in the **Inspector**.

4. In order to use our image as **Source Image** of our UI, we need to change **Texture Type** to **Sprite (2D and UI)** in the **Inspector**. As you learned in the first recipe, if our project is set in 2D, all the images will have already been imported as sprites.

5. Now, in the **Inspector**, there are different import settings. There is no need to change the settings for this recipe; it is important to understand these features so that we can properly import all our images into the project. These features include the format, along with the size and the compression method. If, for instance, we need to make the image file size smaller for performance. You can find references to them in the *See also* section of this recipe. Then, when we are satisfied with our choices, we can click on the **Apply** button so that the import settings are applied. This could take some minutes if you have changed the settings of many different images at once.

6. Next, we need to create the UI image that will be in the UI. In order to add it to the scene, we have to right-click on the **Hierarchy** panel and then navigate to **UI | Image**. We should also ensure that it is inside the **Canvas** object.

UI components that are outside **Canvas** will not be drawn by Unity, so ensure that every UI component is always inside **Canvas**!

If they are not, we can drag and drop them onto the **Canvas** object so that they become children, and they appear again.

7. Inside the **Image (Script)** component, which we can find in the **Inspector**, we drag the image that we have imported inside the **Source Image** variable.

If our image is sliced, as we saw in the first recipe of this chapter, we also need to set **Image Type** to **Sliced**.

8. As a result, our image appears in the UI, but it has taken the dimensions and scaling of the **Image** object that we have created. Therefore, if we need to keep its original dimensions, we can click on **Set Native Size** in order to set them again.

9. So that it is easier to work with the UI, set your scene view to 2D, as shown in the following screenshot, and zoom out and pan until you can clearly see your **Canvas**. At this stage, it is very large, so don't worry if you zoom out too much. Otherwise, you can use the hotkey *F* (or double-click on the image in the **Hierarchy** panel) to focus the camera on it:

In order to scale and place the image, we select the last **Transform Tool**, which we can find in top-left corner of Unity, as shown in the next screenshot. It is called the **Rect Tool**, and it can easily be selected by pressing the hotkey *T*. While we need different tools to translate, rotate, and scale 3D objects, since they have many degrees of freedom, we can perform all of these operations with just one tool when we deal with a 2D object:

10. After we have selected the image from the scene view, four blue points appear on the corners. These are the control points of the **Rect Tool**.

11. We can drag one of them to scale the image.

If you want to keep the images' original proportions, you can hold down *Shift* while you are dragging the blue points.

Furthermore, if you hold down *Alt* instead of *Shift*, you can simultaneously scale the object in two directions symmetrically.

Finally, you can also resize the image by clicking on the edges instead of the corners and dragging them.

12. In conclusion, we can place the image wherever we want to by clicking anywhere inside the rectangle and dragging. Again, keep in mind that all the UI elements, including the image, must be inside the **Canvas** in order to be drawn by Unity and displayed to the player.

How it works...

The new UI system of Unity allows us to add images to the UI in a very simple way. The **Image (script)** component takes a **Source Image** and draws it on the screen. However, this happens only if the object to which this component is attached is inside **Canvas**. In fact, Unity calls functions to draw the UI only if they are inside **Canvas**.

In the preceding examples, we used the **Rect Tool** to scale and place the image, because every UI element is represented as a rectangle for the purpose of this layout.

There's more...

Rotating an image it's crucial in designing good UIs. Moreover, all the rotations depends by the pivot point. Thus, the aim of the following section is to give an overview of the concepts to start to experiment and learn how to use properly this tools.

Rotating the image and changing the pivot point

We can also rotate the image by slightly moving the cursor away from the corners until it looks like a rotation symbol. Then, we can click and drag it in either direction to rotate the image. We can also change the pivot point. After selecting the image in the scene view, just click and drag the blue circle at the center of the image. By doing this, we can rotate images in different ways. You can better understand this concept by paying attention to the following image, which shows the same rectangle rotated with two different pivot points:

 The four black squares are our referring points to understand the difference. Both the rectangles are rotated by the same angle. In the upper rectangle, the pivot point (blue circle) is in the middle, whereas in the lower rectangle, it is moved to the left side.

Furthermore, changing the pivot point could lead to an interesting variation in our UI when this is animated or controlled by scripts. For instance, we should definitely try to experiment with different locations of pivot points in the *Creating an extendable element with a final fade effect* and *Creating an extendable and rotating element with a final fade effect* recipes in *Chapter 5, Decorating the UI*.

Adding a circular mask to an image

Often in games, UI elements are not designed to be rectangular. Thus, a quick way to change their shape is through masking. One of the basic shapes is a circle. Therefore, in this recipe, you will learn how to make an image circular. This could be useful, for example, to surround a character icon circularly or to create special circular buttons. In order to achieve this, we will use the **Mask** component.

How to do it...

1. First of all, we need to create a mask, which in this case should be circular. Since the mask is just another image, let's open a graphic program that we have. Then, we need to create a new image with the same pixels for the height and width so that the drawing canvas is a square.

2. This step and the following step depend on the graphics program that you are using. Now, we have to draw a white circle in the middle of the image.

3. Furthermore, we should also ensure that the background is transparent. From the following screenshot, you can get an idea of what the final outcome will look like (the program used for this is Photoshop):

If you are using Photoshop, you can easy create this mask using the ellipse tool. While holding down the *Shift* key, click on the top-left corner and drag it to the bottom-right corner.

If you don't have a graphics program or you don't want to use a graphics program, you can use the image provided along with the code featured in this book.

4. The next step is to import this mask into the project. To do this, right-click on the **Project** panel and select **Import new asset**.

5. Unity will ask us to select the mask that we have just created. Therefore, locate the folder where you saved it and then import it.

6. In order to see the settings of the imported mask as an image in the **Inspector**, we need to select it in the **Project** panel.

7. Thus, if our project is not set in 2D, we should change the **Texture Type** in **Sprite (2D and UI)** in the **Inspector** and then click on **Apply**.

8. Now, we need to create a new panel. We can do this by right-clicking on the **Hierarchy** panel and then going to **UI | Panel**. We should also ensure that we have it inside the **Canvas** object.

9. Inside the **Image (Script)** component, we need to set our mask to the **Source Image** variable.

10. In order to get the exact shape that we created in our graphics program, we need to bring the image back to its original proportions. This can be done by clicking on **Set Native Size** and then scaling uniformly (keeping *Shift* pressed) if needed.

11. The next thing to do is transform our panel into a mask. So, we need to add the **Mask (Script)** component to our panel.

12. Then, we need an image to put the mask on. Therefore, let's create an image inside the panel. To do this, we need to right-click on the **Hierarchy** panel and then go to **UI | Image**.

13. Inside the **Image (Script)** component of the image, we need to select the picture that we want to mask. This can be done by dragging it into the **Source Image** variable of the component. As a result, it will be masked with a circle.

14. If needed, we can click on **Set Native Size** and scale it uniformly.

15. In this case, by using an ancient map, we can see what the final outcome should look like in the following picture:

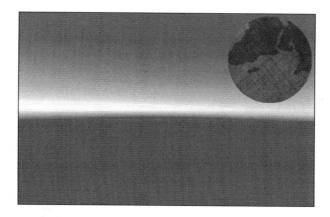

How it works...

As we have seen, Unity uses another image to create the mask. This is the reason the **Mask (Script)** component is attached to the object that has an **Image (Script)** component. As a result, it is possible to create any shape that we want for the mask. In fact, the only thing we need to keep in mind is that the white sections of the mask texture will be the parts that are visible.

See also

▶ If you are looking for more information about the **Mask** component, you can refer to the Unity official documentation at `http://docs.unity3d.com/Manual/script-Mask.html`.

Making an image scrollable

Many fantasy games have huge worlds, along with very large maps, so in order to show them in the UI, they are usually scrollable. This allows the player to explore the map in sections without showing it entirely at once.

This recipe explains how to achieve this using the **Mask (Script)** component, which we have already used in the previous recipe, and the **Scroll Rect (Script)** component. The latter will handle the logic that will allow the UI elements to be scrollable.

How to do it...

1. So that we don't have to start over again, we can use the mask that we created in the previous recipe. In fact, we can change what we have done there to achieve this scrollable effect.

2. To begin, we need to add the **Scroll Rect (Script)** component to the panel.

3. Keeping the panel selected, drag the image that is parented to the panel into the **Content** variable inside **Scroll Rect (Script)**.

4. By default, the image is set to have an elastic effect, which, in most cases, is quite nice. However, since we are using a circle instead of a rectangle, it is better that the image doesn't go out of the circle. This is because the image may appear distorted and affect the overall aesthetic experience, which may even prove to be uncomfortable to the player. Therefore, to solve this, change **Movement Type** to **Clamped**.

5. Finally, it is possible to modify the effect to better suit our needs by changing **Deceleration Rate** and **Scroll Sensitivity**. Thus, take time to test which values are best for you.

6. Once you have finished altering the values, your **Inspector** should look similar to this:

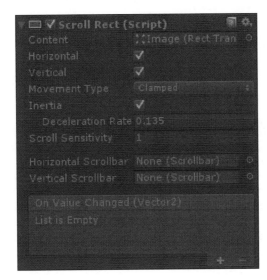

How it works...

First of all, we took the previous image, which is already masked. In fact, scrollable images are often used along with masks. This is because masks allow us to focus on specific locations within large images or text without overwhelming the player, as well as allow larger objects to feature within the UI in more compact ways. Once we had taken the outcome from the previous recipe, we then added a **Scroll Rect (Script)** component to the parent of our image. This component does the work, and it can be controlled by several options or parameters.

For example, we can change the **Movement Type** variable. **Clamped** is where the content is confined to the **Scroll Rect** bounds, **Elastic** means the content bounds when it reaches the edge, and **Unrestricted** means that there are no limitations. In addition to this, we can tweak **Deceleration Rate**, but only if **Inertia** is checked. This determines how much time it takes for the content to come to a complete stop. At a rate of 0, the movement will stop immediately, whereas at a rate of 1, it will never slow down. Among the most important parameters of this component is **Scroll Sensitivity**. This is, as the name suggests, the sensitivity when the content is scrolled.

See also

- ▸ It's always good to refer to the official Unity documentation if you are looking for more information. Besides the previous recipe, you can find more about masks at `http://docs.unity3d.com/Manual/script-Mask.html`.

- ▸ And you can follow the `http://docs.unity3d.com/Manual/script-ScrollRect.html` link to learn about the **Scroll Rect (Script)** component:

Making text scrollable with a vertical slider

Sometimes, we might have a large amount of text, such as a story in a book within our game, and we may want to show this to the player. One solution for improving the accessibility of reading text could be to add a slider so that the player can drag it in order to quickly scroll through text and immediately know which part of the text he is reading. Similar to what we did in the previous recipe, we need to make this text scrollable, and we also need to add the slider, which will be vertical in this example.

By the end of this recipe, we will be able to use the **Scroll Rect (Script)** and **Scrollbar (Script)** components to control scrollable text by using the slider.

How to do it...

1. In the first step, we create a new panel within our UI. Right-click on the **Hierarchy** panel and then go to **UI | Panel**.

2. Next, we should resize the panel until we have a scene view that is similar to this:

3. It's always good practice to have all the files within our project ordered. Hence, we can rename the panel to **Text Scroller**.

4. As we did in the last two recipes, let's add a **Mask (Script)** component. In order to view the scene without visual constraints, for the moment, we can disable it.

5. Next, right-click on **Text Scroller** and then select **Create Empty**. By doing this, we create an empty child game object inside **Text Scroller**. Also, we should rename it to **Text Content**.

6. On this last one, we need to add a **Scroll Rect (Script)** component. Then we need to create the text. This can be done by right-clicking on **Text Content** and going to **UI | Text**.

7. Now we can write (or copy and paste long text) inside the **Text** variable of the component.

8. Using the **Rect Tool**, we should resize the text area in order to obtain a rectangle. This rectangle must have a width narrower than **Text Scroller** and a larger height. We need to continue to increase its height until all of the text is contained inside of the rectangle. You can refer to the screenshot after step 10 to get a better idea of how it should appear at this stage.

9. Now, right-click again on **Text Scroller**, and this time, go to **UI | Scrollbar**. Now our **Hierarchy** panel should look similar to this one:

10. Next, we need to change the **Direction** variable of the **Scrollbar (Script)** component to **Bottom To Up**. Then, resize and place the scroll bar in the remaining space of the panel, as shown in this screenshot:

11. We also need to link the scroll bar to the text. To do this, select **Text Content** and drag the scrollbar inside the **Vertical Scrollbar** variable. We also have to uncheck the **Horizontal** variable in order to force the text to scroll vertically.

12. Finally, we can enable the mask on **Text Scroller** (the one that we have disabled in order to work better) and click on play to test what we have done. If you prefer, you can disable the elastic effect, as was done in the previous recipe. To do this, just change **Movement Type** to **Clamped** on the **Scroll Rect (Script)** component.

13. We are now able to scroll the text within **Text Scroller**. As a result, we should see something like this:

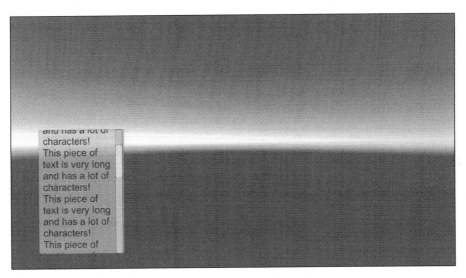

How it works...

The entire process works in a way similar to the previous recipe. In fact, we created a mask for text, instead of images as we had previously done. Then we temporarily hid the mask, which made it easier to place the text. In order to make the text scrollable, we added a **Scroll Rect (Script)**. Ultimately, we had to resize the text to display it correctly on the screen. We also added a scroll bar and linked it to **Scroll Rect (Script)**. Since the **Scroll Rect (Script)** will do the needful for us, we don't need to update the scroll bar. As in this example, the text will scroll vertically, since we have disabled horizontal scrolling on **Scrollbar (Script)**. Finally, we enabled the mask again in order to show only a portion of text at once.

There's more...

The following two sections will introduce us to new ways for scrolling the text so that it can better suit the design of our game.

Scrolling multiple columns at once

What happens if we want different kinds of text, such as a heading or a second column? We need to make a few changes.

First of all, we need to create a new empty game object and parent it with the **Text Scroller**. Next, we add a **Scroll Rect (Script)** component to this object and set the **Text Content** object that we created before in the **Content** variable by dragging it. Then we remove the **Scroll Rect (Script)** component from **Text Content**. Lastly, we can add an arbitrary number of UI text objects inside **Text Content**, and as a result, all of the text will be scrollable. If we add five of them, the **Hierarchy** panel should look like what is shown here:

Remember that in order to properly place the text on the screen, we can temporarily disable the mask attached to **Text Scroller**. By doing this, we are able to see all the objects inside the mask without its constraints.

At the end, we should have something that looks like this:

Resizing all the components could be needed in order to fit the text and the panel properly. As a result, the scroll effect will appear natural and as we have planned.

Scrolling horizontally

Even though using a horizontal slider is unusual, we can transform the slider that we already have and change its orientation. This is often used to implement inventory systems of point-and-click game genres.

To achieve this, we can begin by changing what we did in step 8. This time, we have to stretch the text, making its height a little smaller than the height of **Text Scroller** and the width as long as the text itself. Then, in step 10, instead to selecting **Bottom To Up**, change the **Direction** variable to **Left To Right**. Finally, in step 11, we need to link the **Horizontal Scrollbar** variable (instead of **Vertical Scrollbar**) with our scroll bar, so uncheck the **Vertical** variable.

Since horizontal scrolling becomes hard to read when the width of the **Content** is large, it could be helpful to split the text into more than one column. We can easily achieve this by creating different UI text elements inside the **Content** object and distributing them in order to form as many columns as we like. We can see an example of this in the following screenshot:

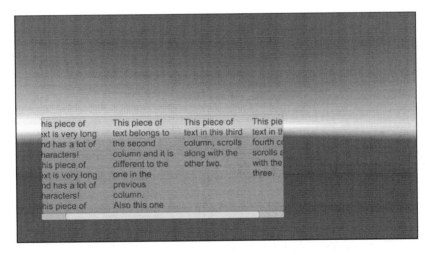

 Again, resizing all the components could be needed in order to fit the text and the panel properly. As a result, the scroll effect will appear natural and as we have planned.

Selecting buttons through the keyboard

Often in games, there are menus that have shortcuts as well. For example, if the player has to use a skill quickly, he needs an easier way to access it. In general, where there is the possibility within the UI to choose more than one selectable element, such as buttons and toggles, it is possible to select them using a keyboard shortcut.

This recipe will teach you how to detect when a key is pressed and select a specific UI element by creating a script that is able to be generic enough to be placed on every UI element without changing the code.

How to do it...

1. To begin, create a new panel. Right-click on **Hierarchy** panel and then go to **UI | Panel**. We can also rename it to keep the project names ordered.

2. Next, we need to create a button inside the panel. We can do this by right-clicking on the panel and then navigating to **UI | Button**.

3. In order to better see, which button is currently selected, let's change some properties of the **Button (Script)** component. For instance, we could choose a different color for **Normal Color**, **Highlighted Color**, and **Pressed Color**. In this example, let's set **Highlighted Color** to red and **Pressed Color** to green, and leave **Normal Color** as white. Finally, we also need to change **Navigation** to **Vertical**.

4. In order to have the ability to choose among different buttons, we need different buttons in the scene. We can achieve this by duplicating the button. This can be done by pressing *Ctrl + D* and then placing the duplicated buttons below the original one. Rename the first of these to **Button 1** and the second to **Button 2**. Repeat the same with the **Text** variable inside the **Text (Script)** component on the child of the button. As a result, we will be able to distinguish buttons on the screen as well. Finally, repeat this step at least two more times to get three buttons. Once we are done, our scene should look similar to the following:

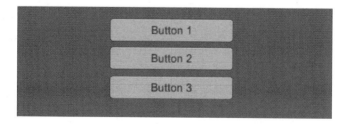

5. Now it's time to create our first script. To begin, in the **Inspector**, go to **Add Component | New Script** and name it **ButtonThroughKeySelection**. Then click on **Create and Add**. While doing this, ensure that the language selected is **C Sharp**.

6. Double-click on the script in order to open it in MonoDevelop.

7. Every time we work with some UI classes, we need to add a using clause on top of our script. This will ensure that we don't have any compilation error when the script is compiled by Unity. Furthermore, since we are also using events, we need to add another using clause. Therefore, at the beginning of our script, we need to get these:

```
using UnityEngine.UI;
using UnityEngine.EventSystems;
using UnityEngine;
using System.Collections;
```

8. Moreover, we need to add a variable for the key that has been chosen. By doing this, we can set that variable in the **Inspector**:

```
public class ButtonThroughKeySelection: MonoBehaviour {

    public string key;
```

9. Since we don't need to set the initial variables, we can erase the Start() function. In order to implement the detection of the pressed key and change the selected button, we need to write the Update() function in the following way:

```
public void Update()
    if (Input.GetKeyDown (key))
    {
        EventSystem.current.SetSelectedGameObject(
                this.gameObject);
    }
}
```

10. Now we can save the script and add it to one of the three buttons.

11. Next, set the **Key** variable with a string that represents a key, for example, **space** for the spacebar. Once we have done this, we should see something like this:

12. Finally, we can click on the play button and see whether everything works. After our button is selected, by pressing the key bounded by the variable, we can move through the others with the arrow keys. However, if we re-press our key, which in this example is the spacebar, the selection returns to our button.

How it works...

To get started, we have created three buttons in the scene, which are our test buttons. We also had to change some of the buttons' properties in order to clearly see the effect that our script had on the buttons. Since we had distributed our buttons vertically, we set the **Navigation** variable to **Vertical**.

At the beginning of the script that we wrote, we added the `using UnityEngine.UI;` and the `using UnityEngine.EventSystems;` statements. The former needs to use UI elements inside our scripts, and it will be the most used through all the recipes of this book. The latter needs to use the **Event System** directly in our script.

As part of the next step in this recipe, we added a `public` string variable. It is public so that it can be set in the **Inspector** later. As a result, we can choose an arbitrary key to bind the specific button where the script is collocated.

Now, in the `Update()` function, we checked through `if (Input.GetKeyDown (key))` to find out whether our key is pressed. In fact, the `Input.GetKeyDown(string)` function returns `true` if the key specified as a string is pressed, and `false` if it is not. It's important to remember that the **Key** variable is set in the **Inspector**, so it could change according to the design of our game. Check out the *See also* section for more information about key press detection.

Finally, if our key is pressed, we need to select a specific button. This can be done with the `EventSystem.current.SetSelectedGameObject(this.gameObject);` line. The first part, `EventSystem.current`, returns the current event system that is used. Then, we call on the `SetSelectedGameObject(gameObject)` function, which selects the game object passed as a parameter. In this case, we use `this.gameobject`, which is the game object where this script is attached, as well as the button that we want to select.

By keeping everything parametric, such as having a **Key** variable that can be set to every instance of the script, we are able to use this script on many buttons at one time and customize it differently without touching the code again.

See also

▶ During the development of this script, we have seen different functions. The most important was the `GetKeyDown()` function. In fact, it allows you to detect whether a particular key is detected. You can find more information about it at `http://docs.unity3d.com/ScriptReference/Input.GetKeyDown.html`.

- However, this function needs a string as a parameter that specifies a key on our keyboard. You can find the complete list of the strings at `http://docs.unity3d.com/ScriptReference/KeyCode.html`.

- Finally, we have also used the `EventSystem`. This is very wide and can be used in different situations within Unity. Therefore, if you are looking for more information about it, you can refer to `http://docs.unity3d.com/ScriptReference/EventSystems.EventSystem.html`.

Using UI layout components

Often, we need to place a lot of objects in their correct and symmetric positions within our UI or in a nested element. Luckily, Unity has an auto-layout system that provides ways to nest UI elements into other UI elements. It is controlled by the UI layouts components that allow us to structure our UI. Learning how to master them is crucial for quickly creating clean UIs and achieving our design goals. In fact, this is the purpose of this recipe.

How to do it...

1. As the first step, we need a panel to apply the layout controllers to, and we have to restructure its children objects. To create this panel, right-click on the **Hierarchy** panel and then go to **UI | Panel**. We should also rename it to **First Panel**.

2. Then, we need to fill in our **First Panel** with some elements. In this recipe, we will use buttons. So let's start creating one of them inside the panel by right-clicking on the panel and then navigating to **UI | Button**.

3. Since just one button is not enough to see how layout controllers work, we need to add more panels. Therefore, we duplicate the button by pressing *Ctrl + D* as many times we want. Of course, we don't worry about the layout; the layout controls will do this for us.

4. Considering the fact that we want to test different layout controllers, we also need to duplicate the panel, using *Ctrl + D*. Finally, rename it to **Second Panel**.

5. We also need a third panel. Therefore, we can rename it to **External Panel** and put inside it the other two panels. Now, we should have the following structure:

6. Next, simply add **Horizontal Layout Group (Script)** to **External Panel** and then **Vertical Layout Group (Script)** to **First Panel**. Finally, add **Grid Layout Group (Script)** to **Second Panel**. Now, we can see the **Auto-Layout** system doing all the work for us. In order to better understand how the system works, just add the buttons, or duplicate them, and watch how the **Auto-Layout** system re-organizes the entire layout for us. As the final result, we should see something similar to this:

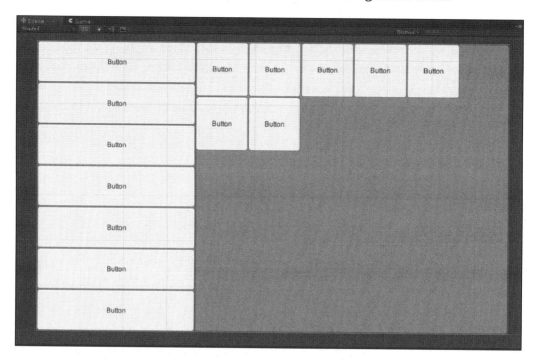

How it works...

The **Auto-Layout** system is composed of two different kinds of elements: **Layout Elements** and **Layout Controllers**. To understand the former, note that every game object that has a **Rect Transform**, and eventually other components, is a layout element. These types have certain knowledge about what size they should be of, but they do not control it directly. Layout controllers, instead, are components that control sizes and also positions of one or more layout elements. They can control their own Layout Element or child Layout Elements of the game object to which they are attached.

In this example, we used **Horizontal Layout Group (Script)**, **Vertical Layout Group (Script)** and **Grind Layout Group (Script)**. They work in similar ways. Furthermore, they take care of the layout of the children inside the game object to which they are attached, and restructure the positions of the UI elements.

See also

If you want to learn more about layout controllers, you can go to the official Unity documentation at the following links:

- **Horizontal layout group**: `http://docs.unity3d.com/Manual/script-HorizontalLayoutGroup.html`

- **Vertical layout group**: `http://docs.unity3d.com/Manual/script-VerticalLayoutGroup.html`

- **Grid layout group**: `http://docs.unity3d.com/Manual/script-GridLayoutGroup.html`

- **Content size fitter**: `http://docs.unity3d.com/Manual/script-ContentSizeFitter.html`

- **Aspect ratio fitter**: `http://docs.unity3d.com/Manual/script-AspectRatioFitter.html`

Downloading the example code

You can download the example code files from your account at `http://www.packtpub.com` for all the Packt Publishing books you have purchased. If you purchased this book elsewhere, you can visit `http://www.packtpub.com/support` and register to have the files e-mailed directly to you.

2

Implementing Counters and Health Bars

In this chapter, we will cover the following topics:

- ▶ Implementing a score counter
- ▶ Implementing lives counter
- ▶ Creating a modular coin counter
- ▶ Creating a symbolic lives counter
- ▶ Implementing a linear health bar
- ▶ Implementing a radial health bar
- ▶ Creating a health bar with armor
- ▶ Using multiple bars to make a multibar
- ▶ Developing a kingdom hearts health bar style

Introduction

This chapter explains how to implement counters for keeping track of variables such as score, coins, and lives, and how to display them through texts or through more complex things such as health bars.

We will start by creating a counter for our score and we will proceed with more complex counters.

Later, we will introduce the concept of health bars and we will also learn how to change their look, so that they are more linear or radial.

Finally, in the last three recipes, we are going to implement very special and complex health bars, which are suitable for bosses, for example.

Implementing a score counter

In this recipe, we are going to create a score counter that displays the score as a number on the screen. To achieve this, we will use the **Text (Script)** component and create a script to handle it. Different functions will be available from this script, that will be called from other scripts to increase the score.

How to do it...

1. First of all, we need to create new UI text to display our score. Thus, right-click on the **Hierarchy** panel and then **UI | Text**. Finally, rename it to **ScoreCounter**.

    To rename an object, right-click on it and select **Rename**. Otherwise, we can change its name in the **Inspector** window.

2. Next, we can change the **Font** and the **Font Size** in the **Inspector** as we wish, to better suit our needs.

3. Furthermore, we should also adjust the **Color**. In this example, we will set it to white in order to be easily visible within the scene.

4. Now, we need to drag the **ScoreCounter** with the **Rect Tool** (the hotkey for this tool is *T*, and we have seen it in the previous chapter) to where we want to place it.

5. We can write in the **Text** variable the word **Score**. In fact, this helps us to visualize what the counter will look like, even though this value will be replaced by the script, which we are going to write in the next steps.

6. Ensure that the **Rich Text** variable is checked. This allows us to use different colors inside the counter.

7. In this step, we need to create a script that manages the score: click on **Add Component | New Script** in the **Inspector** and name it **ScoreCounterScript**, and then press **Create and Add**. In doing this, ensure that the language selected is **C Sharp**.

8. Double-click on the script in order to edit it. Since we are going to use the `Text` class, we need to add the `using UnityEngine.UI;` statement at the beginning of the script.

9. Before we add the functions in our script, we need two `private` variables. Hence, we can write:

   ```
   private Text uiText;
   private long score = 0;
   ```

10. In the `Start ()` function, we can store the **ScoreCounter** in the **uiText** variable so that we can refer to it later in the script. In addition, we need also to update our score, so let's call a function that we will write later. Thus, the `Start ()` function is as follows:

```
void Start () {
   uiText = this.GetComponent<Text> ();
   updateScoreCounter ();
}
```

11. Next, we need a function to add points to our score counter that can be called from other scripts. We pass it an `int` parameter, which is the amount of points the player earned. So we can write the following:

```
public void addPoints(int points){
   score += points;
   updateScoreCounter ();
}
```

12. Finally, since we have called the `updateScoreCounter ()` function twice, it's time to write it down:

```
private void updateScoreCounter(){
   uiText.text = "<color=blue>Score</color>: " + score;
}
```

13. We can save the script and the work is done. We should see something like the following:

How it works...

In the script, there are two variables, `uiText` and `score`, which we've set to `private` because other components do not need to access it. The former stores the reference to the **Text (Script)** component in order to get it later in the script; the latter is the score of the player. This last one is a long variable that allows us to store big numbers since in some games, score points are very huge numbers.

The `Start()` function in Unity is special since it is called only once when the script is enabled for the first time. In this function, we assign the **Text (Script)** component attached in the same game object of this script to `uiText` variable by calling the `this.GetComponent<Text>()` function. Then, we call the `updateScoreCounter()` function in order to update the UIs as well during the first iteration.

Moreover, we added the `addPoints(int points)` function. It takes an `int` as a parameter named `points`. Then, the function adds this value to the `score` variable through `score += points;`. Finally, we call `updateScoreCounter()` to update the interface. The `+=` operator will take the value that score currently is and increase it by whatever is in our points value.

Finally, the `updateScoreCounter()` function changes the `text` variable on the **Text (Script)** component stored in the `uiText` variable. In fact, the new value assigned is a string. In the first part of this function, there is `<color=blue>Score</color>:` that encloses the word `Score` into styling tags to change its color to blue. Of course, we can also change blue to another color, if we prefer. Finally, we added the score. Don't worry that the `score` variable is long because in this case, Unity converts the number in to a string automatically.

There's more...

We have seen how to implement a score counter. However, according to the design of our game, we may want to add new features, such as removing score points or get the score variable to use it in some other script.

Adding a remove points function

In some games, it is possible to lose points, but we should be careful not to have a negative score.

Thus, we can deal with this issue by adding a new function to our script:

```
public void removePoints(int points){
  score -= points;
  if (score < 0)
    score = 0;
  updateScoreCounter ();
}
```

The first line `score -= points;` subtracts the amount of points, passed as parameter to the function, to our score.

Then, with an `if` statement, we verify whether our score is negative: if so, we set it to zero since we don't want negative score.

Finally, we update the score counter by calling the `updateScoreCounter()` function.

Using boldface in the rich text

The rich text of Unity allows us not only to change the color to a specific portion of text, but also to change the style. In order to give more importance to the word `Score`, we can replace this line of code inside the updateScoreCounter() function:

```
uiText.text = "<color=blue>Score</color>: " + score;
```

with this one:

```
uiText.text = "<b><color=blue>Score</color>:</b> " + score;
```

The text inside the `<b>` tag is now shown in boldface. Refer to the *See also* section for more details.

Getting the score

It could also be helpful to retrieve the score. For example, this is useful when we not only display it on the screen but also save the score in a scoreboard. Since we have set the `score` variable as `private`, we cannot access it directly. It's good practice not to change the variable into a `public` one but to add a new `get` function instead. The following is how we can do that:

```
public long getScore(){
   return score;
}
```

We simply return the score value and the job is done.

See also

- ▶ If we want to explore the concept of resolution scaling, we can refer to the following recipe *Resizing the UI according to the screen size and resolution*.

- ▶ Furthermore, if we want to replace the string `Score` on the counter with an icon, see *Creating a modular coin counter* recipe that teaches us also how to add an icon for coins in the counter.

- ▶ Finally, if we are looking for more information about rich text, refer to the official documentation available at `http://docs.unity3d.com/Manual/StyledText.html`.

Implementing a lives counter

This recipe teaches us how to use a **Text (Script)** component, along with a script, to create a counter. It is similar to the counter in the previous recipe; however, instead of keeping track of the score, here we are managing the number of lives that the player has.

How to do it...

1. Like the first step in the previous recipe, we need to create a new UI text to display the number of lives. Right-click on the **Hierarchy** panel and then go to **UI | Text**. Finally, rename it to **LivesCounter**.

2. We can also adjust the appearance, as we have done before with the **ScoreCounter**, so change the **Font** and the **Font size**. We can also set the **Color** of the text to white, and, finally, we place it in the scene through the **Rect Tool**, and so on.

3. Ensure again that the **Rich Text** variable is checked in order to use styling tags.

4. Next, let's create the script that manages the number of lives: click on **Add Component | New Script** in the **Inspector**, name it **LivesCounterScript** and then press **Create and Add**.

5. Double-click on the script in order to edit it. As the previous recipe, we are going to use the `Text` class; therefore, we need to add the `using UnityEngine.UI;` statement at the beginning of the script.

6. Unlike the previous recipe, we need three variables, two `private` and one `public`, so that we can set this last one in the **Inspector**. These three variables are as follows:

    ```
    private Text uiText;
    public intmaxLives;
    private int lives;
    ```

7. In the `Start()` function, we can set the `uiText` and `lives` variables and call our `update` function that we will write later, so:

    ```
    void Start () {
        lives = maxLives;
        uiText = this.GetComponent<Text> ();
        updateLivesCounter();
    }
    ```

8. Now we can write the addLife() function. Since we have set the maximum number of lives in the maxLives variable, we need to pay attention to not exceed that number. As a result, we need to add some more lines to perform this control. Furthermore, when we call this function, we don't know if it takes effect; thus, we need to return a value — in this case Boolean — to let us know if this operation succeeded or not. The function is as follows:

```
public booladdLife(){
    if (lives <maxLives) {
        lives++;
        updateLivesCounter();
        return true;
    }
    return false;
}
```

9. Of course, there is also a function for removing lives; it is as follows:

```
public boolloseLife(){
    lives--;
    if (lives > 0) {
        updateLivesCounter();
        return false;
    }
    lives = 0;
    updateLivesCounter();
    return true;
}
```

10. Finally, our update function:

```
private void updateLivesCounter(){
    uiText.text = "<color=red>Lives</color>: " + lives;
}
```

11. Save the script, and our **LivesCounter** is ready. If we set to 5 the maxLives variable and press play, we should see the following:

How it works...

As in the *Implementing a score counter* recipe, we have created a **Text (Script)** component and adjusted it as we desire, and again we have ensured that we have **Rich Text** checked.

In our script, we have three variables. The uiText stores the reference to the **Text (Script)** component. We store the maximum number of lives that the player can have in the maxLives variable and set its value in the **Inspector**. Finally, the lives contains the number of lives currently possessed by the player.

In the Start() function, we first set the number of lives with the maximum number allowed with this line, lives = maxLives;. Then, we assign the **Text (Script)** component attached in the same game object of this script to the uiText variable by calling the this. GetComponent<Text>() function. Finally, we call the updateLivesCounter() function in order to update the UI, also in the first iteration.

Furthermore, we have also written a addLife() function to add life to the player that returns a Boolean value: true if the life is added, otherwise the number of lives is equal to the maximum number of lives, which are allowed and the function returns false. In fact, at the beginning, there is an if statement that checks whether lives are less than maxLives. If so, we increase the lives by one, lives++;, then we call updateLivesCounter() function to update the interface, and, finally, we return true. Otherwise, we just return false.

Now, we have a function for `loseLife()`, and even this one returns back a Boolean value: `true` if the player has no more lives or `false` if the player has lives remaining. First, we decrease the number of lives by one, `lives--;`, and then we check whether lives are more than zero. If so, we call the `updateLivesCounter()` function to update the interface and, finally, we return `false`. Otherwise, we set `lives = 0;` since we don't want a negative number of lives, and, after `updateLivesCounter()`, we return `true`.

Finally, in the `updateLivesCounter()` function, there is just one line of the code. We assign to the `text` variable inside the **Text (Script)** component a string, with stylistic tags, along with the `lives` variable.

There's more...

We can extend the functionalities of our lives counter by following the next section that will explain how to change the maximum number of lives at runtime.

Changing the number of maxLives

Maybe there are some bonus pick-up items in our game that can temporarily increase the maximum number of lives. In this case, we will need a some other functions in our script; let's add them:

```
public void increaseMaxLives(int value){
   maxLives += value;
}
```

This function is very simple: the following line of code adds an amount equal to the value passed as parameter to the `maxLives` variable:

```
public void decreaseMaxLives(int value){
   maxLives -= value;
   if (maxLives< 1)
     maxLives = 1;
   if (lives >maxLives)
     lives = maxLives;
}
```

The `descreaseMaxLives()` function is a little bit more complex since we have to make more controls. First of all, we decrease the `maxLives` variable with the `maxLives -= value;` line. Then, we have two `if` statements: the first checks whether the `maxLives` is less than 1, since the player must have the possibility to have at least one life, and, if so, the `maxLives` variable is set to 1. The second checks to see that lives doesn't exceed `maxLives`, since the player can't have more lives that the maximum allowed, and, if so, set `lives = maxLives`.

Getting the number of lives

If we need to retrieve the value of the variable lives for any reason, such as to display this value somewhere else or allow the player to engage in a battle only if he has a certain number of lives, we need to add a get function, like the following one:

```
public intgetLives(){
   return lives;
}
```

See also

▸ For more detail about the get function, please refer to *Implementing a score counter* recipe in the *There's more...* section.

▸ Furthermore, if we want to replace the string lives on the counter with an icon, see the recipe *Creating a modular coin counter*, which teaches you how to add an icon for coins in the counter.

▸ Instead, if we are looking for more information about **Rich Text**, the official documentation is the best place to get it: http://docs.unity3d.com/Manual/StyledText.html.

Creating a modular coin counter

This recipe teaches us how to use a **Text (Script)** and **Image (Script)** components along with a script to create a counter with an icon. It is similar to the counters in the two previous recipes, but, instead, to keep track of the score or lives, here we manage the number of coins possessed by the player. In contrast to the first counter that doesn't have an upper bound, or like the second counter that has a maximum for lives, here, when the player has reached a certain number of coins, something will happen. For example, a life will be added and the counter starts from zero, creating modularity.

How to do it...

1. As for the first step of the previous recipe, we need to create a new UI text to show the number of lives. Hence, right-click on the **Hierarchy** panel and then **UI | Text**. Finally, rename it to **Modular Coin Counter**.

2. Let's adjust the settings to suit our needs, such as **Font**, **Font Size**, and **Color**, and also write in the **Text** variable 0 (zero).

3. In order to add an icon to our counter, we need to create an image inside the **Modular Coin Counter**, so right-click on it and select **UI | Image**, and then rename it to **Modular Coin Counter Icon**.

4. The next step is to create the icon, so let's open a graphic program and create our icon:

If we are using Photoshop, you can easy create this by using the ellipse tool: ensure that the main color is on yellow, and, then, while keeping *Shift* pressed, click on the upper left corner and drag to the lower right corner. Finally, select the **Text** tool and type a $, press *Ctrl+T*, then scale, and place it at the center of the circle. Now we have a simple icon for coins.

If you don't have a graphic program or you don't want to open a graphic program, you can use the image provided along with the code of this book.

5. Right-click on the **Project** panel and select **Import new asset**; select the icon that we have just created and import it.

6. If our project is set in 2D, we can skip this step. Otherwise, select the asset just imported in the **Project** panel and, in the **Inspector**, change **Texture Type** into **Sprite (2D and UI)**. Finally, click on **Apply**.

7. We can now add the icon to the **Modular Coin Counter Icon** in the **Source Image** variable and place it near the **Modular Coin Counter**. We should see something like the following:

8. It's time to implement the logic in the script. To begin, let's add it to the **Modular Coin Counter**, select **Add Component | New Script**, and then name it **ModularCoinCounterScript**. Finally, press **Apply**.

9. Double-click on the script to edit it. We are going to use some UI classes, so we need to add the using UnityEngine.UI; statement at the beginning of the script.

10. Before we can add functions, we need three variables, two private and one public, so we can set this last one in the **Inspector**. Thus, we can write:

```
private Text uiText;
public intmaxCoins = 100;
private int coins = 0;
```

11. In the Start() function, we set the uiText variable and then call our update function. The following is the Start() function:

```
void Start () {
  uiText = this.GetComponent<Text> ();
  updateCoinCounter ();
}
```

12. Now, we allow other scripts to add coins through this function:

```
public void addCoins(int value){
    coins += value;
    while (coins >= maxCoins)
        ApplyModularity ();
    updateCoinCounter ();
}
```

13. In the previous function, we called the `ApplyModularity()` function; let's write it down:

```
private void ApplyModularity(){
    coins -= maxCoins;
    GameObject.Find ("LivesCounter").GetComponent<LivesCounterScri
pt> ().addLife ();
}
```

14. Finally, as usual, our `update` function:

```
private void updateCoinCounter(){
    uiText.text = coins.ToString();
}
```

15. As final step, save our work and the job is done.

How it works...

In the script, we have created three variables. The first one is `uiText` and, as usual, it stores the reference to the **Text (Script)** component. The `maxCoins` variable is the number of coins after which the modularity is applied, and we can set its value in the **Inspector**, but as default in our script, it has `100` as value. Finally, the `coins` variable contains the number of coins currently possessed by the player and its default value is `0` (zero).

In the `Start()` function, we assigned the **Text (Script)** component attached in the same game object of this script to the `uiText` variable. We did this by calling the `this.GetComponent<Text>()` function. Then, we called the `updateCoinCounter ()` function in order to update the UI also during the first iteration.

Furthermore, we have written a function to `addCoins(int value)` to the player that takes as an int parameter and it is the number of coins that will be added to the player. In fact, at the beginning, we added value to the coins variable by `coins += value;`. Then, there is a `while` loop: until the number of coins are more than the maximum allowed, we call the `ApplyModularity()` function. Since we don't know how many coins have been added with the `value` parameter, we have to apply the modularity as many times the number of `maxCoins` are into the `coins` variable. At last, of course, we call our `updateCoinCounter ()` function in order to update the UI.

To better understand how the modularity works, let's consider the example of our `ApplyModularity()` function. First of all, this function is private, so only other functions within the same script can call it. Furthermore, it is called only when the number of coins are more than `maxCoins`, at most equal. So we can subtract the value of `maxCoins` from the `coins` variable, without obtaining a negative number of coins, and we do this in the first line of code. Then we can choose the reward for the player since he has reached the `maxCoins` number. In this example, if we have done this in *Implementing a lives counter* recipe, we can add a life to the player. So, let's find the lives counter through `GameObject.Find ("LivesCounter")` and then the script with `GetComponent<LivesCounterScript> ()`. Finally, we can call the `addLife ()` function.

At the end, we have `updateCoinCounter()`, in which we put the value of coins, converted in string through the `ToString()` function, into the **Text** variable contained into **Text (Script)** component in the **Modular Coin Counter**.

There's more...

Some improvements of the modular coin counter can be found in the following sections.

Removing coins

If in our game there is the possibility of losing coins, we can easily implement this feature by adding another function to our script:

```
public void removeCoins(int value){
    coins -= value;
    if (coins < 0)
        coins = 0;
    updateCoinCounter ();
}
```

The first line subtracted the value to the `coins` variable; then the `if` statement checks whether we have a negative coin number and, if so, set the coins variable to zero. Finally, we called our `update` function.

Adding score if the number of lives has reached the maximum

It may happen that the player has reached the maximum amount of lives that he is able to have, and if he reaches 100 coins, it would be unkind not give him a reward. In this case, we can reward him in another way. If we also did the score counter, we can give him some score points so that he doesn't lose the coins gained. Therefore, we need to change the `ApplyModularity()` function in the following way:

```
private void ApplyModularity(){
    coins -= maxCoins;
    if (!GameObject.Find ("LivesCounter").GetComponent<LivesCounterScr
ipt> ().addLife ())
        GameObject.Find ("ScoreCounter").GetComponent<ScoreCounterScri
pt> ().addPoints (230);
}
```

Since the `addLife()` function returns `true` if a life is added or `false` if it is not, we can put it inside an `if` statement with a negation. Therefore, if the life is not added, the next line of code is executed. In fact, this adds 230 score points to the player, in the same way we have added a life, but instead of the `LivesCounter`, we search for `ScoreCounter`.

Getting the number of coins

If we need to retrieve the value of the `coins` variable for any reason, such as displaying them in a virtual shop, we will need to add a `get` function like the following one:

```
public intgetCoins(){
  return coins;
}
```

See also

> ▸ We can refer to the two previous recipes about how to implement a lives counter or a score counter.

> ▸ In addition, for more detail about the `get` function, please refer to the *Implementing a score counter* recipe, in the *There's more...* section.

Creating a symbolic lives counter

This recipe teaches us how to use multiple **Image (Script)** components inside a script in order to create a symbolic lives counter. The number of lives are not displayed as a number, but with heart symbols on the screen. It is similar to the counter in the *Implementing a lives counter* recipe, but the logic to manage different icons is different.

How to do it...

1. To begin, let's create a new empty game object. To do this, right-click on the **Canvas** object, since we want it as parent, and then **Create Empty**. Finally, rename it as **SymbolicLivesCounter**.

 If there isn't the **Canvas** object in the scene, for example, in new scenes, we can create it by right-clicking on **Hierarchy** panel and then go to **UI | Canvas**.

2. Next, click on **SymbolicLivesCounter** and add a new image by selecting **UI | Image**, and then rename the object just created as **Heart1**.

3. Take a heart icon image, or create on our own, and import it in to our project. If our project is not set as 2D, remember to set the **Texture Type** of the icon into **Sprite (2D and UI)** and then click on **Apply**.

4. Let's duplicate **Heart1** with *Ctr+D* as many times as the maximum amount of lives that the player will have. Rename them consecutively, such as **Heart1**, **Heart2**, **Heart3**, and so on. In this example, we have five hearts, and so in the **Hierarchy** panel, we should have the following:

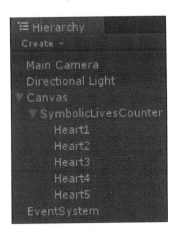

5. Distribute them in the **Scene View**, keeping their order. For example, **Heart2** must be after **Heart1** and before **Heart3**. This order is important because the script that we are going to write uses this order. The following is an image of the correct way to order your hearts:

6. In the **SymbolicLivesCounter**, go to **Add Component | New Script** and name it **SymbolicLivesCounterScript**, and then press **Create and Add**.

7. Double-click on the script to edit it. This time, the `using UnityEngine.UI;` statement at the beginning of the script it is not needed since we will not use any UI classes.

8. Before we add any functions, we need a two variables, one `private` and one `public`, to set this last one in the **Inspector** so that we can write:

```
public GameObject[] hearts;
private int lives;
```

9. In the `Start()` function, we need to set up the lives value, so:

```
void Start () {
   lives = hearts.Length;
}
```

10. As in the *Implementing a lives counter* recipe, we need to write a function to `addLife()`, and also here there is a return value to understand if the life is added or not. The function is as follows:

```
public booladdLife(){
   if (lives <hearts.Length) {
      lives++;
      updateSymbolicLivesCounter();
      return true;
   }
   return false;
}
```

11. And now the `loseLife()` function, again with a return value to check whether the player has finished his life:

```
public boolloseLife(){
   lives--;
   if (lives > 0) {
      updateSymbolicLivesCounter();
      return false;
   }
   lives = 0;
   updateSymbolicLivesCounter();
   return true;
}
```

12. Finally, we need to update our `updateSymbolicLivesCounter()` function. Here the logic is different from the *Implementing a lives counter* recipe. According to the number of lives, we have to either enable or disable the hearts. The following is the function to achieve this:

```
private void updateSymbolicLivesCounter () {
   for (int i=0; i<hearts.Length; i++) {
```

```
     if(i<lives){
        hearts[i].SetActive(true);
     }else{
        hearts[i].SetActive(false);
     }
   }
}
```

13. Let's save the script, but keep in mind that we haven't finish yet. We will have to set up the hearts in the **Inspector**.

14. Now, inside the **Inspector**, set the size of the hearts variable to **5**, then link each **Heart1**, **Heart2**, and so on to fill the array. At the end, you should have something that looks like the following:

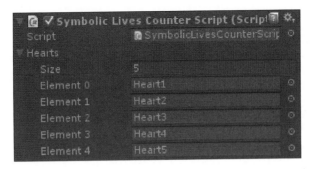

15. Now the **Symbolic Lives Counter** is ready.

How it works...

We have created several hearts icons inside a **GameObject** named **Symbolic Lives Counter**. Finally, we have attached our script to it.

In our script, we have two variables. The first one is an array of game object, called hearts, and as the name suggests us, it will store all the hearts contained in the **Symbolic Lives Counter**. The second one is the number of lives possessed by the player.

This time, we didn't have a variable that stores the maximum number of lives allowed. So, in the `Start()` function, we set the `lives` variable to be equal to the length of the array. Since we will set it in the **Inspector** and it contains all the hearts in the scene, its length represents the maximum number of lives allowed.

Furthermore, we have also written a function called `addLife()` that adds lives to the player that returns back a Boolean value: `true` if a life is added, otherwise `false` if the number of lives is equal to the maximum number of lives allowed and the function. It is quite similar to its homonymous function in implementing a lives counter. In fact, at the beginning, there is an `if` statement that checks whether lives are less than the hearts.Length, which is the maximum number of lives. If so, we increase the lives by one, `lives++;`, then we call `updateSymbolicLivesCounter()` function to update the interface, and, finally, we return `true`, otherwise we just return `false`.

Now, we also have a function for `loseLife()`.This function returns back a Boolean value: `true` if the player has no more lives, otherwise `false`. First, we decrease the number of lives by one, `lives--;`, then we check to see whether lives are more than zero, and, if so, we call the `updateSymbolicLivesCounter()` function to update the interface and finally, we return `false`. Otherwise, we set `lives = 0;` since we don't want a negative number of lives, and, after `updateSymbolicLivesCounter()`, we return `true`.

In the `updateSymbolicLivesCounter()` function, we have to set active or no each heart. In order to do so, we have a for-cycle for every entries of the hearts array. Then, there is an `if` statement that checks if the number of lives is more than the heart of that iteration. For example, if the player has just three lives left, we only want to display the first three hearts on screen and not the last two. Therefore, we enable only the first three hearts, and if there are no hearts in the array, we disable them.

In the last step, we assigned each heart objects to the entries of our hearts array.

See also

> ▸ See *Animating hearts of the symbolic lives counter* and *Changing animation of the hearts of the symbolic lives counter through script* recipes in *Chapter 6, Animating the UI* for animating the hearts on this counter.

Implementing a linear health bar

In this recipe, we are going to create a linear health bar. The health of the player will be displayed as a bar that shortens when the player's health decreases, and extends with the player's health increases. To achieve this, we will use the **Image (Script)** component in a different way than what we have in previous recipes, and develop a script to manage the length of the bar.

How to do it...

1. First of all, we need to create our health bar, so let's open a graphic program and create it. We can create something that should looks like the following:

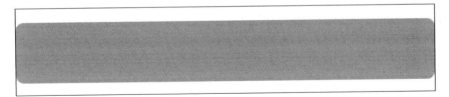

2. Then, import it in to our project. If the project isn't set to 2D, remember to set the **Texture Type** of the imported image to **Sprite (2D and UI)**, and then click on **Apply**.

3. Next, create a new Image. Right-click on the **Hierarchy** panel and then **UI | Image**, and rename it to **Linear Healthbar**.

4. Inside the **Image (Script)** component, we have to change **Image Type** into **Filled**. The component should change a little bit in the **Inspector**.

5. Let's change **Fill Method** into **Horizontal** and **Fill Origin** into **Left**. Of course, we need to add to **Source Image** the health bar that we have created. Finally, we can place the **Linear Healthbar** everywhere we want, always using the **Rect Tool**.

6. In order to keep its original proportion, you can click on **Set Native Size** button on the **Inspector**.

7. The following is how the component should appear:

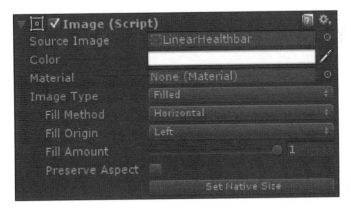

8. Now, in the **Linear Healthbar,** go to **Add Component | New Script** and name it **HealthbarScript**, and then press **Create and Add**.

9. Double-click on the script to edit it and add the `using UnityEngine.UI;` statement at the beginning of the script, since we will use the `Image` class.

10. Before we add any functions, we need a three variables, two `private` and one `public`, so we can set this last one in the **Inspector**. Hence, we can write the following:

```
private Image healthbarFilling;
public intmaxHealth = 100;
private int health;
```

11. In the `Start()` function, we have to set the `health` variable along with the `healthbarFilling` one, thus:

```
void Start () {
  healthbarFilling = this.GetComponent<Image> ();
  health = maxHealth;
}
```

12. As usual, we need a function for add health, so let's write the following:

```
public void addHealth(int value){
  health += value;
  if (health >maxHealth)
    health = maxHealth;
  updateHealth ();
}
```

13. And also, we need to write a `removeHealth(int value)` function:

```
public boolremoveHealth(int value){
  health -= value;
  if (health <= 0){
    health = 0;
    updateHealth ();
    return true;
  }
  updateHealth ();
  return false;
}
```

14. Next, we need to add our `updateHealth()` function to update the health bar on the screen:

```
private void updateHealth(){
  healthbarFilling.fillAmount = health / maxHealth;
}
```

15. Finally, just save the script and we are done.

How it works...

First of all, we created our health bar in one of our graphic programs. After importing the image and setting it to be a **Sprite (2D and UI)**, we created a new image and set its **Fill Method** to **Horizontal** so that the image can disappear or appear gradually, as the health goes down or increases. Finally, we implemented a script for the logic.

Inside it, we have created three variables. The first one is `healthbarFilling` and, as usual, it stores the reference to the **Image (Script)** component. The variable `maxHealth = 100` is the max health that the player can have, and we can set its value in the **Inspector**, but as default in our script, it has `100` as value. Finally, the `health` variable contains the health currently possessed by the player.

In the `Start()` function, we first assigned the **Image (Script)** component attached in the same game object of this script to the `healthbarFilling` variable by calling the `this.GetComponent<Image>()` function. Finally, we set `health` equals to `maxHealth`.

Furthermore, we have written a function to `addHealth(int value)` to the player. It takes an `int` as a parameter, and this `int` is the number of health points that will be added to the player. In fact, at the beginning, we add value to the `health` variable by `health += value`. Then, there is an `if` statement that checks if the health is more than `maxHealth` and, if so, set the health equals to `maxHealth`. At the end, we called our `updateHealth()` function in order to update the UI.

We also have a function to `removeHealth(int value)` from the player that returns back a Boolean value: `true` if the player has no more health, otherwise it returns `false`. The first line subtracts the value to the `health` variable, then the `if` statement checks to see whether we have negative health and, if so, set the `health` variable to zero and, after `updateHealth()`, we return `true`. Otherwise, we call our `update` function and return `false`.

At the end, we have the `updateHealth()` function, in which we put the ratio between `health` and `maxHealth` into the `Fill Amount` variable contained into **Image (Script)** component in the **Linear Healthbar**. In fact, the ratio is the percentage of how much health has the player and also how much longer our health bar should be.

There's more...

We can also consider adding a new image in the scene that encloses the health bar in some graphic elements, such as an artistic border, which also underlines the importance of this UI element. This book does not cover how to do this; however, there are many resources available online that can provide information on how to do this, as well as other UI elements.

See also

▶ For more complex health bars, see *Implementing a radial health bar, Creating a health bar with armor, Using multiple bars to make a multibar*, and *Developing a kingdom hearts health bar style* recipes, all included in this chapter.

Implementing a radial health bar

In this recipe, we are going to create a radial health bar. The health of the player will be displayed as a ring that reduces circularly when health decreases and fills with increasing health. To achieve this, we will use the **Image (Script)** component and develop a script to manage the length of the bar.

How to do it...

1. First of all, we need to create our ring, so let's open a graphic program and create it. It should look like the following:

2. Then, import it in to our project and, if the project isn't set to 2D, set the **Texture Type** of the image to **Sprite (2D and UI)**, and then click on **Apply**.

3. Next, create a new image, so right-click on the **Hierarchy** panel and then **UI | Image**, and, finally, rename it **Radial Healthbar**.

4. Selecting inside the **Image (Script)** component we need to change **Image Type** into **Filled**. The component should change appearance a little bit in the **Inspector**.

5. Ensure that **Fill Method** is set on **Radial 360** and **Fill Origin** on **Bottom**.

6. Since the logic is the same of the previous recipe, we have only to add the **HelathBarScript** created before. To learn how to create it, please refer to *Implementing a linear health bar* recipe. Now, **our Radial Healthbar** is ready to use.

How it works...

First of all, we created our ring in a graphic programs. After importing the image and setting it to be a **Sprite (2D and UI)**, if needed, we created a new image and this time set its **Fill Method** to **Radial**, so the image can disappear or appear gradually, as the health goes down or increases, in a 360° radius. Finally, we added the **HealthBarScript** created in the *Implementing a linear health bar* recipe.

There's more...

The following section provide us another way to let designers to customize the bar in our game.

Having a health bar that isn't necessarily 360°

In order to change how many degrees are between the beginning and the end of the health bar. To do this, let's add a variable to our script called `startingFilling` and set it as `float`:

```
public float startingFilling = 1;
```

Now, take the following line in our function:

```
healthbarFilling.fillAmount = health / maxHealth;
```

Substitute the preceding line with the following:

```
healthbarFilling.fillAmount = (health /
maxHealth)*startingFilling;
```

We multiply the `startingFilling` variable to scale the `health / maxHealth` ratio on the new shorten bar. By doing this, if we want the bar starting at 3/4, we can just set **startingFilling** in the **Inspector** to **0.75**. But remember to not insert a value bigger than 1 in the **startingFilling** variable.

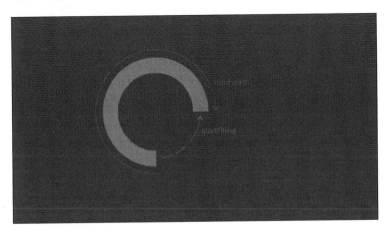

See also

▶ If we want learn how to create the **HealthBarScript**, we can refer to *Implementing a linear health bar* recipe.

▶ For more complex health bars, see *Implementing a linear health bar, Creating a health bar with armor, Using multiple bars to make a multibar*, and *Developing a kingdom hearts health bar style* recipes, all included in this chapter.

Creating a health bar with armor

In this recipe, we are going to create a health bar, similar to the one in *Implementing a linear health bar* recipe, but there is an armor that protects the player. In fact, if the player is attacked, he or she will first lose the armor, then the health. To achieve this, we will use multiple **Image (Script)** components, both for the health bar and for the pieces of armor, and develop a script to manage the entire logic.

How to do it...

1. To begin, let's create an image, so right-click on the **Hierarchy** panel and then **UI | Image**, and rename it **HealthBar with Armor**.

2. Let's change **Fill Method** into **Horizontal** and **Fill Origin** into **Left**. Of course, we need to add the **Healthbar** that we have just created to **Source Image**. Finally, we can place the **Healthbar with Armor** everywhere we want, always using the **Rect Tool**.

3. In order to keep its original proportion, you can click on the **Set Native Size** button in the **Inspector**.

4. Next, right-click on **Healthbar with Armor** and add a new image by selecting **UI | Image**, and again rename the object just created as **Armor1**.

5. Take an icon image to represent the pieces of the armor, or create on our own, and import it in our project. If our project is not set to 2D, remember to set the **Texture Type** of the icon to **Sprite (2D and UI)**, and then click on **Apply**.

6. Let's duplicate **Armor1** with *Ctrl+D* as many times as lives the player will have. Rename them consecutively, such as **Armor1, Armor2, Armor3**, and so on.

7. Distribute them in the **Scene View** while also keeping their order. For instance, **Armor2** must be after **Armor1** and before **Armor3**. This order is important because the script that we are going to write uses this order.

8. Now, in the **Healthbar with Armor**, click on **Add Component | New Script** and name it **HealthbarWithArmorScript**, and then press **Create and Add**.

9. Double-click on the script to edit it. Since we are going to use the `Image` class, we need to add the `using UnityEngine.UI;` statement at the beginning of the script.

10. Before to add any functions, we need five variables, three `private` and two `public`, so that we can set these last ones in the **Inspector**. Therefore, we can write:

```
public GameObject[] armor;
private intpiecesOfArmor;
private Image healthbarFilling;
public intmaxHealth = 100;
private int health;
```

11. In the `Start ()` function, we have to set up our variables, so let's write:

```
void Start () {
   healthbarFilling = this.GetComponent<Image> ();
   health = maxHealth;
   piecesOfArmor = armor.Length;
}
```

12. If the player loses his pieces of armor, there should be a way to regenerate them. We can achieve this by creating the following function:

```
public void addArmor(){
   if (piecesOfArmor<armor.Length) {
     piecesOfArmor++;
     updateArmor();
   }
}
```

13. Next, we need to write the `damage(int value)` function that takes how many health points are taken away from the damage that is applied to the player as a parameter:

```
public bool damage(int value){
   if (piecesOfArmor> 0) {
     piecesOfArmor--;
     updateArmor();
     return false;
   }else{
     return damageIgnoringArmor(value);
   }
}
```

14. Furthermore, it could be helpful to have also a function to applied damage ignoring the armor of the player. This is used in games, for instance, for some magic attacks, which hit the player directly. Thus, we can have the following function:

```
public booldamageIgnoringArmor(int value){
   health -= value;
   if (health <= 0){
     health = 0;
```

```
        updateHealthbar ();
        return true;
    }
    updateHealthbar ();
    return false;
}
```

15. As we have functions to damage the player, we should also have functions to regenerate life to the player. Therefore, we need to write an addHealth(int value) function, which takes as parameter how many health points will be restored to the player health. The following is the function:

```
public void addHealth(int value){
    health += value;
    if (health >maxHealth)
        health = maxHealth;
    updateHealthbar ();
}
```

16. Instead of the other recipes that we have seen so far, we need two update function, one for the health and one for the armor. The following one is for the health:

```
public void updateHealthbar(){
    healthbarFilling.fillAmount = health / maxHealth;
}
```

17. And this other one is for the armor:

```
public void updateArmor(){
    for (int i=0; i<armor.Length; i++) {
        if(i<piecesOfArmor){
            armor[i].SetActive(true);
        }else{
            armor[i].SetActive(false);
        }
    }
}
```

18. To finish, save our work. We only need to assign the pieces of the armor into the entries of the armor variable, as we did with *Implementing a symbolic lives counter* recipe.

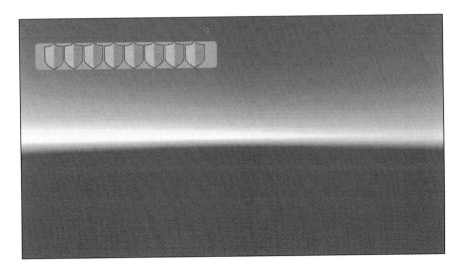

How it works...

We have created a linear health bar and named **Healthbar with Armor**. Then, we created different pieces of armor. Then, we attached our script to **Healthbar with Armor**.

In the script, we have created five variables. The first one is `healthbarFilling` and it stores the reference to the **Image (Script)** component. `maxHealth = 100` is the max health that the player can have, and we can set its value in the **Inspector**, but as default in our script, it has a value of `100`. Furthermore, the `health` variable contains the health currently possessed by the player. The `armor` variable is an array of game object and it will store all the pieces of armor contained in the **Healthbar with Armor**. Finally, the `piecesOfArmor` variable stores the number of pieces of armor currently possessed by the player.

In the `Start()` function, we set up some variables. In the `healthbarFilling` variable, we store the **Image (Script)** component attached in the same game object of this script by calling the `this.GetComponent<Image>()` function. Then, we set the health variable equal to `maxHealth`. Finally, we haven't created a `public` variable that stores the maximum number of pieces of armor directly, so we set the `piecesOfArmor` variable equal to the length of the `armor` array, and since we will set this array in the **Inspector**, it contains all the pieces of armor in the scene. Therefore, its length represents how many pieces of armor there are on this health bar.

The `addArmor()` function increases the `piecesOfArmor` variable by one if it has not reached the maximum amount allowed. Then, it calls the `updateArmor()` function.

The `damage(int value)` function includes the parameter of how many health points will be taken away from the player after the damage is applied. In fact, it first checks whether the player has some `piecesOfArmor`, and, if so, decreases it by one, independently from the parameter value and, after calling the `updateArmor()` function, returns `false`; this means that the player is still alive. Otherwise, it will call the `damageIgnoringArmor(int value)` function passing value as a parameter.

The `damageIgnoringArmor(int value)` function includes the parameter of how many health points will remain when the damage applied. Then, it decreases health by value and checks to see whether the player is still alive. If the player is still alive, it will return `false`, otherwise return `true`. After this, the `updateHealthbar()` function is called to update the user interface.

There is also a function to `addHealth(int value)` to the player. It increases health by value, if it exceeds `maxHealth`, then it set `health` equal to `maxHealth`, and, finally, calls the `updateHealthbar()` function to update the user interface.

In the `updateHealthbar()` function, we set `healthbarFilling` equal to the ratio between `health` and `maxHealth`.

Finally, in the `updateArmor()` function, we set active or no each pieces of armor according to the `piecesOfArmor` variable, through a for-cycle, very similar to the one in *Implementing a linear health bar* recipe.

As last step, we assigned each pieces of armor we have created to the entries of our armor array.

See also

- If the design of our game doesn't require a health bar with an armor, we should have a look at *Implementing a linear health bar* and *Implementing a radial health bar* recipes.
- For other kind of health bars, see *Using multiple bars to make a multibar* and *Developing a kingdom hearts health bar style*.

Using multiple bars to make a multibar

In this recipe, we are going to create a very special kind of health bar, since we are combining multiple bars of *Implementing a linear health bar* type together. This may be the case when the player has to face a boss in our game who has multiple health bars. Once the player reduced one health bar to zero, there is another one behind .To achieve this, we will use multiple **Image (Script)** components, one for each health bar, along with a script to manage all these bars within only one health points system.

How to do it...

1. To begin, let's create a new empty game object. Right-click on **Canvas** object, since we want it as a parent, and then **Create Empty**. Finally, rename it to **MultiBar**.

 If there isn't the **Canvas** object in the scene, for example, in new scenes, we can create it by right-clicking on **Hierarchy** panel and then go to **UI | Canvas**.

2. Now, right-click on **Multibar** and add a new image by selecting **UI | Image**, and again rename the object just created as **HealthBar1**.

3. Take an image for a linear health bar; we can use the one created in *Implementing a linear health bar* recipe.

4. Import it in to our project. If this one is not set in 2D, remember to set the **Texture Type** of the image to **Sprite (2D and UI)**, and then click on **Apply**.

5. Let's change **Fill Method** into **Horizontal** and **Fill Origin** into **Left**. Of course, we have to add to **Source Image** the health bar that we have imported. Finally, we can place the **HealthBar1** everywhere we want, always using the **Rect Tool**.

6. Let's duplicate **HealthBar1** with *Ctrl+D* as many times as health bars the player will have. Rename them also in progression, such as **HealthBar1**, **HealthBar2**, **HealthBar3**, and so on.

7. As next step, we need to differentiate them. The easiest way to do this is to change their colors. Otherwise, we can even import different images and assign them to all the health bars.

8. Place them in order to have one above the other in the **Scene View**, keeping their order: **HealthBar2** must be after **HealthBar1** and before **HealthBar3**. This order is important because the script we are going to write will use this order.

9. Now, in the **Multibar**, click on **Add Component | New Script** and name it **MultibarScript**, and then press **Create and Add**.

10. Double click on the script to edit it and, as always, add the `using UnityEngine.UI;` statement at the beginning of the script. By doing this, we can use UI classes inside our script.

11. Before to add functions, we need a couple of variables, one `private` and two `public`, so we can set these last ones in the **Inspector**. Thus, the following are the variables:

```
public Image[] bars;
public intmaxHealth = 1000;
private int health;
```

12. In the `Start()` function, we need to set up the `health`, therefore:

```
void Start () {
   health = maxHealth;
}
```

13. Our script should include an `addHealth(int value)` function that takes how many health points will be added to the player health as a parameter. So we can add the following:

```
public void addHealth(int value){
   health += value;
   if (health >maxHealth)
     health = maxHealth;
   updateMultibar ();
}
```

14. A `removeHealth(int value)` function should also be included so that the boss of our game can be damaged:

```
public boolremoveHealth(int value){
   health -= value;
   if (health <= 0){
     health = 0;
     updateMultibar ();
     return true;
   }
   updateMultibar ();
   return false;
}
```

15. Now, the most difficult part of the script is to design our `update` function. In fact, we need to pay attention to how we can fill every bar correctly given only one health points system. But we can do it the following way:

```
private void updateMultibar () {
   float absolute = health*1f/maxHealth;
   float perBars = 1f / bars.Length;
   for (int i=0; i<bars.Length; i++) {
     float minrange = i*perBars;
     float maxrange = (i+1)*perBars;
     if(absolute >minrange){
       if(absolute <maxrange){
         bars[i].fillAmount = (absolute-minrange)*bars.Length;
       }else{
         bars[i].fillAmount = 1;
       }
```

```
        }else{
          bars[i].fillAmount = 0;
        }
      }
    }
```

16. Save our work. Then, we have to assign the health bars to the bars array variable in the **Inspector** by dragging each health bar in the entry of the array. Remember to maintain the order.

17. Finally, the work is done! During a gameplay session we could get the following scenario, in which the health is slightly reduced and it is therefore possible to see the other bar under the first one.

How it works...

We have created several health bars inside a game object named **Multibar**. Then, we developed a script to handle all of this bars.

Inside this script, we have created three variables. The first one is an array of image called bars, and it will store all the bars contained in the **Multibar**. The second is maxHealth = 100 and it is the max health that the player can have; we can set its value in the **Inspector**, but as default in our script, it has 1000 as value. Furthermore, the third is health and it contains the amount of health that is currently possessed by the player.

In the Start() function, we have made health equal to maxHealth. This will ensure that at the beginning, whichever character has this health bar will start with all the health.

We have also created a function to `addHealth(int value)` to the player. It increases health by value, if it exceeds, `maxHealth` set `health` equals to `maxHealth`. This is because we cannot have more health the maximum. Finally, we have called the `updateMultibar()` function to update the user interface.

Then, we developed a function to `removeHealth(int value)` that has a parameter, which determines how many health points are removed from the character that has this **Multibar**. This function decreases the health by value and checks whether the player is still alive. If he or she is, it will return `false`, otherwise it will return `true`. But before we return a value, in both branches, the function calls the `updateMultibar()` function in order to update the users interface.

Finally, we have written the `updateMultibar()` function. Here, we had to set every single bar to the right proportion. To begin, we created a couple of variables. The absolute stores the ratio between `health` and `maxHeath`. The `perBars` stores how much, in percentage, every bar represents the health. Then, we use a for-cycle to set every bar to the right proportion. For every bar, we set up two variables. One is the `minRange` and the other is the `maxRange`, displayed as a percentage of where that bar is collocated if every bar is concatenated to be only one long bar. Now, if the absolute is more than this range, the `fillAmount` of that bar is set to `1`. If the absolute is less than that range, the `fillAmount` variable of that bar is set to `0`. Otherwise, the absolute is inside the range, and we set the `fillAmount` variable of that bar to its relative percentage, that is, `(absolute-minrange)*bars.Length`.

Before running the game, we assigned each bar that we have created to the entries of our bars array so that our script can have the right reference to them.

See also

▸ If the design of our game doesn't fit with a **Multibar**, we can refer to *Implementing a linear health bar* and *Implementing a radial health bar*.

▸ For other kinds of health bars, see *Creating a health bar with armor* and *Developing a kingdom hearts health bar style* recipes.

Developing a kingdom hearts health bar style

In this recipe, we are going to create a very special kind of health bar, since we are combining the linear bar of *Implementing a linear health bar* with the radial one of *Implementing a radial health bar* in order to create a kingdom hearts health bar style. This style is like a typical horizontal health bar that is rounded at the end. To have a better idea, let's have a quick glance at the picture ahead of this recipe.

How to do it...

1. To begin, let's create a new empty game object, so right-click on **Canvas** object, since we want it as parent, and then **Create Empty**. Lastly, rename it as **KHHealthbar**.

> If there isn't the **Canvas** object in the scene, for example, in new scenes, we can create it by right-clicking on **Hierarchy** panel and then **UI | Canvas**.

2. Next, right-click on **KHHealthbar** and add a new image by selecting **UI | Image**, and again rename the object just created as **Linear Part**.

3. Repeat the previous step and rename the new image to **Radial Part**.

4. Create one image for the linear part of the health bar and another for the radial part.

> We can use also the image used in *Implementing a linear health bar* and *Implementing a radial health bar* recipes.

5. Then, import them in to our project. If it is not set in 2D, remember to set the **Texture Type** of the images to **Sprite (2D and UI)**, and then click on **Apply**.

6. For **Linear Part**, let's change **Fill Method** into **Horizontal** and **Fill Origin** into **Left**. Of course, we need to add to **Source Image** the health bar that we have imported.

7. For **Radial Part**, let's change **Fill Method** into **Radial 360** and **Fill Origin** into **Left**. Again, we need to add to **Source Image** the health bar that we have imported. Finally, set **Fill Amount** to **0.75**.

8. Place them in order, and now we should see something that looks like the following:

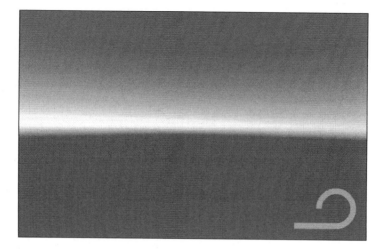

9. Now, in the **KHHealthbar**, click on **Add Component | New Script** and name it as **KHHealthbarScript**, and then press **Create and Add**.

10. Double click on the script to edit it. Since we are going to use UI classes, we need to add the using `UnityEngine.UI;` statement at the beginning of the script.

11. We need four variables, one `private` and three `public`, so we can set these last ones in the **Inspector**. The following are the variables:

```
public Image linearBar;
public Image radialBar;
public intmaxHealth = 1000;
private int health;
```

12. In the `Start()` function, we need to set up the health so that at the beginning it is equal to the maximum:

```
void Start () {
   health = maxHealth;
}
```

13. Then, we can add a function to `addHealth(int value)` to the player, which takes how many health points will be added to the player's health as a parameter. Hence, let's write it:

```
public void addHealth(int value){
   health += value;
   if (health >maxHealth)
     health = maxHealth;
   updateKHHealthbar ();
}
```

14. Since there must be a way to apply a damage, we should add a `removeHealth(int value)` function, as the following one:

```
public boolremoveHealth(int value){
    health -= value;
    if (health <= 0){
        health = 0;
        updateKHHealthbar ();
        return true;
    }
    updateKHHealthbar ();
    return false;
}
```

15. Now, the most difficult part of the script is to design our update function. In fact, we have to be careful to make sure that we properly fill the two health bars. On the contrary of the previous script, our main issue is that the radial part of the bar starts it's filling from `0.75` and not from `1`, and also it represents 3/5 of the health and not 1/2. But we can face this in the following way:

```
private void updateKHHealthbar () {
    float ratio = health*1f / maxHealth;
    Debug.Log (ratio);
    if (ratio > 0.6) {
        linearBar.fillAmount = (ratio - 0.6f) * 2.5f;
        radialBar.fillAmount = 0.75f;
    } else {
        linearBar.fillAmount = 0;
        radialBar.fillAmount = 0.75f *ratio * 10f / 6f;
    }
}
```

16. Save our work. Then, we need to assign the two health bars to the `linearBar` and `radialBar` variables in the **Inspector** by dragging the **Linear Part** and the **Radial Part** in their own variables.

17. Finally, the work is done!

How it works...

We started by creating two health bars: one linear and the other one radial. Then, we can parent them to a **GameObject** called **KHHealthbar**. Furthermore, we have set them to look like the kingdom hearts health bar style. Finally, we have implemented our logic within the script.

Inside the script, we have created four variables. The first two are image, called `linearBar` and `radialBar`, and they will store the **Image (Script)** component attached on `LinearPart` and `RadialPart`, respectively. `maxHealth = 1000` is the max health that the player can have: we can set its value in the **Inspector**, but in our script, `1000` is set as the default value. Furthermore, the `health` variable contains the health currently possessed by the player.

In the `Start()` function, we have set up `health` equal to `maxHealth`. This ensure us that at the beginning, whoever (or whatever) will have this health bar will start with full health.

We have also created a function to `addHealth(int value)` to the player. It increases health by value, and if it exceeds `maxHealth`, it sets `health` equals to `maxHealth`. Finally, it calls the `updateKHHealthbar()` function to update the user interface.

Moreover, we also need to have a function to `removeHealth(int value)` from the player. The function takes how many health points have to be removed as a parameter. Then, it decreases health by value and checks whether the player is still alive. If he or she is, the function will return `false`, otherwise it will return `true`. Before a value is returned, in both branches, it calls the `updateKHHealthbar()` function to update the user interface.

Finally, we have written the `updateKHHealthbar()` function. All the numbers that we are going to see in the script are set up in order to give to the **Linear Part** the 2/5 of the health of the player, and to the **Radial Part** the 3/5 of the health. We created a ratio variable and store in it the ratio between `health` and `maxHealth`. Then, check through an `if` statement whether the ratio is more than 3/5 for performance in the script `0.6`. If so, we set the `fillAmount` of `linearBar` to the proportion of how long the bar should be, which in this case is `(ratio - 0.6f) * 2.5f`, and the `fillAmount` of `radialBar` to its maximum filling, that is, `0.75`. Otherwise, we set the `fillAmount` of `linearBar` to zero and the `fillAmount` of `radialBar` to the proportion of how long the bar should be. In this case, `ratio * 10f / 6f` and then also multiply for `0.75f` since its maximum filling is `0.75`.

As a last step, we assign `linearBar` and `radialBar` in the **Inspector** with **Linear Part** and **Radial Part**, respectively.

See also

- If the design of our game doesn't fit with a kingdom hearts heatlhbar style, we can refer to *Implementing a linear heath bar* and *Implementing a radial heath bar* recipes.
- For other kinds of health bars, see *Creating a health bar with armor* and *Using multiple bars to make a multibar* recipes.

3
Implementing Timers

In this chapter, we will cover these recipes:

- ▶ Implementing a numeric timer
- ▶ Creating a linear timer
- ▶ Implementing a radial timer
- ▶ Creating a mixed timer
- ▶ Creating a well-formatted timer
- ▶ Developing a well-formatted countdown that changes

Introduction

In this chapter, we are going to implement different kinds of timers and countdowns. These serve many different purposes in games, such as indicating to the player how much time he has left to complete a level or after how long he will be able to use a certain ability again. Timers are also a good way for players to experience flow throughout the game. On the other hand, countdowns can indicate how much time is remaining to complete a task, depending on the aspect of gameplay that we are trying to represent with a timer — for example, to let a player know how much time is remaining to complete a task, or how much time has elapsed since the task began. Both timers and countdowns are effective methods of altering the dynamics of gameplay.

We will begin this chapter by seeing how to create a numeric timer. From this, you will learn how to create graphic timers and, finally, how to implement a countdown that changes over time.

Implementing a numeric timer

In this recipe, we are going to create a timer that displays the time (as a number) on the screen. This may be a useful element when attempting to inform the player how much time has passed during an objective. In some cases, if the player is aware of how much time he is taking with a task, it may encourage him to be more efficient and considerate about his choices throughout the gameplay. To create a timer, we will use the **Text (Script)** component as well as develop a script to implement the logic of the timer.

How to do it...

1. First of all, we need to create a new UI text to show our timer. To do this, right-click on the **Hierarchy** panel and then navigate to **UI | Text**. Next, rename it to **Numeric Timer**.

2. We can change the **Font** and the **Font Size** fields as we wish so that they suit our needs.

3. We can also adjust **Color**. In this recipe, we will set the color to light gray, but feel free to change it to a color that better suits your design.

4. Now, we can drag **Numeric Timer** with **Rect Tool** where we want to place it. In some cases, it is important to make a timer properly to a player. In other instances, it is a nice, subtle addition to the UI.

5. To display the timer better in the scene view, we can write in the **Text** variable the word `time`, even if this value will be replaced by the script. This is so that we have a better approximation of how it will look. This will help us to better gauge whether its placement will be effective or will inhibit or distract the player during gameplay.

6. Next, we want to ensure that the **Rich Text** variable is checked. This is important in order to display the color of the text and also for us to observe the appearance of the timer within the game space.

7. Then, we have to create a script that manages the time. To do this, navigate to **Add Component | New Script**, then name it **NumericTimerScript**, and finally click on **Create and Add**.

8. Double-click on the script to edit it and, as always, add the `using UnityEngine.UI;` statement at the beginning of the script. This allows us to handle the UI elements within the script.

9. Before we add any functions to the timer, we need to add two variables and make sure that we set them to `private`. So, we can write this:

```
private Text uiText;
private floattime;
```

10. Next, we can set up the `uiText` variable in the `Start()` function. In fact, this is the ideal function for assigning the initial value to our variables, since it is called when the script runs for the first time in the game environment. Therefore, we can assign the reference to the **Text (Script)** component to the variable just before the timer starts, in the following way:

```
void Start () {
    uiText = this.GetComponent<Text> ();
}
```

11. Now, we need to update our timer for each frame. This can be done by writing the following lines in the `Update()` function:

```
void Update () {
    time += Time.deltaTime;
    uiText.text = "<color=blue>Time</color>: " + time.
ToString("F2");
}
```

12. Finally, we can save the script and the work is done. When we run the script, we should see something like this:

How it works...

First of all, we created a new UI text, and then adjusted it to suit our needs. We changed **Font**, **Font Size**, and also **Color**. In addition, we ensured that **Rich Text** was checked. In this way, it is possible to use different colors in the text of the timer. Then, we wrote a script to handle the timer.

In the script, there are two private variables: `uiText` and `time`. The `uiText` variable stores the reference to the **Text (Script)** component, so we can get access to it and modify its text. The `time` variable stores the amount of time that has passed since the timer started.

In the `Start()` function, we assigned the reference to the **Text (Script)** component, which is attached to the same game object of this script, to the `uiText` variable by calling the `this.GetComponent<Text>()` function.

Keeping in mind that the `Update()` function is called at every frame, we added `Time.deltaTime`, which is the time that has elapsed from the last frame to the `time` variable. We did this to accumulate the time that has passed since this script/timer started. In the second line, we updated the `text` variable on the **Text (Script)** component, which we can have access to through the `uiText` variable, with the new time value. Since we don't want all the decimal points, we have to change it to `float` by calling `ToString("F2")` on it.

There's more...

The next section will teach us how to retrieve the value of our variable.

Getting the time variable

For some reason, we may want to retrieve the value of the `time` variable, such as when we want to trigger an event in our game environment, or pass its value to another script. We can achieve this by implementing a `get` function, like this:

```
public float getTime(){
    return time;
}
```

See also

- For more details about the `get` function, refer to the *Implementing a score counter* recipe in *Chapter 2, Implementing Counters and Health Bars*, inside the *There's more...* section

- However, if you are looking for more information about rich text, the official documentation is the best place to visit at `http://docs.unity3d.com/Manual/StyledText.html`

Creating a linear timer

In this recipe, we are going to create a linear timer. In this instance, the timer is shown as a long bar that shortens over time. An example of this would be when we want a player to make a decision within a short period of time, such as during a dialog choice to progress the narrative. In this case, the timer may feature above or even below the choices to indicate the amount of time that the player has left to decide. To achieve this, we will use the **Image (Script)** component and develop a script to manage the length of the bar according to the time remaining.

How to do it...

1. First of all, we need to create a bar for our timer. To do this, we can open a graphics program to create it. Alternatively, we can just use the bar that we created in the *Implementing a linear heath bar* recipe in the previous chapter.

2. Next, we need to import the bar into our project and set **Texture Type** to **Sprite (2D and UI)** so that it can be set as **Source Image** in our UI components. Then click on **Apply**. Of course, this is not needed if our project is set to work in 2D mode.

3. Now, we can create a new UI image inside Unity. To do this, right-click on the **Hierarchy** panel and then navigate to **UI | Image**. Next, rename it to **Linear Timer**.

4. Inside the **Image (Script)** component, we have to change **Image Type** to **Filled**. As a result, we can decide how much of the image is filled. Furthermore, the component should change a little in the **Inspector**.

5. Let's change **Fill Method** to **Horizontal** and **Fill Origin** to **Left**. Of course, we have to add the bar that we previously created to **Source Image**. Finally, we can place **Linear Timer** wherever we want, using **Rect Tool** or the keyboard shortcut *T*.

6. If we want to maintain the original proportion of the bar, we can click on the **Set Native Size** button in the **Inspector**.

7. Then, in **Linear Timer**, navigate to **Add Component | New Script**, name it **BarTimerScript**, and then click on **Create and Add**.

8. Double-click on the script to edit it and, as always, add the `using UnityEngine.UI;` statement at the beginning of the script. This ensures that we are able to manipulate the UI elements within the script.

9. Before we add any functions, we need three variables: two private and one public. We will set the last one in the **Inspector**. To do this, we can write the following code:

```
private Image barFilling;
public float timeAmount;
private float time;
```

10. In the `Start()` function, we have to set up the `time` variable along with the `barFilling` one, by adding these lines:

```
void Start () {
   barFilling = this.GetComponent<Image> ();
   time = timeAmount;
}
```

11. Finally, in our `Update()` function, we have to decrease the `time` variable by the time that has elapsed from the last frame, and update the filling of the bar so that it can reflect the amount of time that has elapsed. Therefore, we can script the following:

```
void Update () {
   if (time > 0) {
      time -= Time.deltaTime;
      barFilling.fillAmount = time / timeAmount;
   }
}
```

12. Now, once we have finished the script, we can save our work. If we click on play, we should have something that looks like this:

How it works...

After we have imported the image, we can set it to **Sprite (2D and UI)** (this is not needed if the project is in 2D). Next, we can change its **Fill Method** field to **Horizontal** and set **Fill Origin** to **Left** so that the image can disappear gradually as the time decreases, starting from the right-hand side.

Then, we have created three variables in our script. The first variable, `barFilling`, stores the reference to the **Image (Script)** component, which is attached in the same game object of this script. The second variable, `timeAmount`, is the starting value of time for the countdown, in seconds. Finally, the third variable, which is `time`, contains the time that is remaining.

In the `Start()` function, we first assigned the `barFilling` variable by calling the `this.GetComponent<Image>()` function. Then, we set the time to `timeAmount` so that the countdown begins with a specific starting time.

Finally, in the `Update()` function, we set the ratio between `time` and `timeAmount` to the `fillAmount` variable. This is contained in the **Image (Script)** component of **Linear Timer**. In fact, the ratio is the percentage of time left and also how much longer our linear timer should be.

There's more...

The first of the next two sections will explain to us how to improve our timer by running some code after the timer expires. The second one, instead, will give us an idea about how to quickly change the design of our timer.

Running code when the timer expires

In order for something to happen after the time has expired, such as loading the game on the screen, or triggering the sound of a closing door because the player shouldn't be able to reach it after the time limit, we have to add a new variable to our script:

```
private bool isOver;
```

Also, add an `else` branch inside the `Update()` function after the `if` statement, in the following way:

```
else{
  if(!isOver){
    isOver = true;
    //DO SOMETHING
  }
}
```

We use the `isOver` variable to trigger the time elapsed event only once after the time expires. In order to test it, we can write something in the debug console by calling this function:

```
Debug.log("Timer expired!");
```

Creating a double-sided timer

In some cases, we might want a timer that animates on both ends, adding intensity to the game by providing the player with a heightened sense of urgency. To achieve this, we can use two linear timers that are synchronized; just make one specular to the other.

See also

> ▸ For different kinds of timers or countdowns, refer to the *Implementing a numeric timer, Implementing a radial timer, Creating a mixed timer, Creating a well-formatted timer,* and *Developing a well-formatted countdown that changes* recipes, which are all contained in this chapter

Implementing a radial timer

In this recipe, we are going to create a radial timer. The time that is remaining will be displayed as a ring that reduces circularly over time. To achieve this, we will use the **Image (Script)** component, along with a script to manage the length of the circular bar. A timer like this can be useful when it is relating to something in particular. For instance, if a character has a special ability and we want the timer to represent the duration that the ability can be used for, a radial timer can be implemented. In this way, we are able to add an icon that then represents the ability. It can be centered in the middle of the radial timer, keeping the UI concentrated and contained.

How to do it...

1. First of all, we need to create a circular bar for our timer. We can do this by opening a graphics program to make it, or by implementing the one that we previously created in the *Implementing a radial heath bar* recipe in the previous chapter.

2. Next, import the bar into your project, and remember to set its **Texture Type** field to **Sprite (2D and UI)** (only if the project is not in 2D) in order to use it as part of the UI elements. Lastly, click on **Apply**.

3. Now, we need to create a new UI image. Right-click on the **Hierarchy** panel and then navigate to **UI | Image**. Rename it to **Radial Timer**.

4. Inside the **Image (Script)** component, we have to change **Image Type** to **Filled**. The component should change a little in the **Inspector**.

5. Ensure that **Fill Method** is set to **Radial 360** and **Fill Origin** to **Bottom**.

6. Since the logic is the same as that of the previous recipe, we only have to add **BarTimerScript** that we created before. This is because it contains what we need. To learn how to create it, you can refer to *Creating a linear timer* in the previous recipe.

7. After completing all of these steps, our radial timer is ready to use.

How it works...

First of all, you have either imported the image from the *Implementing a radial health bar* recipe or created a new one with a graphic program. If the project isn't in 2D, we have to set it to **Sprite (2D and UI)**. Then, we added a new UI image to the scene; this time, we set **Fill Method** to **Radial 360** and **Fill Origin** to **Bottom**. We did this so that the image can disappear or appear gradually in 360 degrees in an anticlockwise direction, starting from the bottom, according to the amount of time remaining. Finally, we attached **BarTimerScript** that we developed in the *Creating a linear timer* recipe. It works fine, since it implements the same logic.

See also

▶ If you want learn how to create **BarTimerScript**, you can refer to the *Creating a linear timer* recipe

▶ For different kinds of timers or countdowns, you can take a look at the *Implementing a numeric timer, Creating a linear timer, Creating a mixed timer, Creating a well-formatted timer,* and *Developing a well-formatted countdown that changes* recipes, all contained in this chapter

Creating a mixed timer

In this recipe, we are going to mix the radial timer with the numeric one. Like in the previous recipe, the time remaining will be displayed as a ring that reduces circularly over time. Furthermore, inside the ring, we will display the time remaining as a number. A mixed timer can serve many different purposes, especially when a number of timers have to be viewed at once. For instance, imagine a strategy game where we have a number of resources that we wish to use. Each of these resources takes time to regenerate after it has been used. At a glance, the radial timer can indicate how much time, across a range of different resources, any single resource has left. In addition, incorporating a numeric timer can specify exactly how much time is remaining until that resource is available again. In this way, using both a radial timer and a numeric timer in combination can provide the player with both an overview and a specific indication of time remaining. To create a mixed timer, we will use the **Image (Script)** and **Text (Script)** components and develop a script to manage the length of the circular bar, synchronized with the time shown as a number inside the ring.

How to do it...

1. First of all, we need to create a circular bar for our timer, so we can open a graphic program and create it, or just use the one we created in the *Implementing a radial health bar* recipe from the previous chapter.

2. Then, we should import it into our project and set its **Texture Type** to **Sprite (2D and UI)** (only if our project is not 2D) so that we can use it within the UI elements. Next, click on **Apply**.

3. Now, let's create a new UI image. To do this, right-click on the **Hierarchy** panel and then navigate to **UI | Image**. Rename it to **Mixed Timer**.

4. Inside the **Image (Script)** component, we have to change **Image Type** to **Filled**. The component should change a little in the **Inspector**.

5. Ensure that **Fill Method** is set to **Radial 360** and **Fill Origin** to **Bottom**. We have to drag the bar that we previously imported into **Source Image**. Finally, we can place **Mixed Timer** wherever we want, remembering to use **Rect Tool** as we do this or the keyboard shortcut *T*.

6. We may want to keep its original proportions. In this case, we can click on the **Set Native Size** button in the **Inspector**.

7. Furthermore, we need to create a new UI text to display the time as a number inside the ring. Right-click on **Mixed Timer** in the **Hierarchy** panel, and then navigate to **UI | Text**.

8. We can change the **Font** and the **Font Size** fields as we want so that they better suit our needs.

9. We can also adjust **Color**. For this example, we will set it to light gray, but feel free to use a color that better suits your design.

10. Now we can drag **Text** with **Rect Tool** inside our timer, or again use the keyboard shortcut *T*.

11. To see it better in the scene view, we can write something in the **Text** variable — for instance, the word `time`, even if this value will be replaced by the script.

12. Make sure that the **Rich Text** variable is checked. We do this to ensure that different parts of the text in our timer can have different colors.

13. Now, we have to create the script that manages the timer. After selecting **Mixed Timer**, navigate to **Add Component | New Script**, name it **MixedTimerScript**, and then click on **Create and Add**.

14. Double click on the script to edit it, and then add the `using UnityEngine.UI;` statement at the beginning of the script so that we can use UI elements within the script.

15. Next, we need to add five variables; three are private and two are public. These will be set in the **Inspector**. We write the following:

```
private Text uiText;
private Image barFilling;
public float timeAmount = 18f;
private float time;
```

16. In the `Start()` function, we can set the `time` variable along with `barFilling` and `uiText` as well:

```
void Start () {
    barFilling = this.GetComponent<Image> ();
    time = timeAmount;
    uiText = this.GetComponentInChildren<Text> ();
}
```

17. Finally, in our `Update()` function, we need to decrease the time by `Time.deltaTime` and then update the `fillAmount` variable of the bar accordingly. We can do this by writing the following:

```
void Update () {
  if (time > 0) {
    time -= Time.deltaTime;
    if(time < 0 )
      time = 0;
    barFilling.fillAmount = time / timeAmount;
    uiText.text = "<color=blue>Time</color>: " + time.
ToString("F2");
  }
}
```

18. Save the script and test it by clicking on the play button. We should see the following result:

How it works...

After importing the image, we set it to **Sprite (2D and UI)** (only for 2D projects) so that we could use it in the UI. Then we created a new image and changed its **Fill Method** value to **Radial 360** and **Fill Origin** to **Bottom**. In this way, the image can disappear gradually in an anticlockwise direction starting from the bottom, as the time decreases. Furthermore, we created another game object nested in the **Mixed Timer** object, with a **Text (Script)** component, in order to display the time as a number. Finally, we implemented a script for the logic.

In the script, we have four variables. The first one is `barFilling` and stores the reference to the **Image (Script)** component attached to the same game object of the script. The second one is `uiText`, and it stores the reference to the **Text (Script)** component, which is attached to the child game object of the mixed timer. The third variable is `timeAmount`, which is the amount of time set at the start, and from which the countdown begins to decrease. Finally, the fourth variable is `time` and contains the amount of time remaining.

In the `Start()` function, we began by assigning the **Image (Script)** component, which is attached to the same game object of this script, to `barFilling`. We did this by calling the `this.GetComponent<Image>()` function. We assigned the **Text (Script)** component, which is attached to the child of the game object where this script is, to the `uiText` variable by calling the `this.GetComponentInChildren<Text>()` function. We did this to get the reference that we need in order to quickly access that component. Finally, we set the time to `timeAmount` so that the countdown begins with that specific starting time.

In `Update()`, we check at every frame whether `time` is more than zero. If so, we subtract `Time.deltaTime` from `time`, since the coupon decreases. If `time` is less than zero, then we set it to zero. Finally, we put the ratio between `time` and `timeAmount` into the **Fill Amount** variable, which is contained in the **Image (Script)** component of the mixed timer. In fact, the ratio is the percentage of the time remaining, which also indicates how much longer our linear timer needs to be. In the last line, we also updated the text inside our timer so that it could be displayed correctly inside the ring.

There's more...

The following section will teach us how to improve the aesthetic of our timer to better suit our needs.

Changing the number of decimal points shown

We can easily change the script so that it displays a certain number of decimal points in the timer. In order to do that, let's add a variable called `decimalDigits` into our script and set its default value to 2:

```
public int decimalDigits = 2;
```

Then we have to look for this line inside the `Update()` function:

```
uiText.text = "<color=blue>Time</color>: " +
time.ToString("F2");
```

And we can replace it with the following:

```
uiText.text = "<color=blue>Time</color>: " +
time.ToString("F"+decimalDigits);
```

To decide how many decimal points will be shown, we need to set the `decimalDigits` variable in the **Inspector**. In fact, by setting this variable in the **Inspector**, we are changing the parameter of the `ToString` function. We do this in order to return a string that represents the float as a string, with as many decimal points as we have decided in `decimalDigits`.

Using a linear timer instead of a radial timer

Instead of using a radial timer, we can also use a linear timer and put the text inside the bar. In this example, it would be nice to add some borders to the bar. In fact, this helps to better integrate the timer with the rest of the UI. To do this, you can refer to the *Implementing a linear health bar* recipe contained in the previous chapter, inside the *There's more...* section.

To change the radial timer to a linear one, we have to change the **Fill Method** of the mixed timer to **Horizontal** and change **Fill Origin** to **Left**. Of course, we also have to change the **Source Image** with the linear bar. If needed, we can use the **Set Native Size** function and/ or change the size of the text of the timer to better fit the bar. Once we have done all of these steps, we should have something that looks like this:

See also

▶ For different kinds of timers or countdowns, check out the *Implementing a numeric timer, Creating a linear timer, Implementing a radial timer, Creating a well-formatted timer,* and *Developing a well-formatted countdown that changes* recipes, all contained in this chapter

Creating a well-formatted timer

In this recipe, we are going to create a timer that displays time on the screen in minutes and seconds. The benefit of using a more precise timer is the ability to provide the player with a more precise indication of time. This is particularly helpful when there are moments during the game that can take up a considerable amount of time. Having time displayed in a familiar format also assists the player to easily recognize and respond to the amount of time remaining. We will use **Text (Script)** and develop a script to achieve this goal.

How to do it...

1. First of all, we need to create new UI text that will display our timer. Right-click on the **Hierarchy** panel and then navigate to **UI | Text**. Rename it to **Well Formatted Timer**.

2. We can change the **Font** and the **Font Size** values as we wish so that they can better suit our needs.

3. Next, we can adjust **Color**; for this example, we will set it to light gray, but feel free to use another color that better suits your design.

4. Now we can drag **Well Formatted Timer** with **Rect Tool** to where we want to place it.

5. To have the timer better displayed in **Scene View**, we can write the word `time` in the **Text** variable, even if this value will be replaced with the real amount of time remaining after every frame by our script. We have to ensure that the **Rich Text** variable is checked so that we can have the advantage of changing colors in different parts of the text.

6. Then, we have to create the script that manages the timer. To do this, navigate to **Add Component | New Script** and rename it to **Well Formatted Timer Script**. Then click on **Create and Add**.

7. Double click on the script to edit it, and then add the `using UnityEngine.UI;` statement at the beginning of the script. This allows us to use UI elements within our script.

8. Before we can add any more functions, we need two private variables:

```
private Text uiText;
private float time;
```

9. Now, we have to set the `uiText` variable in order to use it. We can do this in the `Start()` function:

```
void Start () {
    uiText = this.GetComponent<Text> ();
}
```

10. In order to update the timer, we need to write a couple of lines in the `Update()` function. To do this, let's write the following:

```
void Update () {
    time += Time.deltaTime;
    string minutes = Mathf.Floor(time / 60).ToString(""00"");
    string seconds = (time % 60).ToString(""00"");
    uiText.text = "<color=blue>Time</color>: "" + minutes + ":" +
    seconds;
}
```

11. Let's save the script, and our work is done. We should see something like this:

How it works......

First of all, we created a new UI text and adjusted it to suit our needs by changing **Font**, **Font Size**, and also **Color**. We also ensured that the **Rich Text** option was checked.

In the script, there are two private variables, `uiText` and `time`. The `uiText` variable stores the reference to the **Text (Script)** component, and `time` stores the amount of time remaining.

In the `Start()` function, we assigned **Text (Script)**, which is attached in the same game object of this script component, to the `uiText` variable by calling the `this.GetComponent<Text>()` function.

Finally, in the `Update()` function, we added `Time.deltaTime` to the `time` variable. This indicates the amount of time that has elapsed from the last frame, when this function was called the last time.

Next, we calculated the minutes by dividing `time` by 60, and then removed its decimal part using the `Mathf.Floor(float f)` function. Finally, we transformed the result into a string that is stored in the `minutes` variable. In order to get the seconds remaining, we did the same and divided the time by 60. However, this time, we took the remainder of the division. We transformed this value into a string and stored it inside the `seconds` variable.

In the last line of the script, we updated the text variable on the **Text (Script)** component, which was stored in the `uiText` variable. We put onto it a formatted string in which minutes are separated from seconds.

There's more...

This section reminds us how to retrieve the time from our timer.

Getting the time variable

As we have previously done in the first recipe, it is possible to retrieve the value of the `time` variable. We just have to add a `get` function, like this:

```
public float getTime(){
   return time;
}
```

See also

▶ For more details about the `get` function, refer to the *Implementing a score counter* recipe in the *There's more...* section

▶ However, if you are looking for more information about rich text, the official documentation is the best place to get it, at `http://docs.unity3d.com/Manual/StyledText.html`

Developing a well-formatted countdown that changes

In this recipe, we are going to create a countdown that displays the time on the screen as minutes and seconds. However, to take this display a step further, as the time elapses, it will change color. Just as the radial timer graphically represents the time that passes, a colored numeric timer provides a similar function. For example, in moments during gameplay when there is intense action, a player may not necessarily have the time to focus on the timer, or he may actually lose track of the time that has elapsed. Whatever the case may be, another good way to indicate to the player the time as it is decreasing is through color. Therefore, as the player is engaged in gameplay, the color of the time can provide a quick indication of how close he is to running out of time. We will use the **Text (Script)** component and develop a script to achieve our goal.

How to do it...

1. First of all, we need to create a new UI text to display our timer. To do this, right-click on the **Hierarchy** panel and then navigate to **UI | Text**. Rename it to **Well Formatted Countdown**.

2. We can change **Font** and **Font Size** as we wish so that they suit our needs better.

3. Next, we can adjust **Color**. For this example, we will set it to to light gray, but feel free to use another color that better suits your design.

4. Remember that the color will also be changed from our script.

5. Now, we drag **Well Formatted Countdown** with **Rect Tool** to where we want to place it on the **Canvas**.

6. To see it better inside **Scene View**, we can add some text to the **Text** variable. Even though this value will be replaced by the script, it will show us an approximation of how the timer will be displayed during runtime.

7. Furthermore, ensure that the **Rich Text** variable is checked to be able to use different colors in the text.

8. Then, we have to create a script that manages the timer. To do this, navigate to **Add Component | New Script**, name it **Changing Countdown Script**, and then click on **Create and Add**.

9. Double click on the script to edit it, and add the `using UnityEngine.UI;` statement at the beginning of the script. As a result, we will be able to handle UI elements within our script.

10. Before we start adding any more functions, we need two private variables. So, we can write this:

```
private Text uiText;
private floattime;
```

11. Now, we need to set the `uiText` variable in order to use it. We can do this in the `Start()` function:

```
void Start () {
   uiText = this.GetComponent<Text> ();
}
```

12. Next, we will need to write a few lines in the `Update()` function in order to update the timer:

```
void Update () {
   time -= Time.deltaTime;
   if (Mathf.Floor (time / 60) >= 1) {
     string minutes = Mathf.Floor (time / 60).ToString ("00");
     string seconds = (time % 60).ToString ("00");
     uiText.text = "<color=blue>Time</color>: " + minutes + ":" +
seconds;
   } else {
     if(time>=10){
       uiText.text = "<color=blue>Time</color>: " + time.
ToString("FOR");
     }else{
```

```
    uiText.text = "<color=blue>Time</color>: <color=red>" +
time.ToString("F0")+"</color>";
      }
    }
  }
```

13. We can save the script, and now our work is done. When the countdown has more than one minute remaining, it should look like this:

14. When the countdown has less than 1 minute but more than 10 seconds remaining, it should look like the following:

15. When the countdown has fewer than 10 seconds remaining, it should look like this:

How it works...

First of all, we created a new UI text and adjusted it to suit our needs. We did this by changing **Font**, **Font Size**, and also **Color**. We even ensured that **Rich Text** was checked. Finally, we wrote a script to handle all of these changes depending on the amount of time remaining.

In the script, there are two private variables, `uiText` and `time`. The `uiText` variable stores the reference to the **Text (Script)** component. The `time` variable stores the amount of time that has elapsed since the countdown began.

In the `Start()` function, we assigned the **Text (Script)** component, which is attached to the same object of the script, to the `uiText` variable by calling the `this.GetComponent<Text>()` function.

In contrast to what we did with the timers, in this case we subtracted `Time.deltaTime` from the `time` variable in the `Update()` function. This was because we were implementing a countdown. Therefore, we had to decrease the amount of time remaining.

In the first `if` statement, we check the number of minutes that are calculated by `Mathf.Floor (time / 60)`. If it is more than 1, we format our countdown like the timer in the previous recipe. Otherwise, we can use the formatting from the first recipe in this chapter. In this last branch, we calculated the minutes by dividing `time` by `60`, and removing its decimal points with the `Mathf.Floor(float f)` function. Consequently, we transformed the number of minutes into a string, which is stored in the `minutes` variable. In order to get the seconds, we divided `time` again by `60`.

However, this time we took the remainder of the division. Again, we transformed this value into a string and stored its value inside the `seconds` variable. Finally, we updated the text variable of the **Text (Script)** component, which is stored in the `uiText` variable. We had to set a formatted string where minutes are separated from seconds to text. In the `else` branch, we check whether the countdown had less than 10 seconds remaining. If so, then the time is displayed in the same format as in the first recipe of this chapter. However, in this case, we changed the color of the text to red. Otherwise, if we do the same as in the first recipe, it would have retained its original color.

There's more...

The following sections will give us some new concepts that can be applied to our countdown.

Getting the time variable

As we have seen before, in some cases it's useful to retrieve the value of the `time` variable. To do this, we need to add a `get` function, like this:

```
public float getTime(){
    return time;
}
```

Running code when the time expires

If we place a countdown in our game, it's probably because we want to trigger an event when it expires, such as making the player lose the level. Despite the reason, we can achieve this by changing our script slightly. First, we need to add a new variable:

```
private bool isOver;
```

Then, we should add this line in the `Update()` function:

```
uiText.text = "<color=blue>Time</color>: <color=red>" + time.
ToString("F0")+"</color>";
```

Replace it with the following lines:

```
if(time <= 0){
    uiText.text = "<color=blue>Time</color>: <color=red>0</
color>";
    if(!isOver){
        isOver = true;
        //DO SOMETHING
    }
}else {
    uiText.text = "<color=blue>Time</color>: <color=red>" +
time.ToString("F0")+"</color>";
}
```

As we can see from the code, the `bool` variable is needed to trigger the countdown expired event only once. In fact, now we are able to implement or call a function when the time expires.

Furthermore, in order to test it, we can write something that indicates when the time has expired. For instance, we can do this in the debug console by calling this function:

```
Debug.log("Timer expired!");
```

Increasing tension by adding decimal points when the time is close to expiring

By combining what we did before with the *Creating a mixed timer* recipe, when the timer has fewer than 10 seconds remaining, the timer could display the number with decimal points to increase tension in the player. In this way, as each second draws closer to the time of expiry, the player can see with more precision and at a faster rate how much time is left (in milliseconds). Ultimately, this increases the tension between the current moment and the moment when the timer expires.

See also

- For more details about the `get` function, refer to the *Implementing a score counter* recipe in the previous chapter, inside the *There's more...* section

- However, if you are looking for more information about rich text, the official documentation is the best place to get it, at `http://docs.unity3d.com/Manual/StyledText.html`

4
Creating Panels for Menus

In this chapter, we will cover the following recipes:

- ▶ Creating a toggle group
- ▶ Showing the slider value as a percentage
- ▶ Adding upper and lower bounds to the slider
- ▶ Making UI elements affected by different lights
- ▶ Making a draggable panel
- ▶ Making a resizable panel
- ▶ Creating a drag-and-drop element
- ▶ Developing an MP3 player

Introduction

In this chapter, we are going to learn how to make different kinds of panels to create interactive menus. These menus will feature elements such as sliders and draggable and resizable features. This chapter will conclude by showing you how to create a simple MP3 player.

Creating a toggle group

In this recipe, you will learn how to create a toggle group. Often in menus, there is an opportunity to choose between different options, but the player can choose only one of them. A toggle group allows users to select just one of its toggles. To achieve this, we will use the **Toggle (Script)** component along with the **Toggle Group (Script)** component.

How to do it...

1. First of all, we need to create a panel in which our toggle elements will be placed. To do this, right-click on the **Hierarchy** panel and then on **UI | Panel**. Rename it to **Toggle Group**. Of course, it is possible to resize and place the panel as we wish.

2. The next step is to add a **Toggle Group (Script)** component to our **Toggle Group** panel. To do so, click on **Add Component | UI | Toggle Group**.

3. Now, we have to add our toggles. We can do this by right-clicking on the **Toggle Group** panel in the **Hierarchy** panel and selecting **UI | Toggle**. We can rename it to **Toggle01** and duplicate it as many times as we want by pressing *Ctrl + D*. Each time we duplicate it, Unity will update the name for us in **Toggle02**, **Toggle03**, and so on.

4. The toggles are all in the same place and with the same text. Therefore, we can change the text of the toggles to **Option A**, **Option B**, and so on. Finally, we need to displace the toggles in the panel – in order to separate them – until we have obtained something that looks like this:

5. Next, we have to link all of these toggles together and make them act as a toggle group. To do this, we need to select all of them so that we can then drag the **Toggle Group** panel in the **Group** variable. This last variable can be found inside the **Toggle (Script)** component in the **Inspector**. As a result, for each toggle, we should have something that should appear like the following:

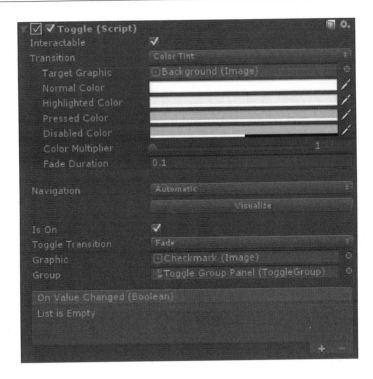

6. As a final step, we need to leave just one toggle checked. To do this, we can select all the toggles except the one we want to leave checked, and uncheck their **Is On** variable from the **Inspector**. Now, we can press play and test whether everything works.

How it works...

By default, each toggle element is separated from all others. For this reason, we need to create a toggle group. This is a script that checks whether one of its elements changes state and consequently modifies the state of the other elements accordingly. For example, if a toggle becomes checked, and since we want exactly one toggle checked at a single point in time, we need to uncheck the already checked toggle, if any. Luckily, we don't need to write this script from scratch. Unity offers a component called **Toggle Group (Script)** that handles this kind of interaction for us. Therefore, we only need to link each toggle to this component to create a toggle group.

There's more...

The following section will show us how we can remove the constraint to necessarily chose one of the options.

Giving the player the privilege not to choose one of the options

Removing the possibility to select an option from a toggle group for the player is an important design decision that needs to be made carefully, but it doesn't have any impact from a programming perspective. In fact, **Toggle Group (Script)** also takes care of this possibility. Thus, we need to select the **Toggle Group** panel from the **Hierarchy** panel, and inside the **Toggle Group (Script)** component in the **Inspector**, we need to check the **Allow Switch Off** variable. As result, if the player clicks on the currently checked toggle, it becomes unchecked as well as all other toggles.

Furthermore, we can set the default option of our toggle group to **no choose**, which means that at the beginning, no toggles are checked. We only need to uncheck the **Is On** variable from the toggle that we left in step number 6.

See also

 ▸ Since the **Toggle (Script)** and **Toggle Group (Script)** components are a part of Unity, for more information about them, we can check out the official Unity documentation here:

 ❏ http://docs.unity3d.com/Manual/script-Toggle.html

 ❏ http://docs.unity3d.com/Manual/script-ToggleGroup.html

Showing the slider value as a percentage

Sliders are used a lot in video games. As a result, we have to display some percentage of the slider to give the player a better visual idea of what he is changing. For example, when the player is tweaking an ability parameter, it could be useful if the amount remaining is displayed as a percentage. The goal of this recipe is to create a script that shows the value of the slider in percentage. As such, we will develop a script that will use both the **Slider (Script)** and **Text (Script)** components.

How to do it...

1. First of all, we need to create a new UI text to display the value of our slider in percentage. Therefore, we can right-click on the **Hierarchy** panel and then click on **UI | Text**. Rename it to **Slider Shower**. Furthermore, to customize the look or suit our needs, we can change **Font** and **Font Size** as well.

2. Now, we need a script that receives the value of the slider, as data, which we will learn how to do later, and then show it as a number in percentage. So, let's click on **Add Component | New Script**, name it **ShowSliderValueScript**, then click on **Create and Add**.

3. To edit the script, double click on it. Add the `using UnityEngine.UI;` statement at the beginning of the script. Before the class, we can also add the following line: `[RequireComponent(typeof(Text))]` (without the semicolon at the end). In this way, we are saying that, in order to use this script, it requires a **Text (Script)** component attached to the same game object of this script.

4. We just need a private variable to keep track of the **Text (Script)** component, without needing to find it every time we have to update its text. So, we can add `private Text uiText;`.

5. Next, we can write a function that takes `float` as a parameter (the value of the slider) and changes it to `string` that represents that number in a percentage. To do this, we multiply the value by 100 and round it off using the `Mathf.RoundToInt()` function. In addition, by doing this, we get to see all percentages with decimals. Finally, add `%` at the end of the string. We put this string into the `text` variable of the `Text (Script)` component. Therefore, we can write the function in the following way:

```
public void updateValue(float value){
    uiText.text = Mathf.RoundToInt (value * 100) + "%";
}
```

6. Let's save the script and come back to Unity from MonoDevelop. The next step is to add a slider to our scene. Hence, we can right-click on the **Hierarchy** panel and then click on **UI | Slider**. If we want to organize things better in our project, we should rename it as well.

7. As you can see from the following screenshot, at the bottom of the **Slider (Script)** component, there is the **On Value Change (Single)** panel. Click on the **+** sign in the bottom-right corner of the panel.

8. As result, we have just added an element to the tab. As we can see in the next screenshot, we need to drag **Slider Shower** into the **object** variable. Now, the drop-down menu should be enabled. Therefore, we can click on it and select **ShowSliderValueScript | updateValue**. In fact, there are two of them listed, and we need to select the first one, under **Dynamic float**. By doing this, when the value of the slider changes, the **updateValue()** function from our previous script is called and the value of the slider is passed as a parameter.

9. Finally, we can press the play button and perform a test to see whether everything works as we have planned, as shown in the following screenshot:

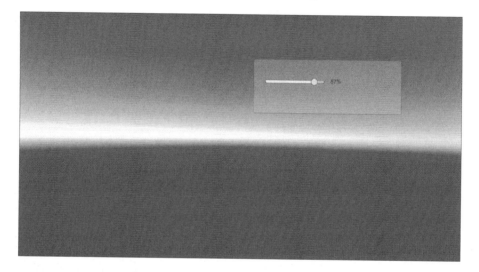

How it works...

The **Slider (Script)** component has a variable called `value` that stores the position of the slider as `float` between 0 and 1. In order to show this number, we passed it through an event — **OnValueChange**. This happens every time the player changes the value of the slider, that is, every time the slider is dragged. When this event happens, a value is passed to our script. This first transforms the number into an integer between 0 and 100, and then converts it into a formatted string to show it as a percentage. Finally, this string is shown in the **Text (Script)** component.

Adding upper and lower bounds to the slider

Unity allows us to add lower and upper bounds to sliders in a very simple way. Inside the **Slider (Script)** component, there are two variables named **Min Value** and **Max Value**. If we take the slider from the previous recipe and change the values of these variables, we'll see that we can drag the handle of the slider to the end and the value has an upper bound, as we can see in the following screenshot:

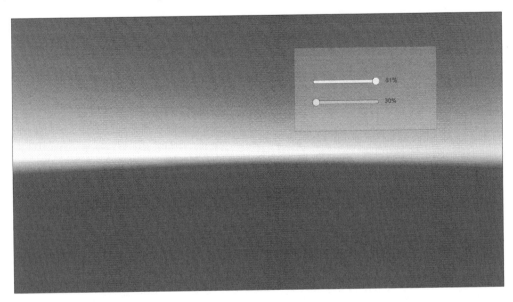

In this recipe, we will write a script to block the handle of the slider as well in order to make the player perceive a real upper or lower bound.

How to do it...

1. So that we don't recreate another slider, we can take the one from the previous recipe; thus, we can also see the value as a percentage. Otherwise, simply right-click on the **Hierarchy** panel and then click on **UI | Slider**.

2. For the next step, we need to create our script on the slider. So, click on **Add Component | New Script**, name it **UpperAndLowerBoundsForSlidersScript**, and then click on **Create and Add**.

3. Now, double click on the script in order to edit it. As usual, we need to add the `using UnityEngine.UI;` statement at the beginning of the script so that we can handle UI elements within the script. We can also add the following line before the class: `[RequireComponent(typeof(Slider))]` (without the semicolon at the end). By doing this, the script requires a **Slider (Script)** component attached to the same game object of it in order for it to work. In fact, if it is not present, Unity will add it for us.

4. We need a private variable to keep track of the **Slider (Script)** component without seeking it every time that we want to check its upper and lower bounds. We also need two public variables. They can be set in the **Inspector** or via the script for the lower and the upper bound, respectively. So, we can write these lines:

```
private Slider slider;
public float lowerBound;
public float upperBound;
```

5. In the `Awake()` function, we have to link the `Slider` to our variable and then carry out our first check. To improve performance, future checks will be done only if the value of `Slider` changes. We can perform our check by calling the `checkBounds()` function, which we will write in the next step. Thus, we can write the `Awake()` function as follows:

```
void Awake () {
   slider = GetComponent<Slider> ();
   checkBounds ();
}
```

6. In the `check` function, we have to ensure that the value of `Slider` is between the lower bound and the upper bound. If not, we have to change its value to the closer bound, like this:

```
public void checkBounds () {
   if (slider.value>= upperBound) {
      slider.value = upperBound;
   } else {
      if (slider.value<= lowerBound) {
         slider.value = lowerBound;
      }
   }
}
```

7. Save the script and come back to Unity from MonoDevelop. As in the previous recipe, we can see this at the bottom of the **Slider (Script)** component, the **On Value Change (Single)** panel. By clicking on the **+** sign in the bottom-right corner of the panel, we add a new element (the second one if you took the slider from the previous recipe).

8. Next, we have to drag the **Slider** itself into the **object** variable. Now the drop-down menu should be enabled, so click on it and select **UpperAndLowerBoundsForSliders Script | checkBounds**. In this way, when the value of the slider is changed, the `checkBounds()` function from our script is called, and it will check whether the new value of the slider is inside the bounds. If we have taken the slider from the previous recipe, we should see this:

9. Finally, we can press the play button and perform a test to see whether everything works as it should.

How it works...

Since Unity doesn't allow us to block the handle of the slider directly, we need a script that controls it within the bounds. In fact, every time the `OnValueChange` event occurs, the value of the slider is passed to our script. This checks whether the slider value is between the bounds. If it isn't, the script changes the value of the slider to the closest bound limit. For example, if the player tries to move the slider further than the bound, our script will make the slider come back to that bound. Finally, our script stores the bound limits in a couple of public variables so that we can change them during the gameplay with other scripts. This is useful because the player will perceive this as a block of the slider. Therefore, we can change the bounds to give more power to the player over time.

There's more...

The following sections will give us some interesting suggestions on how to improve our **Slider Shower**.

Changing the color when a bound is reached

Sometimes in games, we not only want to block the slider by creating bounds, but also to make the player feel the bounds. One way of doing this is by changing the color of the **Slider Shower**. To achieve this, we need to modify the script slightly. First, we should add the reference to the **Slider Shower** inside our script. Thus, we can add a new public variable into our script:

```
public Text uiText;
```

This will store the **Text (Script)** component attached to **Slider Shower**. Furthermore, we need to change the checkBounds() function in the following way:

```
public void checkBounds () {
    if (slider.value>= upperBound) {
        slider.value = upperBound;
        uiText.color = Color.red;
    } else {
        if (slider.value<= lowerBound) {
            slider.value = lowerBound;
            uiText.color = Color.red;
        }
    }
    uiText.color = Color.white;
}
```

By doing this, if a bound is reached, we change the color of **Slider Shower** to red. Otherwise, we can assign the color white to it. Finally, we need to drag and drop **Slider Shower** into the **uiText** variable of our script in the **Inspector**.

Expressing bounds as a percentage

Sometimes, it's better to express the parameters in a different way, especially if designers have to tweak them. In fact, another way might be more understandable and comfortable. For example, instead of expressing a result in decimal points, we can display it more simply as a percentage. Here, you are going to learn how to express bounds as a percentage within the **Inspector**; this is easy to understand for designers. Therefore, let's start changing our script a little.

First of all, we need to change our variables. Consider these lines:

```
public float lowerBound;
public float upperBound;
```

Replace them with the following lines:

```
[Range(0,100)]
public int lowerBound;
[Range(0,100)]
public int upperBound;
```

In this way, we have changed the type of our variable in int and added a Range attribute in order to limit the possible values (between 0 and 100) that can be set in the **Inspector**.

Now, since the slider value is a float between 0 and 1, we also need to convert the percentage value into a decimal one in the checkBounds () function. In fact, if we divide the value by 100f, we obtain the decimal value. Therefore, we can rewrite the entire function in the following way:

```
public void checkBounds () {
    if(slider.value>= upperBound/100f){
       slider.value = upperBound/100f;
    } else {
       if(slider.value<= lowerBound/100f){
          slider.value = lowerBound/100f;
       }
    }
}
```

As in the original function, we need to check whether the slider is exceeding the bounds, and if so, restore it to the closest bound.

Limiting the value that we can set in the Inspector

If we want to limit the possible values that can be set in the **Inspector**, we have to add a Range attribute to our variables. This prevents designers or us from setting a wrong number.

If we have expressed the value as a percentage, we can add the [Range(0,100)] line before our variable in this way:

```
[Range(0,100)]
public int lowerBound;
[Range(0,100)]
public int upperBound;
```

In fact, they are int, and the percentage can be a number between 0 and 100.

Otherwise, if we still express the bounds as floats in the Inspector, the Range attribute is [Range(0,1)]. Therefore, we can write the following:

```
[Range(0,1)]
public float lowerBound;
[Range(0,1)]
public float upperBound;
```

In this case, the value of our variable can be a float number between 0 and 1.

See also

▸ Since we have better tested the bounds by displaying the value of the slider in percentage, you can find more details about this in the previous recipe, *Showing the slider value as a percentage.*

Making UI elements affected by different lights

To give a professional touch to our user interface, we can add lights to it. This could be effective if we want to create a specific type of atmosphere or emphasize an element. In fact, Unity allows us to alter UI elements by light. In this recipe, you will learn how to create two UI elements and, using layers, how to have them affected by different lights. In order to do this, we will add two new layers, create a new UI material, and of course play with lights.

How to do it...

1. We need to create two panels that are slightly separated, as shown in the following screenshot. From this, you can learn how to affect different UI elements with different lights. To create the panels, right-click on the **Hierarchy** panel and then click on **UI | Panel**. Furthermore, to be more ordered, we can rename them as **Panel01** (the one on the left) and **Panel02** (the one on the right).

2. Now, we have to change the render mode of our canvas. Hence, select it from the **Hierarchy** panel, and inside the **Canvas** component in the **Inspector**, change the **Render Mode** variable to **World Space**.

3. If we switch to the **Game** view, we will not be able to see our panels anymore. This is because we have to move our camera to frame them. To do this, we can select it from the **Hierarchy** panel and, in the **Scene** view, move it in front of our panels.

Switching to **3D** mode will allow us to better observe where our camera is placed. To do this, uncheck the **2D** icon at the top of your **Scene** view, as shown in this screenshot:

In the end, we should have something like this:

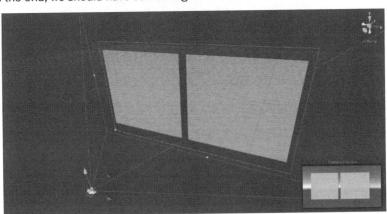

4. Now select one of the two panels and click on **Layer | Add Layer** at the top of the **Inspector**. The **Inspector** should change. If this is a new project, we can add two different layers onto **User Layer 8** and **User Layer 9** by typing the names of the new layers next to them. In this case, we can call them **UI1** and **UI2**. So, we should see something like the following:

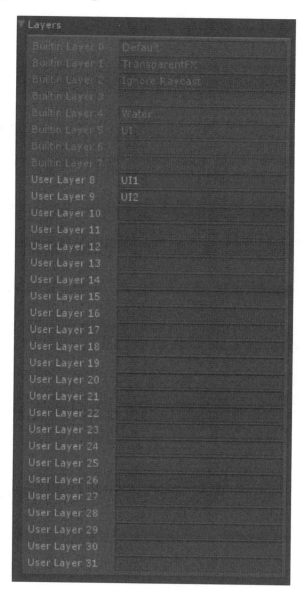

5. Select **Panel01** and click on **Layer | UI1**. Then select **Panel02** and click on **Layer | UI2**. By doing this, we have put the panels on different layers.

6. The next step is to create a new UI material to allow our panel to be affected by light. In order to do so, right-click somewhere in the **Project** panel, select **Create | Material**, and rename it to **UIMaterial**. Select it, and in the **Inspector**, click on **Shader | UI | Lit | Detail**.

7. Select **Panel01** along with **Panel02** and drag and drop **UIMaterial** inside the **material** variable in the **Inspector**.

8. Now we can create a light; right-click on the **Hierarchy** panel and then on **Light | Point Light**.

9. We can change the light as we want, but let's ensure that in **Culling Mask**, only one layer is selected (**UI1** or **UI2**), and that the range of the light is very long (maybe around 2000). We do this so that we can see the effect on our panels. Lastly, we can place the light wherever we want it.

10. We can create as many lights as we wish and then decide which panel to affect by changing its **Culling Mask**.

How it works...

Unity allows us to cause UI elements to be affected by lights, but they must be in **World Space** and must have the right material. This is because lights belong to the 3D world, and so the UI also needs to stay there. Furthermore, it also needs a material that can respond to lights. In fact, we have created a material so that our panels can be affected by lights. Additionally, we have created different layers so that we can affect only some UI elements by a certain light.

See also

▶ It could be great if we can make interactive lights. This will increase the realism of the lights and thus also enhance how the player perceives the UI. Therefore, you should definitely take a look at the *Creating a slider that changes colors gradually* and *Creating sliders that change single channels of a light* recipes in *Chapter 7, Applying Runtime Customizations*.

▶ Furthermore, using light becomes very easy when all of the system is integrated in a 3D UI. In fact, when the UI moves into the third dimension, we can see the reflection, the position, or other effects of the lights changing. Therefore, to increase the visual impact in this recipe, you should integrate with the recipes contained in *Chapter 9, Diving into 3D UIs*.

Making a draggable panel

In same cases, UI elements require some kind of interaction with the player, and the next three recipes will teach you how to create interactive panels. In this recipe, you will learn how to make a panel draggable. For instance, the player will be able to move the panel all around the screen by dragging it. This is useful when we want to allow the player to organize his UI with his logic and order. In order to do this, we will use the **Event Trigger (Script)** component and develop a script to handle the interaction.

How to do it...

1. To begin, we can create a panel by right-clicking on the **Hierarchy** panel and then on **UI | Panel**. We should also resize it so that we can see the entire panel on the screen.

2. Now we need to create our script on the panel, so we click on **Add Component | New Script**, name it **DraggablePanelScript**, and then click on **Create and Add**.

3. Double-click on the script to edit it. This time, we don't need to add the using UnityEngine.UI; statement at the beginning of the script.

4. In the next step, we need to create just one public function. This will be called from the **Event Trigger (Script)** component that will be attached to the panel. In this function, we change the position of the transform where the script is attached to the mouse by calling Input.mousePosition. Therefore, we can write this:

```
public void OnDrag(){
    transform.position = Input.mousePosition;
}
```

5. Let's save the script and add an **Event Trigger (Script)** component to the panel. Click on **Add Component | Event | Event Trigger**.

6. Then click on **Add New Event Type | Drag**. A new menu that is similar to the one in the previous recipes should appear in the **Inspector**. By clicking on the **+** sign in the bottom-right corner of the panel, we can add a new event.

7. Furthermore, we need to drag **DraggablePanelScript** itself into the **object** variable. As result, the drop-down menu should now be enabled. Click on it and select **DraggablePanelScript | OnDrag**. In this way, when the player drags the panel, the OnDrag() function from our script is called, and therefore the position of the panel will change.

8. Finally, we can press the play button and make sure that everything works as it should.

How it works...

Each time the player drags the panel, **Event Trigger (Script)** calls our script, and it will change the position of the panel with the mouse. As a result, the panel will move according to the player's dragging.

There's more...

In the following section, we can learn how to drag the panel only from a specific area.

Creating a draggable area for the panel

We may want to allow the player to drag the panel from just some specific parts or areas of it — for instance, only at the top of the panel, where the name of the window is usually placed. In this context, the panel can be considered a window. Therefore, we need to create another game object, which will be our draggable area, and follow the steps in the _How to do it..._ section. After we have completed this, we also need to modify the script. Instead of changing the position of the transform of the game object that is attached to the script, we move an arbitrary transform that we want — in this case the entire panel.

See also

> ▶ We may want to give the player more power to structure his UI. So, we can make the panel not only draggable but also resizable. Therefore, we can include the technique that we will cover in the next recipe, _Making a resizable panel_, by providing the player with more options to customize his experience.

Making a resizable panel

Sometimes, UI elements require some kind of interaction with the player. This recipe, along with the previous and the following ones, will teach you how to create interactive panels. Furthermore, we will see how to make a panel resizable. For instance, the player will be able to resize the panel by dragging one of its corners. This is useful when the UI is full of panels and windows and we want to let the player choose their dimension to suit his needs. To do this, we will use the **Event Trigger (Script)** component and develop a script to handle the interaction.

How to do it...

1. First, we can create a panel by right-clicking on the **Hierarchy** panel and then clicking on the **UI | Panel**. Rename it to **ResizablePanel**. We should also resize it so that we can see the entire panel on the screen.

2. We need to create another panel inside the first one. To do this, right-click on **ResizablePanel** in the **Hierarchy** panel and then choose **UI | Panel**. We should rename it as **ResizeArea** in order to reduce confusion. Finally, place it in the bottom-right corner of the first panel, in this way:

3. Now we have to change **Anchor** of **ResizeArea**. To do this, select **Anchor**. Then, in the **Inspector**, click on the icon with two squares and four blue arrows inside. Now, a drop-down menu should appear, with **Anchor Presets**. Let's select the bottom-right one. After doing this, you should see what is shown in the following screenshot:

4. Now, we need to create our script on **ResizablePanel**. Therefore, click on **Add Component | New Script** and name it **ResizablePanelScript**. Then click on **Create and Add**.

5. Double-click on the script in order to edit it. As usual, we need to add the `using UnityEngine.UI;` statement at the beginning of the script.

6. Before we add functions, we need three private variables. Two of them are `Vector2`, respectively, for keeping track of the original mouse position and the original `DeltaSize` of `RectTransform` when the player begins resizing. The third one is a `RectTransform`, so we can get access to the `RectTranform` of `ResizablePanel`. Therefore, we can write the following lines:

```
Vector2 initialMousePos;
Vector2 initialDeltaSize;
RectTransform rectTransform;
```

7. In the `Start()` function, we assign the `RectTransform` component, attached to the same game object of this script, to the `rectTransform` variable. We can do this by writing these lines:

```
void Start () {
   rectTransform = (RectTransform)this.transform;
}
```

8. Then we have to write a function that will be called every time the player starts resizing the panel. We will call this function `onDragBegins()` because in order to resize, we will be dragging `ResizeArea`. Here, we just assign the initial start position of the mouse to `initialMousePos` and the current `deltaSize` to `initialDeltaSize`:

```
public void onDragBegins(){
   initialMousePos = Input.mousePosition;
   initialDeltaSize = rectTransform.sizeDelta;
}
```

9. The next step is to have a function that is called during the dragging of `ResizeArea`; means resizing the panel according to how the player moves the mouse. Therefore, we need to create a function called `OnDrag`, which will look like this:

```
public void OnDrag(){
   Vector2 temp = (Vector2)initialMousePos - (Vector2)Input.
mousePosition;
   temp = new Vector2 (-temp.x, temp.y);
   temp += initialDeltaSize;
   rectTransform.sizeDelta = temp;
}
```

10. Save the script and select **ResizeArea** from the **Hierarchy** panel. Then, in the **Inspector**, click on **Add Component | Event | Event Trigger**.

11. Now we have to add two event types. To add the first, click on **Add New Event Type | BeginDrag**. Then, click on the + sign in the bottom-right corner of the panel to add a new event. Next, we have to drag **ResizablePanel** itself into the **object** variable. Subsequently, the drop-down menu should be enabled. Hence, click on it and select **ResizablePanelScript | onDragBegins**. As a result, when the player starts to drag **ResizeArea**, the OnDragBegins() function from our script is called.

12. To add the second event, click on **Add New Event Type | Drag**. Then click on the + sign in the bottom-right corner of the panel to add a new event. Again, we have to drag **ResizablePanel** itself into the **object** variable. From the drop-down menu, select **ResizablePanelScript | onDrag**. As a result, when the player drags **ResizeArea**, the OnDrag() function from our script is called.

13. Finally, we can check whether everything works as it should by clicking on the play button.

[

Keep in mind that all the elements within the panel will be resized as well. Thus, ensure that you have placed all the anchors correctly within the elements inside your panel, if any.
]

How it works...

Each time the player drags **Resize Area, Event Trigger (Script)** calls our script. In particular, two functions are called: the OnDragBegins() function, in which we initialize our variables, and the OnDrag() function. In the latter, we first create a temporary variable that stores the difference of initialMousePos and the current mouse position, Input.mousePosition. This means the distance between where the player started to drag and the current mouse position. Since in this case the difference between vectors is ambiguous, we need to make an explicit cast. Then, we have to invert the x coordinate of the temporary vector if we want to resize the panel coherently. Finally, after adding the initialDeltaSize to our new vector, we assign it as the new sizeDelta of rectTransform.

See also

▶ Keep in mind that rarely, and only in specific designs, can the player resize a panel without moving it around. Therefore, if this is not our design, we should integrate the resizable panel with what we have covered in a previous recipe, *Making a draggable panel*, to create a more immersive, interactive menu.

Creating a drag-and-drop element

Often, UI elements require some kind of interaction with the player. This recipe, along with what we have done in the previous two recipes, will teach you how to create interactive panels. In particular, you will learn how to create two panels: one from which we can drag an element (such as a coin or an item) and one on which we can then place it. This is useful when we are developing a system wherein we need to drag objects from one place to another. For instance, it's common to find this system in a shop menu, where the player can decide what to buy and drag what he wants into his inventory. In order to do this, we will use the **Event Trigger (Script)** component and develop a script to handle the interactions.

How to do it...

1. To begin, we can create a panel by right-clicking on the **Hierarchy** panel. Then click on **UI | Panel** and rename it to **CoinPanel**. We should also resize it in order to see the entire panel on the screen.

2. Next, we need to create a script for **CoinPanel**. Therefore, click on **Add Component | New Script** and name it **DragAndDropScript**. Then click on **Create and Add**.

3. Double-click on the script in order to edit it. As usual, we have to add the `using UnityEngine.UI;` statement at the beginning of the script. This allows us to handle UI elements within our script.

4. Before we add functions, we need two variables. The first one is a public variable and it will store the original `GameObject`. We will use this to instantiate new game objects every time the player drags from this panel. The second variable is a private one and is required to keep track of our new `GameObject` during the dragging process:

```
private GameObject temp;
public GameObject original;
```

5. Now, we can add the `onDragBegins()` function. This is where we initiate a new `GameObject` from the original one and store it inside the `temp` variable. Furthermore, in order to display a UI element, it must be a child of `Canvas`. Therefore, we need to change its parent to `Canvas`:

```
public void onDragBegins(){
  temp = (GameObject) GameObject.Instantiate (original, this.
transform.position, Quaternion.identity);
  temp.transform.SetParent (GameObject.Find ("Canvas").transform);
}
```

6. In the onDrag() function, we just change the position of temp with the one on the mouse:

```
public void OnDrag(){
    temp.transform.position = Input.mousePosition;
}
```

7. In the onDragEnd() function, we can perform our checks and finally destroy temp:

```
public void onDragEnd(){
    //Check if temp is dropped as you want and perform what you want
    GameObject.Destroy (temp);
}
```

8. Let's save the script and add an **Event Trigger (Script)** component to the panel. To do this, click on **Add Component | Event | Event Trigger**.

9. Moreover, we need to add two types of events. To add the first event, click on **Add New Event Type | Drag**. As in the previous recipe, a new menu should appear in the **Inspector**. By clicking on the **+** sign in the bottom-right corner of the panel, we can add a new event. Then, we have to drag the **DragAndDropScript** itself into the **object** variable. As result, the drop-down menu should be enabled. Click on it and select **DragAndDropScript | OnDrag**. By doing this, we ensure that, when the player drags, the OnDrag() function in our script is called.

10. To add the second event, click on **Add New Event Type | Begin Drag** and then click on the **+** sign in the bottom-right corner of the panel. Again, we have to drag the **DragAndDropScript** itself into the **object** variable. From the drop-down menu that was just enabled, select **DragAndDropScript | onDragBegins**. By doing this, we ensure that, when the player starts dragging, the OnDragBegins() function from our script is called.

11. To add the last event, click on **Add New Event Type | End Drag**. Next, click on the **+** sign in the bottom-right corner of the panel. Again, we have to drag the **DragAndDropScript** itself into the **object** variable. As before, select **DragAndDropScript | onDragEnd** from the drop-down menu. As a result, when the player finishes dragging, the OnDragEnd() function from our script is called.

12. As a final step, we can draw a new image and use it as an **Icon**. Alternatively, we can take the one created in the *Creating a modular coin counter* recipe from *Chapter 2, Implementing Counters and Health Bars*. After we have created a new prefab, we drag and drop this image into the prefab. Then, we drag and drop the prefab into the original variable of our script.

13. Finally, we can click on the play button and check whether everything works as it should, as shown here:

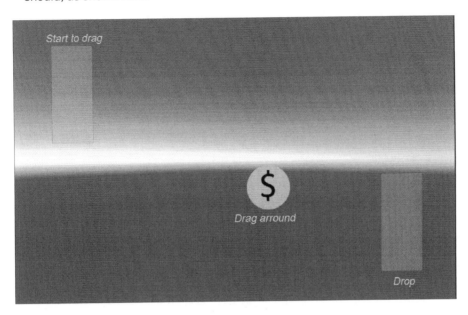

How it works...

Every time the player starts dragging, drags, or finishes dragging, the **Event Trigger (Script)** will call our script. It creates a new GameObject and moves it accordingly.

There's more...

It is possible to learn how to perform a check for the objects that have been dropped, in the next section.

Checking for dropped objects

When the player drops the temp object, we may want to check whether it is inside another panel. In order to do this, we need to add a new variable and some lines of code to our onDragEnd() function.

Let's add a variable that stores the reference to the panel where we want to check whether our temp is dropped. It has to be public so that designers can set it in the **Inspector**. Therefore, we can write this line:

```
public RectTransform dropPanel;
```

Now, we need to change the onDragEnd() function in the following way:

```
public void onDragEnd(){
  Vector3[] worldCorners = new Vector3[4];
  dropPanel.GetWorldCorners(worldCorners);

  if(Input.mousePosition.x>= worldCorners[0].x
&&Input.mousePosition.x<worldCorners[2].x
  &&Input.mousePosition.y>= worldCorners[0].y
&&Input.mousePosition.y<worldCorners[2].y) {
    Debug.Log ("Dropped");
  }
  GameObject.Destroy (temp);
}
```

We used the GetWorldCorners() function, which allows us to retrieve the corners of our dropPanel. Furthermore, along with an if statement, we have to check whether temp is inside the boundaries of the dropPanel when the player drops it. Since we set the temp position to the same position of the mouse in the onDrag() function, we can use the mouse position to perform the check. Therefore, if this check is true, it means the item has been dropped inside the dropPanel, and we print a message through the Debug.Log() function. Of course, feel free to perform whichever action is adequate for your game.

Developing an MP3 player

In this recipe, we will see how to create a simple MP3 player with the **Play, Pause, Stop, Next**, and **Previous** buttons. Here, the focus will be on how to learn the interaction between **UI** and the **Audio Source (Script)** component within a script. Furthermore, we will see how to use the **Event Trigger (Script)** component to call all the functions in our script. These will actually implement the logic behind the MP3 player.

How to do it...

1. First, we can create a panel by right-clicking on the **Hierarchy** panel and then clicking on **UI | Panel**. Rename it to **MP3Panel**. We should also resize it so that we can see the entire panel on the screen. This is the panel that will contain all the buttons of our player.

2. Next, we need to create five buttons inside the panel. To do this, we can right-click on **MP3Panel** in the **Hierarchy** panel and then click on **UI | Button**. We can easily duplicate it four times by pressing *Ctrl + D*. Each time, place the button on the screen as shown in the following screenshot. We should rename them to **PlayButton, PauseButton, StopButton, PrevButton**, and **NextButton**, and also change the text of these buttons respectively to **Play, Pause, Stop, Prev**, and **Next**. Finally, we should have something that looks like this:

3. We also need to add an **Audio Source (Script)** component to **MP3Panel**. To do this, click on **Add Component | Audio | Audio Source**. As a result, our player can now act as an audio source. This means that it is able to reproduce music.

4. Now, we need to create our script on **MP3Panel**. Therefore, click on **Add Component | New Script** and name it **MP3PlayerScript**. Then click on **Create and Add**.

5. Double-click on the script in order to edit it. This time, we don't need to add the `using UnityEngine.UI;` statement at the beginning of the script. But before the class, we add this line: `[RequireComponent(typeof(AudioSource))]` (without the semicolon at the end). In this way, we are saying that, to use this script, an **Audio Source (Script)** component attached to the same game object of this script is required. If it is not present, it will be added automatically.

6. Before we add any functions, we need four variables. The first is a private variable for storing `AudioSource`, where all the sounds will be reproduced. The second one is an array of `AudioClip` for storing our entire playlist, and it is public, so we can set the music from the **Inspector**. The third one is `private int`, and it stores the index of the current song. The last one is `private bool`, and it stores information on whether the player has stopped the music or not. So, we can write these lines:

```
private AudioSource audioSource;
public AudioClip[] musicList;
private int index=0;
private bool isStopByPlayer;
```

7. In the `Start()` function, we assign the **Audio Source (Script)** component that is attached to the same game object of this script to the `audioSource` variable:

```
void Start () {
   audioSource = GetComponent<AudioSource> ();
}
```

8. Now, we have to write one public function for each button, which means five functions in total. The first one is the `Play()` function, in which we call the `Play()` function on `audioSource` and set the `isStopByPlayer` variable to `false`, since the player has just pressed play and not one of the stop buttons. So, we can write the following:

```
public void Play(){
   audioSource.Play ();
   isStopByPlayer = false;
}
```

9. The second one is the `Pause()` function, in which we call the `Pause()` function on `audioSource`. Also, since the player has just pressed one of the stop buttons, we set the `isStopByPlayer` variable to `true`:

```
public void Pause(){
   audioSource.Pause ();
   isStopByPlayer = true;
}
```

10. The `Stop()` function is similar to the previous one. It calls the `Stop()` function on `audioSource` and, since the player has just pressed one of the stop buttons, we set the `isStopByPlayer` variable to `true`:

```
public void Stop(){
   audioSource.Stop ();
   isStopByPlayer = true;
}
```

11. In the `Next()` function, we need to take care with the index of the playlist and play the next song that is on the list. If the current track is the last one, we play the first one. Therefore, we start increasing `index` by 1. Then we check whether `index` has reached the last track, and if so, we change `index` to 0 in order to make it point to the first track. Finally, we assign the track pointed by `index` in the music list to the `clip` variable of `audioSource`. After that, in the final line, we call the `Play()` function, which we have written before:

```
public void next(){
   index++;
   if (index == musicList.Length)
      index = 0;
   audioSource.clip = musicList [index];
   Play ();
}
```

12. As we did in the preceding function, in the `previous()` function, we have to worry about the index of the playlist and reproduce the previous track of the list. Thus, if the current track is the first one, we need to play the last one. Therefore, we start decreasing `index` by `1`. Then we check whether `index` has reached the first track, and if so, we change `index` to make it point to the last track. Finally, we assign the track pointed by `index` in the music list to the `clip` variable of `audioSource`. And in the final line, we call the `Play()` function, which we have written before:

```
public void previous(){
    index--;
    if (index == -1)
        index = musicList.Length-1;
    audioSource.clip = musicList [index];
    Play ();
}
```

13. In the `Update()` function, we check whether the track is finished and is not stopped by the player. If so, we call the `next()` function that we wrote before. It will play the next track from the music list:

```
void Update () {
    if (!audioSource.isPlaying && !isStopByPlayer)
        next ();
}
```

14. Save the script and come back into Unity. Now, we need to set the events. We select all the five buttons so that we can multi-edit them, and click on the **+** sign in the bottom-right corner of the `OnClick` event panel in the **Inspector**. Then drag **MP3Panel** into the `object` variable.

15. For the next step, we need to set the event differently for each button. So, for each of them, select in the drop-down menu **MP3PlayerScript** and the corresponding function: **PlayButton** with the `Play()` function, **PauseButton** with the `Pause()` function, **StopButton** with the `Stop()` function, **NextButton** with the `next()` function, and finally **PrevButton** with the `previous()` function.

16. Since we don't want the player to press **PlayButton** while a track is being played, we have to enable and disable it dynamically. To do this, we select **PlayButton**, **StopButton**, and **PauseButton** so that we can multi-edit them. In the **OnClick** event panel, click again on the **+** sign in the bottom-right corner to add a new event. Drag **PlayButton** in the **object** variable. Finally, in the drop-down menu, select **Button | Interactable**.

17. By default, the boolean value should be `false` (not checked), and it is fine for **PlayButton** but not for the other two. Therefore, select **StopButton** and **PauseButton** and check the boolean to make it `true`.

18. Since the MP3 player will start at the beginning of the scene, we have to disable **PlayButton** even at the start. Hence, after we have selected it, we can uncheck the **Interactable** variable from the **Inspector**.

19. The final step is to load some nice tracks into the **MP3Panel** inside the **Inspector**. Click on the play button to test the scene and listen to some nice music.

How it works...

Each button has an attached **Event Trigger (Script)** that will call the respective function of our script. In fact, our script contains a function for every component. This last one will control the **Audio Source (Script)** component to create an MP3 player.

There's more...

The next section teaches us how to display the name of the song in our MP3 Player, to the player.

Showing the name of the song

It would be a great improvement for the MP3 player if we displayed the name of the song that is currently being played, providing the player with more information during his experience. We can achieve this by using a **Text (Script)** component and modifying our script a little.

First, select **MP3Panel** in the **Hierarchy** panel. Then select **UI | Text** and rename it to **MP3Text**.

Before we modify our script, we need to add the `using UnityEngine.UI;` statement at the beginning of the script. In fact, here we are going to use the `Text` class.

Then, we add a new `public` variable to our script:

```
public Text uiText;
```

This will store the reference to the **Text (Script)** component of **MP3Text** so that we can keep track of it.

After this, let's add these lines at the end of the `Update()` function:

```
uiText.text = audioSource.name;
```

By doing this, we display the name of the song (the name of **AudioClip**) in the **text** variable of the **Text (Script)** component on **uiText**.

Finally, we can click on play to verify that everything works as expected.

Since the name of the song could be longer than the **text** component, ensure that **MP3Text** is long enough. We can stretch it with the **Rect tool**.

Otherwise, we can implement other solutions. Let's explore three of them. The first is the easiest, and it requires us to use the **Content Size Fitter** to make the text dynamically fit within **MP3Text**. Another solution, which is a bit more effective, is to write a script that truncates the name of the song, if it is too long. For instance, we can add ... at the end of the name. Finally, if it is important to show the entire name, we can make the name scroll gradually, by programming this behavior within our script.

5
Decorating the UI

In this chapter, we will cover the following recipes:

- ▶ Creating an extendable element with a final fade effect
- ▶ Creating an extendable and rotating element with a final fade effect
- ▶ Creating bars that randomly go up and down
- ▶ Making a floating UI element
- ▶ Adding shadows to text
- ▶ Adding outlines to text

Introduction

In this chapter, we will see how to create dynamic elements to decorate our UI. We will start with elements used to decorate the background, such as fading and rotating effects. This may perhaps include some with a very low alpha value. Then, we will demonstrate how to create elements for the foreground of our UI, such as sci-fi bars or a floating UI element. At the end of this chapter, we will explore the **UI Effect** component, the **Shadow (Script)** component, and the **Outline (Script)** component, and see how we can use them to decorate our UI.

Creating an extendable element with a final fade effect

In this recipe, you will learn how to create an extendable UI element with a final fade effect. These kinds of decorative elements are useful in the background with smaller graphics such as nice images or simple shapes. Often, they are used in main or pause menus in order to make the background dynamic and give more life to the menu. Additional techniques about how to animate the menu itself can be found in *Chapter 6, Animating the UI*.

How to do it...

1. First of all, we need to create a UI element. In this example, we will use a square, but you can also use a decorative star or another shape that you prefer. To do this, right-click on the **Hierarchy** panel and then navigate to **UI | Image**. Rename it to **Extendable Element**. Of course, it is possible to resize, change the source image, and place an image that we have chosen.

2. Next, we need to create a script that extends our image on the screen and gradually decreases the alpha channel of the color. By decreasing the alpha channel, it will begin to fade away. So, let's go to **Add Component | New Script** and name it to **ExtendableElementScript**. Then click on **Create and Add**.

3. Now, double-click on the script in order to edit it. Since we are going to use the Image class, we have to add the using UnityEngine.UI; statement again at the beginning of the script. Before the beginning of the class, we can add this line: [Req uireComponent(typeof(Image))] (without the semicolon at the end). By doing this, we are saying that in order to use this script, it requires an **Image** component that is attached to the same game object of this script. In addition, this prevents designers from using this script without an **Image (Script)** component.

4. We need two public variables to be shown in the **Inspector** so that designers can tweak them, one for the speed and another for the amount of time the UI element continues to expand before it is destroyed. Thus, we can add the following lines to our script:

```
public float speed;
public float surviveTime;
```

5. Furthermore, we need three private variables, two of them to keep track of the RectTransform component, and the third one to keep track of the original SizeDelta without seeking it every time. In addition, a couple of other variables are used to accumulate the time for every frame. So let's add the following:

```
private float x, y;
private RectTransform rectTransform;
private Vector2 originalSizeDelta;
```

6. As usual, in the Start() function, we will store the reference of the game elements inside our variables. We assign RectTransform, attached to the same game object in which this script is placed, by calling the GetComponent<RectTransform>() function, to the rectTransform variable. Furthermore, we will set the originalSizeDelta variable. Therefore, we can write this code:

```
rectTransform = GetComponent<RectTransform> ();
originalSizeDelta = rectTransform.sizeDelta;
```

7. Inside the `Start()` function, we have to start the fade effect by calling `CrossFadeAlpha()` and then passing some parameters. One is the final alpha value, which is `0f` in this case. Another is the time of the fading, which in this case is the entire span of time before the object is destroyed:

```
GetComponent<Image>().CrossFadeAlpha(0f, surviveTime,
false);
```

8. In the last line of the `Start()` function, we call the `GameObject.Destroy()` function to destroy the game object in which this script is attached after the time that we have specified in the **Inspector** through the `surviveTime` variable:

```
GameObject.Destroy(gameObject, surviveTime);
```

9. Now, in the `Update()` function, we have to increase the x and y variables by the time from the last frame multiplied by the speed. Finally, we set new `sizeDelta` of `rectTransform` equal to a `Vector2` with x and y as coordinates plus `originalSizeDelta`:

```
x += speed * Time.deltaTime;
y += speed * Time.deltaTime;
rectTransform.sizeDelta = new Vector2(x, y) +
originalSizeDelta;
```

10. For the next step, we can save the script and come back to Unity. From the **Inspector** window we can tweak `speed` and `surviveTime`. These values depend on what we are trying to achieve, but let's set them to 20 and 10 respectively. We can test the script and see whether everything works as it should. In this screenshot, we can see a frame of the effect:

How it works...

In the `Start()` function, we launch two Unity coroutines. The first one is launched from the `GetComponent<Image>().CrossFadeAlpha(0f, surviveTime, false);` line, and the second one is launched from `GameObject.Destroy(gameObject, surviveTime);`.

The first coroutine gradually changes the `Alpha` value to create the fade effect. The second destroys the game object when it is no longer required. As a result, it improves the performance of our game, because the scene doesn't contain futile objects.

There's more...

By changing this effect, it is possible to achieve very interesting variations of it. This is what we are going to learn in the following sections.

Changing the speed for each axis

We may want to let designers customize the effect more, for instance, by having different speeds for each axis. In order to implement this, we need to modify our script. Instead of a common `speed` variable, we need a `speed` variable for each axis. Therefore, we need a couple of variables. So, let's consider this line:

```
public float speed;
```

We replace it with these two lines:

```
public float speedX;
public float speedY;
```

Now, in the `Update()` function, we have to change the way the x and y variables are updated. Thus, we can rewrite the code in the following way:

```
x += speedX * Time.deltaTime;
y += speedY * Time.deltaTime;
```

When we do this, x and y change accordingly to different speeds. We can set the variables again in the **Inspector** and check whether everything works.

Fade-in instead of Fade-out

We may want to reverse the process and have an element that appears instead of one that fades away. This could be a useful way of decorating our UIs differently. It is possible for us to mix the two ways in order to create a more decorative UI, where there are both elements that enter and elements that fade away. In order to do this, we need to change a couple of lines of code. Keep in mind that at the end, the object will be destroyed anyway.

First, we need to consider the `CrossFadeAlpha()` function:

```
GetComponent<Image>().CrossFadeAlpha(0f, surviveTime, false);
```

Change it to these two lines:

```
GetComponent<Image>().CrossFadeAlpha(0f, 0f, false);
GetComponent<Image>().CrossFadeAlpha(1f, surviveTime, false);
```

In order to understand the previous lines, we need to remember that the
`CrossFadeAlpha()` function doesn't take care of the initial `Alpha` value of the **Canvas
Renderer** component. Therefore, the first function sets **Alpha** of the **Canvas Renderer**
component to `0` immediately so that the image is not visible at the beginning. The second
function increases the `Alpha` value until `1f` over the time specified in the `surviveTime`
variable, creating the fade-in effect.

See also

▶   We may want to increase the effectiveness of our effect by rotating the image while
    it is expanding. For this case, we are going to extend this script in the *Creating an
    extendable and rotating element with a final fade effect* recipe.

Creating an extendable and rotating element with a final fade effect

In this recipe, you will learn how to create an extendable and rotating UI element with a
final fade effect. This recipe is an extension of the previous one. In fact, we will add some
controllers to the rotation. By extending the script that we made in the previous recipe,
we can create more complex decorating elements for our UIs.

How to do it...

1. To begin, we need to create a UI element. In this example, we will use a square, but
    you can also use any other image, such as a decorative star or a circle. To do this,
    create the UI element, right-click on the **Hierarchy** panel, and then navigate to **UI
    | Image**. Finally, rename it **Extendable and Rotating Element**. Of course, it is also
    possible to resize it, change its source image, and place it wherever we wish.

2. Now, we need to create a script that extends and rotates our image on the screen,
    and gradually decreases the alpha channel of the color. By doing this, we ensure
    that the image will gradually fade away. So, let's navigate to **Add Component | New
    Script**, name it **ExtendableElementWithRotationScript**, and then click on **Create
    and Add**.

3. Since this script is very similar to the one in the previous recipe, we can copy the
    body of **ExtendableElementScript** into it.

4. We must remember to add the `using UnityEngine.UI;` statement at the beginning of the script, since we are going to use the `Image` class, and it is not included within the body of script that we just copied. As before, we can also add `[RequireComponent (typeof (Image))]` to say that to use this script, it requires an **Image** component attached to the same game object of this script.

5. Next, we need to add a new public variable so that we can set it in the **Inspector**. In fact, this variable will store the speed of rotation. So, let's write the following line:

   `public float rotationSpeed;`

6. Then, in the `Update()` function, we have to change not only `SizeDelta`, but also its rotation. For this reason, we add this line at the bottom of the function:

   ```
   rectTransform.Rotate (0,0 , Time.deltaTime *
   rotationSpeed);
   ```

7. We can save the script and come back to Unity. From the **Inspector**, we can tweak `rotationSpeed` as well as the speed and `surviveTime`, if we didn't do it before. Just to test, we can set the speed to `20`, `rotationSpeed` to `30`, and `surviveTime` to `10`. Finally, we can check whether everything works as it should. In the following screenshot, you can see a frame that shows this effect:

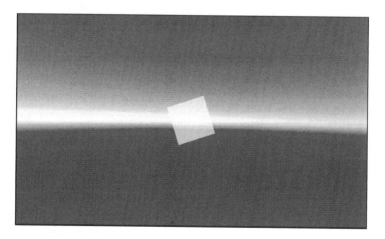

How it works...

This script works in the same way as the one in the previous recipe. However, here we can also change the rotation. With the `rectTransform.Rotate()` function, we can modify the orientation of the object within the space. This is done according to these variables: `Time. deltaTime`, which is the time passed since the last frame, and `rotationSpeed`. If the latter has a positive value, the UI element will rotate clockwise. But if it has a negative value, the element will rotate anticlockwise. Therefore, designers can choose which is best for the UI. This is because the sign of the variable changes the direction of the rotation made by the `rectTransform.Rotate()` function.

There's more...

We can definitely improve the effect with slight variations, which can be learnt in the following sections.

Creating a shining effect

In order to create a shining effect, we can use an image of a shining star. We also need a transparent background for this image. After we have placed the image in **Extendable and Rotating Element**, let's rescale the image and place it in our UI, where we want to have the shining effect. Set speed to 10, rotationSpeed to 30, and surviveTime to 1. Next, press the play button to see the shining effect. If our image is unique, or if we are not completely satisfied with the effect, we can tweak the variables until we reach a good effect that suits our needs. Otherwise, we can refer to the following section.

Creating a better shining effect

In this section, we will see how to improve our shining effect by making it appear and then disappear. To do this, we need to rewrite the code using a coroutine.

To begin, let's add a new public bool variable. Thus, we can set it in the **Inspector**. It will store information on whether we want to reverse the rotation or not. Therefore, we can add this line:

```
public bool reverseRotation;
```

In the Start() function, let's consider this line:

```
GetComponent<Image>().CrossFadeAlpha(0f, surviveTime, false);
```

Substitute it with these two:

```
GetComponent<Image>().CrossFadeAlpha(0f, 0f, false);
GetComponent<Image>().CrossFadeAlpha(1f, surviveTime, false);
```

The explanation of this can be found in the previous recipe, in the *Fade in instead of fade out* section.

Next, we have to double the time before the object is destroyed, so we rewrite the Destroy() function in this way:

```
GameObject.Destroy(gameObject, surviveTime*2);
```

Finally, at the end of the Start() function, we have to call our coroutine, even if we haven't created it yet, like this:

```
StartCoroutine ("fadeAway");
```

After we have done this, we need to write our coroutine. Hence, we can add this portion of code at the end of our script:

```
IEnumeratorfadeAway(){
    yield return new WaitForSeconds(surviveTime);
    GetComponent<Image>().CrossFadeAlpha(0f, surviveTime, false);
    if(reverseRotation)
        rotationSpeed = -rotationSpeed;
}
```

The first instruction waits for the initial fade effect to finish. Then, in the second line of the script, we launch another fade effect to make our extendable and rotating UI element fade away. In the `if` statement, we check whether the variable that we have set in the **Inspector** is `true`, and if it is, it will reverse the sign of the `rotationSpeed` variable in order to change the direction of rotation.

Let's save the script and finally test whether everything works as expected.

Using more than one axis to create 3D effects

We are not limited to using only one axis of rotation. In fact, we can substitute the following line with the next one:

```
rectTransform.Rotate (0, 0 , Time.deltaTime * rotationSpeed);
```

Here is the line that we can use instead of the preceding one:

```
rectTransform.Rotate (Time.deltaTime * rotationSpeed, 0 ,
Time.deltaTime * rotationSpeed);
```

In this case, we are rotating the object along the x axis as well. But feel free to test different combinations as you wish, such as this one:

```
rectTransform.Rotate (Time.deltaTime * rotationSpeed,
Time.deltaTime * rotationSpeed , 0);
```

In the preceding case, we are rotating only on the x and y axes.

Having control over each axis

We may want to make the effect more customizable in order to get very nice variations. To do this, we can add more variables to be set in the **Inspector**, and control each axis of rotation. Along with the *Changing the speed for each axis* subsection in the *There's more...* section of the previous recipe, this allows us to gain full control over the effect. If we use our imagination, the number of beautiful effects that we can create is endless.

Let's start! First of all, we have consider the following variable:

```
public float rotationSpeed;
```

Substitute it with these:

```
public float rotationSpeedX;
public float rotationSpeedY;
public float rotationSpeedZ;
```

By doing this, we can control each axis independently of the others, whereas this didn't happen in the previous section.

Now, let's look at the following line in the `Update()` function:

```
rectTransform.Rotate (0, 0, Time.deltaTime * rotationSpeed);
```

Substitute it with this one, in which the `speed` variable is different for each axis:

```
rectTransform.Rotate (Time.deltaTime * rotationSpeedX,
Time.deltaTime * rotationSpeedY , Time.deltaTime *
rotationSpeedZ);
```

Save the script, and try different numbers along all the rotation speed variables. Of course, don't forget to use a nice image. Refer to the next section to get an idea on how to use this script.

Creating a butterfly

If we made the changes in the previous section, creating a butterfly should not be a problem. In fact, simply use a symmetric image of a butterfly and set both `rotationSpeedX` and `rotationSpeedZ` to 0. Now, just set a positive number for `rotationSpeedY`, maybe more (around `300`). Remember that the higher the value, the faster the butterfly's wings flap.

See also

▶ Since this recipe is an extension of an effect that has already been implemented, you may want to find the original script. You can find it in the previous recipe, *Creating an extendable element with a final fade effect*.

▶ Furthermore, we have seen how it is possible to create a butterfly. You can improve it to make it fly around the UI using a script that you will learn in another recipe. Hence, you can refer to the *Making a floating UI element* recipe, specifically the *Create a better butterfly* section.

Creating bars that go up and down

In this recipe, you will learn how to create a bar that goes up and down. This decorative UI element is often used in sci-fi HUDs. In fact, it gives a touch of life to our UI. Bars that go up and down can be a nice addition when we are trying to provide the player with an atmosphere in which many different things are dynamic and are being measured, such as a character gaining or even losing an ability over time during a battle, as if monitoring various statistics of a player to demonstrate a dynamic and quite living atmosphere.

How to do it...

1. First of all, we have to create a UI image that should be like a decorative bar for a sci-fi HUD. In this recipe, we are going to use the bar that we used in *Chapter 2*, *Implementing Counters and Health Bars*. To start, right-click on the **Hierarchy** panel, then navigate to **UI | Image**, and finally rename it **HUDBar**. Of course, it is possible to resize it and place the image as we wish. Lastly, we change **Source Image** with the bar that we created in the second chapter, or design one.

2. After we have changed **Source Image**, we need to change **Image Type** to **Filled**.

 If we have a vertical bar as the graphic, we have to set **Fill Method** to **Vertical** and **Fill Origin** to **Bottom**. Otherwise, if we have a horizontal bar, like the one that we are using for this example, we have to rotate it. In the **Rect Transform** component, change the rotation along the **z** axis to **90**. Then, change **Fill Method** to **Horizontal** and **Fill Origin** to **Left**.

3. Then, we need a script that controls the movement of the image and changes its `fillAmount` variable. Thus, let's navigate to **Add Component | New Script**, name it **HUDBarScript**, and then click on **Create and Add**.

4. Now, double-click on the script in order to edit it. Since we are going to use the `Image` class again, we need to add the `using UnityEngine.UI;` statement at the beginning of the script. Before the beginning of the class, we can add this line: `[RequireComponent(typeof(Image))]` (without the semicolon at the end). By doing this, we are saying that to use this script, it requires that an **Image** component be attached to the same game object as that of this script.

5. We don't need any `public` variable, but we need one `private` variable. This is for storing the reference to the **Image (Script)** component. We can write the following line:

```
public Image uiImage;
```

6. As usual, in the `Start()` function, we store the reference of the game elements inside our variables, in this case only the `uiImage` variable. By calling the `GetComponent<Image>()` function, we take the **Image(Script)** component attached to the same game object in which this script is placed. Therefore, we can code the following:

```
uiImage = GetComponent<Image> ();
```

7. Next, in the `Update()` function, we have to change the `fillAmount` variable of our **Image(Script)** component . Let's add this code:

```
uiImage.fillAmount = ((Mathf.Sin (Time.time) + 1f) / 2f);
```

8. Save the script, and click on the play button to verify that everything works as it should. Here, you can see a screenshot of the effect:

How it works...

The `Mathf.Sin()` function returns a value between -1 and +1, and this depends on upon the parameter.

If we plot the function, we get the following graph:

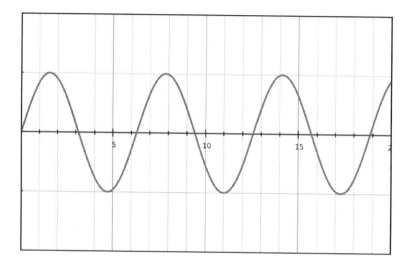

As we can see from the graph, by increasing x, which is also a parameter of the `Mathf.Sin()` function, the value of y goes up and down. Therefore, if we pass `Time.time` as the parameter, the output will be a value that changes over time. Since the function has a value between -1 and 1, we have to crop its returning value. To do so, we added 1f; thus, its value was now between 0 and 2. Finally, we divided it by 2f, so its value was between 0 and 1, as we wanted.

There's more...

This decoration is quite nice when used multiple times in the same screen. But to make the effect pleasant for the player, we need to add a phase or some bounds.

Adding a phase to use more than one bar

In many sci-fi HUDs, there is often more than one bar. If we duplicate the one that we created in this recipe, all of them will appear the same. For this reason, we need to introduce a displacement phase in our script.

To do so, let's add a new `public` variable so that we can set it in the **Inspector**:

```
public floatphase;
```

Now modify the code line in the `Update()` function in the following way:

```
uiImage.fillAmount = ((Mathf.Sin (phase + Time.time) + 1f) / 2f);
```

In fact, if we set different values for each bar in the **Inspector**, they will be displaced.

In the following screenshot, we can see the final effect:

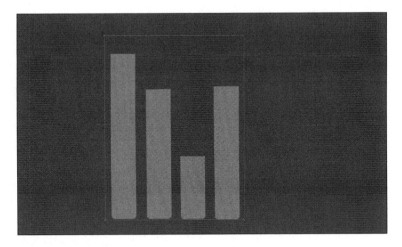

Adding bounds to our bar

We may want to limit the bar movement, so that we can try different aesthetic variations within our UI. We can do so by adding a couple of variables to our script:

```
public float startFilling;
public float maximumStretch;
```

In fact, as the name suggests, one stores the initial point and the other stores the amount by which the bar is stretched. So, when we set these in the **Inspector**, we need to pay attention to the fact that the sum of their values should be less than 1.

In the `Update()` function, we need to modify our code to include these two variables in the `Sin()` function, like this:

```
uiImage.fillAmount = startFilling + ((Mathf.Sin (Time.time) + 1f)
/ 2f) * maximumStretch;
```

Now, the minimum value that can be assigned to `uiImage.fillAmount` is `startFilling`, and the maximum is `startFilling` summed to `maximumStretch`.

In this screenshot, there is a visual explanation of the effect of our variables on the bar:

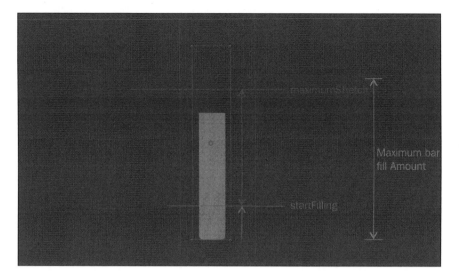

Adding bounds and a phase

To gain more control over our bars, we can combine the effects of the two previous sections. This is particularly useful when we are designing a complex sci-fi HUD in order to customize it to better suit our needs.

After we have added all the variables from both sections, we can write this line in the `Update()` function:

```
uiImage.fillAmount = startFilling + ((Mathf.Sin (phase +
Time.time) + 1f) / 2f) * maximumStretch;
```

As a result, we are able to create different decorative bars for our UI.

See also

> ▶ If you are looking for more information about the `Mathf.Sin()` function in Unity, you should refer to the official Unity documentation at `http://docs.unity3d.com/ScriptReference/Mathf.Sin.html`.

> ▶ Other than this, if you want to understand the *sin* function from a mathematical point of view, any book about trigonometry should be fine.

Making a floating UI element

In this recipe, you will learn how to make a floating UI element. This is a nice effect to use within every kind of user interface. If you are going to use a very slow movement with a small amplitude, you can use this effect even on menus to give them more life and a professional look. A floating element can add yet another type of dynamic element to the UI, ultimately breaking the usually rigid nature that UI elements tend to have.

How to do it...

1. First of all, we need to create an UI element. In this example, we will create a panel that can be the background of a menu. To do this, right-click on the **Hierarchy** panel and then navigate to **UI | Panel**. Finally, rename it **Floating Panel**. Of course, it is possible to resize and place the panel as we wish.

2. Next, we need a script that moves our panel on the screen in such a way that it seems to float. Thus, navigate to **Add Component | New Script** and name it **FloatingUIScript**. Then, click on **Create and Add**.

3. Now, double-click on the script in order to edit it. Since we are going to use only the `RectTransform` class, we don't need to add the `using UnityEngine.UI;` statement at the beginning of the script this time. Before the beginning of the class, we can add this line: `[RequireComponent(typeof(RectTransform))]` (without the semicolon at the end). By doing this, we are saying that to use this script, it requires a **Rect Transform** component that is attached to the same game object of this script.

4. We need only a `private` variable to keep track of the **Rect Transform** component, without seeking it every time we have to update its position. Then we also need four public variables. These will be set in the **Inspector**. There are two variables for the speed, one for each axis, and two variables for the amplitude of the floating movement, again, one for each axis. So, we can write this:

```
private RectTransform rectTransform;
public float xspeed,xAmplitude, yspeed, yAmplitude;
```

5. As usual, in the `Start()` function, we store the reference of the game elements inside our variables; in this case, it is only `rectTransform`. By calling the `GetComponent<RectTransform>()` function, we take the **Rect Transform** attached to the same game object in which this script is placed:

```
void Start () {
  rectTransform = GetComponent<RectTransform> ();
}
```

6. In the `Update()` function, we need to implement our logic. We change the local position of `rectTransform` to new `Vector3` wherein the `z` component is zero. The `x` and `y` components depend on `Sin`, the `math` function that creates the floating movement for us. We can control this function through our four public variables. Therefore, we can adjust the amplitude and speed for each axis:

```
void Update () {
    rectTransform.localPosition = new Vector3(xAmplitude*Mathf.
Sin(Time.time*xspeed), yAmplitude*Mathf.Sin(Time.time*yspeed), 0);
}
```

7. Save the script and come back to Unity from MonoDevelop. The next step is to tweak the values of our variables in the **Inspector**. We can create different effects with them, but for a nice floating effect, we can set them in the following way:

8. Finally, we can press the play button and see if everything works as expected.

How it works...

We use the `Mathf.Sin()` function to create a soft and natural movement over time. In fact, it is a periodic function and is continuous. More information about it can be found in the previous recipe, or in any general textbook about trigonometry. We use one of them on each axis, and through our variables we can set the parameters of the movement. In particular, we can change the amplitude of the movement and its speed.

There's more...

By setting the parameters of this script properly, it is possible to create many different effects. So that we will have an idea of these effects, we will see some of them in the following sections.

Creating a shaking effect

From this script, we can create a shaking effect. We only need to move the image faster than our eyes can notice. In order to do this, let's set **Xspeed** to **500**, **XAmplitude** to **300**, **Yspeed** to **80**, and **YAmplitude** to **350**. In the end, the component should look like the following settings:

Creating a sparkle effect

We can also create a sparkle effect, and again the trick is to move the image faster than our eyes can notice, although this time it should be along both axes and not just one. Therefore let's set **Xspeed** to **20**, **X Amplitude** to **10**, **Yspeed** to **50**, and **Y Amplitude** to **180**. Finally, the component should look like this:

Creating a better butterfly

After creating a butterfly in the *Creating an extendable and rotating element with a final fade effect* recipe, we can improve it using the float script. By doing this, we can give the butterfly the illusion that it is moving around our UI.

To do this, we need to modify `ExtendableElementWithRotationScript`. Of course, we need to start from the version of the script created in the *Having control over each axis* section. In fact, we need to remove the fade effect along with the destruction of the object.

If we don't want to override the script, we can duplicate it by selecting it and pressing *Ctrl* + *D*. Once we have duplicated it, we can rename it to **ButterflyWingsScript**. Don't forget to rename the class with the same name inside the script.

Therefore, from the `Start()` function, remove these two functions:

```
GetComponent<Image>().CrossFadeAlpha(0f, surviveTime, false);
GameObject.Destroy(gameObject, surviveTime);
```

As a result, the object will not change its alpha, and also it will not be destroyed. Furthermore, we can remove the `surviveTime` variable and the `using UnityEngine.UI;` statement, since they are no longer required.

Now let's save the script and create new `Image`. Right-click on the **Hierarchy** panel and then select **UI | Image**. Rename it **Butterfly**. Of course, it is possible to resize it and place the butterfly as we wish. Finally, change the **Source Image** to an image of a butterfly, but remember that it has to be symmetric.

The next step is to add this new script to our **Butterfly**. As in the *Having control over each axis* section of the *Creating extendable and rotating elements with a final fade effect* recipe, we need to set both `rotationSpeedX` and `rotationSpeedZ` to `0`, and assign a positive number to `rotationSpeedY`, maybe a high value (around `300`). Keep in mind that the higher the value, the faster the butterfly's wings will be.

Moreover, add the **FloatingUIScript** as well and set **XAmplitude** and **YAmplitude** both to **100**, **Xspeed** to **1**, and **Yspeed** to **2**.

The last step is simply to test the scene by clicking on play and to make sure that our butterfly comes to life.

See also

- If you are looking for more information about the `Mathf.Sin()` function, you should check out the official documentation on Unity at `http://docs.unity3d.com/ScriptReference/Mathf.Sin.html`.

- If you are looking for more information about the *sin* function from a mathematical point of view, any book about trigonometry should be fine. In addition, we have a brief explanation of why this function is used with time. It is in the previous recipe, in the *How it works...* section.

Adding shadows to text

In this recipe, you will learn how to add a shadow to a **Text (Script)** component. In order to achieve this, you will learn how to use a **UI Effect** component of the new UI system of Unity — the **Shadow (Script)** component. This kind of effect can add a dramatic touch to text and, as a result, make it stand out among other elements that may be in the UI. In addition to this, when there are many elements in the background, it is possible that a piece of text may seem lost. As such, adding a shadow to the text can also improve its legibility.

How to do it...

1. First of all, we need to create a new UI text. To do this, right-click on the **Hierarchy** panel and then navigate to **UI | Panel**. Finally, rename it **Text with Shadow**.

2. Then, we can regulate all the parameters in the **Inspector** as we want. However, in order to make sure that we notice the nice effect, we can enlarge **Text with Shadow** with **Rect tool** (which can be used quickly with the *T* hotkey), increase the **Font Size** variable to **100**, and change its **Color** to cyan. Of course, we can change the **Text** variable, such as in **Text with Shadow**.

3. The next step is to add the **Shadow (Script)** component. So, let's navigate to **Add Component | UI | Effects | Shadow**.

4. Now, we can leave the **Effect Color** variable as default and change **Effect Distance**. For the **X** axis we, can enter **-7**, and for the **Y** axis, **-3**. In the end, the **Shadow (Script)** component should appear like this:

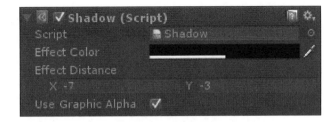

5. If we look at the scene view panel, we can see the final effect, as follows:

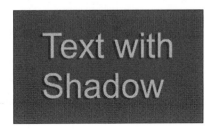

How it works...

The **Shadow (Script)** component replicates the text that it is attached to. It changes its color to the one that is specified in the **Effect Color** variable, and moves it from the center with a phase displacement specified in the **Effect Distance** vector. Therefore, if this displacement is not too far, which means small values for the **Effect Distance** vector, the new text will form a shadow of the original text.

We can also use this component to quickly create 3D letters, which we will explain in the following section.

Creating 3D letters

With this component, it is also easy to create an illusion of 3D letters. This method doesn't work every time. It depends on the font we use, but most of the time we can achieve nice 3D letters without other graphical efforts.

To use this trick, we need to change the **Effect Color** variable to almost the same color that we set for the original text, but this time just a little darker. Then, change the **Alpha** channel of the color to a lower level of the one in the **Text** component. For instance, if the **Alpha** channel of the text is at **255**, it is probably a good compromise to set the **Alpha** of the shadow to **60**. The only reason for using this number is that it is empirical. In fact, it produces a nice effect, but we need to tweak this value according to our needs.

Therefore, you can achieve this kind of effect:

▶ This is not the only **UI Effect** component that we can find in Unity. Therefore, to obtain more information about other **UI Effect** components, you can refer to the next recipe, *Adding outlines to text*.

▶ The official documentation with all the UI effects can be found at `http://docs.unity3d.com/Manual/comp-UIEffects.html`.

▶ Furthermore, in order to create better 3D letters, you should check out the *Creating better 3D letters* section in the next recipe.

Adding outlines to text

In this recipe, you will learn how to add an outline to a **Text (Script)** component. In order to achieve this, you will have to learn how to use a **UI Effect** component of the new UI system of Unity, the **Outline (Script)** component. Similar to text shadows, text outlines can also add an element of boldness to text that is displayed on the screen. This can be useful when there are many elements on the screen, or even if you just want a certain text element to appear more dominant than others. There are many uses for text outlines, and they can be useful to experiment with in order to find out what suits your game the most.

How to do it...

1. First of all, we need to create a new UI text. In order to do this, right-click on the **Hierarchy** panel and then navigate to **UI | Panel**. Finally, name it **Text with Outline**.

2. After this, we can regulate all the parameters in the **Inspector** as we want. However, in order to be sure that we notice the nice effect, we can enlarge **Text with Outline** with **Rect tool** (which can be used quickly with the *T* hotkey), increase the **Font Size** variable to **100**, and change its **Color** in cyan. Of course, we can change the **Text** variable to **Text with Outline**, for instance.

3. The next step is to add the **Outline (Script)** component. To do this, navigate to **Add Component | UI | Effects | Outline**.

4. Now we can leave the **Effect Color** variable as default and change **Effect Distance**. For the **X** axis, we can enter **-2**, and for the **Y** axis **-2**. Then, **Outline (Script)** should appear like this:

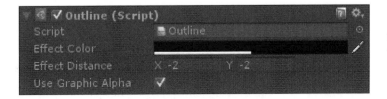

5. If we look at the scene view panel, we can see the final effect, as displayed in this screenshot:

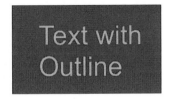

How it works...

The **Outline (Script)** component replicates the text to which it is attached, in particular, four times. It changes the color of each of these four copies to the one specified in the **Effect Color** variable. Furthermore, it moves them symmetrically from the center with a phase displacement specified in the **Effect Distance** vector. If this displacement is not too far, which means small values in the **Effect Distance** vector, all the new text copies will form an outline around the original text.

There's more...

Nice and soft outlines can be created by using this component. Furthermore, by combining this also with the Shadow component, we can create better 3D letters than in the previous recipe.

Creating a nice, soft outline

Through this component, we can also improve the graphical appearance of text very easily by adding a soft outline. In fact, this outline marks the text to make it more important without being visually overwhelming. We can achieve this by setting the distance on one axis in **Effect Distance** to zero. For instance, if we set the **x** axis to **0** and the **y** axis to **-2**, we obtain this effect:

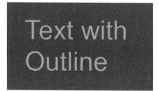

Creating better 3D letters

We can extend the creation of 3D letters that we saw in the last recipe using both the **Outline (Script)** component and the **Shadow (Script)** component. In fact, if we add a soft outline to our text (as in the previous section) and a shadow component (as the one described in the *Creating 3D letters* section of the *Adding shadows to text* recipe), we can obtain a very nice and cool effect. Of course, this is without any graphical efforts. You can see the final result in the following screenshot:

See also

▸ This is not the only **UI Effect** component that you will find in Unity. Therefore, for more information about these components, you should refer to the previous recipe, *Adding shadows to text*.

▸ Other than this, the official documentation with all the UI effects can be found at `http://docs.unity3d.com/Manual/comp-UIEffects.html`.

6
Animating the UI

In this chapter, we will cover the following recipes:

- Appearing and disappearing menu
- Creating a menu with an entrance transition
- Creating a menu with an idle animation
- Animating a button when the cursor is over it
- Creating a pop-up menu
- Animate the hearts of the symbolic lives counter
- Changing the animation of the hearts of the symbolic lives counter through the script

Introduction

In this chapter, we will see how to animate our UI. We will start by making a menu appear and disappear, using only the **OnClick()** event. Then, we will create new animations for the UI through the **Animation** window. Next, we will deal with the **Animator** controller as well. Finally, we will see how we can animate the lives counter that we made in the second chapter, using all that we have covered about animations.

Appearing and disappearing menu

Since the UI does not need complex animations, you will learn that it is not necessary to use the **Animator** controller and/or the **Animation** files. In fact, in this recipe, we are going to use only the **OnClick()** event, which is already implemented inside the **Button (Script)** component, to handle the menu appearing and disappearing.

How to do it...

1. First of all, we need to create our menu. We are going to create a simple menu to show how we can make it disappear and then reappear. However, feel free to construct the entire menu for your game with all the elements that you need in it. Thus, we can right-click on the **Hierarchy** panel and then go to **UI | Panel**. Next, we can rename it **Appearing Menu**. Of course, it is possible to resize, change **Source Image**, and place the panel wherever we wish.

2. The next step is to add at least one button to our menu. To do this, right-click on **Appearing Menu**, go to **UI | Button**, and then rename it **Resume Button**. We can also change the **text** variable of the **Text (Script)** component, attached to the child of our button, to the **Resume** string. For instance, we can construct a menu like this:

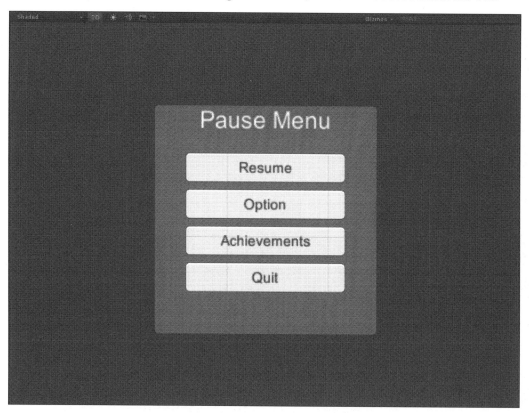

3. Now, we need to add outside of our menu another button that opens the pause menu that we have just created. Thus, instead of right-clicking on **Appearing Menu**, right-click on **Canvas** and then go to **UI | Button**. Again, we should rename it **PauseMenuButton** and change the text inside it to **Pause**. After we have placed it in a location in which we want to use it, such as the top-right corner, we should have something that looks like this:

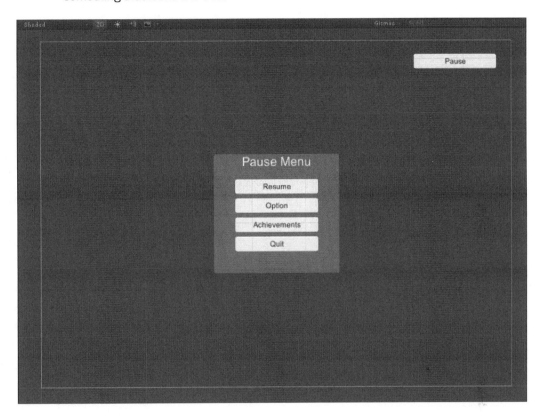

4. When the **Pause** button is clicked we want **PauseMenuButton** to disappear and the **Pause** menu to appear instead. In order to do this, we need to use events. Select **PauseMenuButton** and, in the **Inspector**, click on the small **+** sign in the **OnClick** tab inside the **Button (Script)** component. A new event should appear in the **Inspector**.

5. Drag **Appearing Menu** into the **Object** variable, and then click on the drop-down menu on which **no function** is written. Select **GameObject | SetActive(bool)**. Finally, check the **bool** variable. Once we have done all of this, when we click the **PauseMenuButton**, the **Pause** menu will appear.

6. Now, we have to do the same again. We need to add a new event, but instead of dragging **Appearing Menu** into the **Object** variable, let's set it to **PauseMenuButton**. At the end, remember to uncheck the **bool** variable. Therefore, when we click the **PauseMenuButton**, it will disappear. After completing the last two steps, we should have something that looks this:

7. We also need to repeat the same two steps with **Resume Button**, but invert the **bool** variables. As a result, we have something that looks like this:

8. Since we probably don't want to have the **Pause** menu active at the start of our game, let's select **Appearing Menu** and set it to inactive. We can do this by clicking on the **bool** variable next to the name of **GameObject**.

9. Finally, we can click the play button and check whether our **Pause** menu works.

How it works...

We used events instead of **Animator** controllers to handle the menu. In fact, we have set four events. Two of them are in **PauseMenuButton**, and both trigger our UI elements when the button is clicked on. The former makes **Appearing Menu** appear by calling the **setActive()** function and passing the **true** boolean value to it. The latter disables **PauseButton** by calling the same function. By doing this, we ensure that the player cannot use **PauseButton** anymore when the **Pause** menu appears. The other two events are symmetric, but they are on the **ResumeButton**. These can be triggered only when the **Resume** button is clicked on, and this can happen only if **Appearing Menu** is visible. That means that it can occur only after the player has clicked the **PauseButton**. Again, the first one makes **PauseButton** appear by calling the setActive() function, and the second one makes **Appearing Menu** disappear.

There's more...

Since we have implemented a **Pause** menu, there are a few things to keep in mind beyond the animations. Usually, we have pause menus for allowing the player to stop temporarily playing or to tweak some settings. In order to do this, the whole game needs to be frozen so that it can be resumed once the player is ready to play our game again. Thus, the next subtopic is going to explain how to really pause the game.

Freezing time

Usually, when the **Pause** menu appears in a video game (unless it is an online game), the game will freeze, even if this is not strictly part of the animation system of the menu. We can make the menu freeze quite easily in Unity.

To do this, we need to create a script that changes the time scale of our game. We can rename it **FreezeTimeScript**.

Just a public function is required — the following one, which we can add to the script:

```
public void setTimeScale(float timeScale){
   Time.timeScale = timeScale;
}
```

In this line of code, we change the time scale of the game by the one passed as a parameter. Keep in mind that a time scale equal to **0** means that the game is frozen, and a timescale equal to **1** means that the game has no time distortions. Now, we need to call this function when **PauseMenuButton** or **ResumeButton** is clicked on. To do this, select **PauseMenuButton** from the **Project** panel and then add a new event in the **OnClick()** tab. Furthermore, add **FreezeTimeScript** to **PauseMenuButton** and drag it into the **object** variable of the new event. From the drop-down menu, go to **FreezeTimeScript | setTimeScale(float)** and set the float variable to **0**.

Repeat this process with **ResumeButton**, but instead of setting the float variable to **0**, set it to **1**.

Since **timeScale** is set to **0**, when we click on the button, all of our game freezes. Alternatively, when **timeScale** is set to **1** and we click on **Resume**, the game starts again. It's important to keep in mind that animations may or may not be affected by **timeScale**, depending on how they are implemented.

Creating a menu with an entrance transition

We may want a more complex animation than simply an appearing/disappearing effect as covered in the previous recipe. In this case, we need to use an **Animator** controller along with the **Animation** window in order to create animations. In this recipe, you will learn how to create an entrance transition. However, feel free to change the animation when performing the following steps to fit the needs of your game. Furthermore, we will still be using the **OnClick()** event to cause **PauseMenuButton** to disappear.

How to do it...

1. First of all, we need to create our menu. To do this, just follow the first three steps of the previous recipe, *Appearing and disappearing menu*.

2. Next, we need to place **Appearing Menu** slightly outside **Canvas**, as shown in the following screenshot:

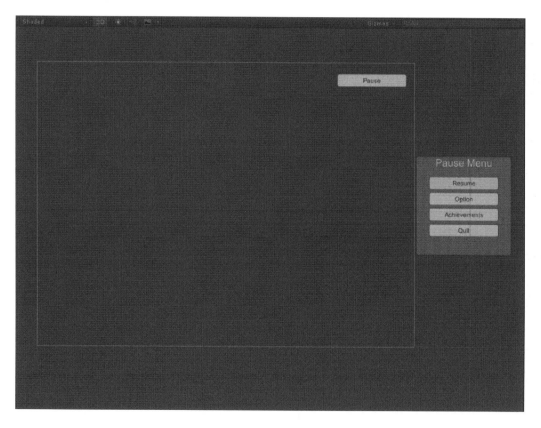

3. After we have selected **Appearing Menu**, we can click on **Add Property** in the **Animation** window. Unity asks us to choose a folder and a name for our animation. For now, let's name it **MenuEntryTransition**.

4. Next, we are going to create the animation. To do this, click on the **Rec** button and then move the red bar to **1** second, that is, to the sixtieth key frame if the sample is set to **60.** Using the **Rect** tool, we can move the menu inside **Canvas**, where we want it to be. For instance, we can place it to the right of the screen.

5. Then, click on the drop-down menu, find **MenuEntryTransition**, and select **[Create new Clip]**.

6. Again, Unity will ask us to save the animation. Hence, let's select the same folder as that of the previous one and rename it **MenuExitTransition**.

7. This time, we need to make the same animation, but in reverse. After clicking on the **Rec** button at **0** seconds, which means that the vertical red bar is at the zeroth key frame, we have to place the menu where it was at the end of the previous animation. Then, at **1** second (which is the sixtieth key frame for **60** samples), place the menu where it was at the beginning of the previous animation.

8. The next step is to put the animations that we have just created together using a controller. If we search in the same folder in which we saved the animations, we can find a controller called **Appearing Menu**. Double-click on it to open the **Animator** window with the controller already loaded.

9. One more step about the animation is to select them one at a time in **Project Panel**, since multi-editing of animations is not supported by Unity. In addition, we will also need to uncheck the **Loop Time** variable for both in the **Inspector**. By doing this, we are setting the animation as a single shot and not as a loop.

10. Since we will call the animation directly by its name, we don't need any graph transition. Therefore, we need to be sure that we have both the animations inside the graph, like this:

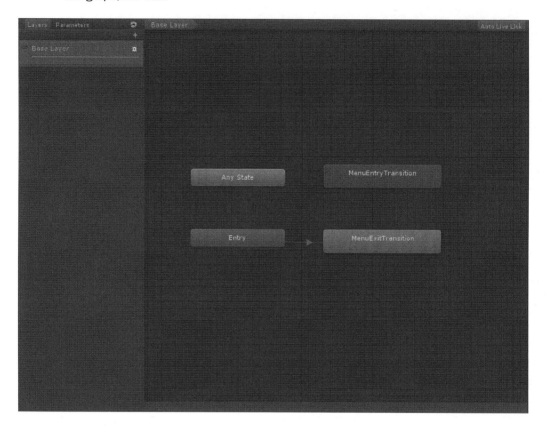

 If they are not inside the graph, just drag and drop them from the **Project** panel.

11. Now, we want **PauseMenuButton** to disappear when the pause button is clicked on, and then we want the pause menu to appear with our transition. To do this, select **PauseMenuButton** and, in the **Inspector**, click on the small **+** sign in the **OnClick** tab inside the **Button (Script)** component.

12. A new event should appear in the **Inspector**. Now drag **PauseMenuButton** into the **object** variable. Then, click on the drop-down menu in which you see **no function**, and go to **GameObject | SetActive(bool)**. Finally, uncheck the **bool** variable.

13. Add a new event again, but this time, drag **Appearing Menu** into the **object** variable. Navigate to **Animator | Play(string)** from the dropdown and put it inside the **string** variable called **MenuEntryTransition**. Finally, the **OnClick()** tab should look like this:

14. Again, we have to add a couple of events to **ResumeButton**. However, we need to change the string variable of the transition in **MenuExitTransition**, and check the **bool** variable to make **PauseMenuButton** appear. So far, it should look as follows:

15. Finally, we can click on **Play** and see if our transitions work.

How it works...

First, we created our menu. We began by creating a couple of animations with the **Animation** window, and then we placed them inside an **Animator** controller. Here, we used the controller just as a set of animations, since they are triggered by the **OnClick()** events from our buttons. When the trigger arrives, **Animator** plays the animation, which is specified by us.

There's more...

As we did in the previous recipe, it is possible to freeze the game, as a pause menu should do.

Freezing time

Usually, when the **Pause** menu appears in a video game, the game should freeze, unless it is an online game. In order to do this, we can use the same script and the same steps that we performed in the homonymous section of the previous recipe, *Appearing and disappearing menu*.

Creating a menu with an idle animation

The previous recipes taught you how to make a menu appear or create a transition that allows the menu to enter the screen. We are now going to see how to make an idle animation, where the object just cycles through a general animation, such as hovering or pulsing. To do this, we need to create an animation that can be played as a loop. In this recipe, we will see how to change the color background of the pause menu that we created in the first recipe, *Appearing and disappearing menu*.

How to do it...

1. First of all, we need to create a menu. We can follow the first three steps of the previous recipe, *Appearing and disappearing menu*.

2. Next, select **Appearing Menu** and then click on **Add Property** inside of the **Animation** window. Once again, Unity asks us to save the animation, so we can simply select a folder and save the animation by naming it **IdleAnimation**.

3. Now, in the **Animation** view, select the **Rec** button if it is not already selected in Unity. Also select **Appearing Menu**. Go to **Inspector | Image (Script)** component and change the color. For now, we will set it to green.

4. At the beginning of the **Animation** window, at **0 key frame**, there is now the color key frame. Just move the red bar to **1** second, which means **60th key frame** for **60** samples, and change the color again in the **Inspector**. In this example, we will use blue.

5. Now, select the first key frame at the beginning and press *Ctrl + C* to copy it. Next, move the red bar to **2** seconds, which means **120th key frame** for **60** samples, and press *Ctrl + V* to paste it. By doing this, we can be certain that the last key frame is the same as the first one. Now, the animation is ready to be played as a loop.

6. Since **IdleAnimation** is set as a loop by default and the autogenerated animator has to handle just one animation, we don't need to do anything other than clicking on the **Rec** button again to deactivate the recording mode. Finally, we can click on play to see that our menu changes its background color over time.

How it works...

Here, we created an animation that is ready to be played as a loop. This means that the last key frame is equal to the first one. In fact, when Unity plays the animation and it reaches the last frame, it is restarted from the beginning. So once it starts again, it's important to give an illusion of continuity. Therefore, since standing animations are always played as a loop, this is an important step. In fact, we also copied the key frame so that the first and the last key frames are identical.

Furthermore, for creating an idle animation, we are not limited to changing just the color of the background. In fact, we can create anything that we wish; our only limitation is our imagination. Just keep in mind that the animations need to be ready to be played as a loop.

The first key frame equals the last one.

Animating a button when the cursor is over it

In this recipe, you will learn how to animate a button when the cursor is over it. You will also learn how to use an **Animator** controller to handle generated animations from the **Button (Script)** component and how to change these animations.

How to do it...

1. First of all, we have to create a UI button. Right-click on the **Hierarchy** panel, then go to **UI | Button**, and rename it **Animated Button**. Of course, it is possible to resize, change **Source Image**, the text, and place it as we wish.

2. Now, we need to change the **Transition** mode in order to use a controller to animate it. In the **Button (Script)** component, click on **Transition** and select **Animation**. If you don't want to create a controller from scratch, click on the **Auto Generate Animation** button that has just appeared in the **Inspector**, as shown here:

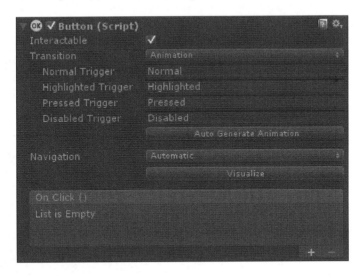

3. Now, Unity will ask us where to save the new controller, and we have to give it a name. Let's choose a folder in our **Project**, rename it **AnimatedButton.controller** and then click on **Save**.

4. We should notice that an **Animator** component has just been added and the **Controller** variable is set with the controller that we just saved. In order to open it, double-click on **AnimatedButton** inside the **Controller** variable.

5. Unity opens the **Animator** window, as shown in the following screenshot. If some nodes are overlapping, we can just drag them around to make the graph clearer. The four nodes emanating from the **Any State** node denote the different states that our button can be in: **Normal**, **Highlighted**, **Pressed**, or **Disabled**. The others, including the **Any State** node, are special nodes, and they need to handle some transition:

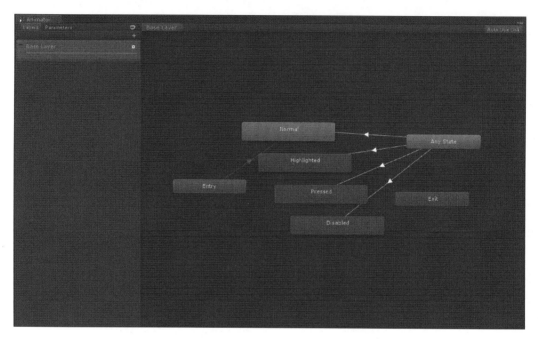

6. The next step is to select the **Animation** window. Click on **Normal** and a drop-down menu will appear. Let's select **Highlighted**, since we are going to animate the button when the mouse is over it. Finally, click on the **Rec** button in the top-left corner (the one with a circle), as shown in the following screenshot:

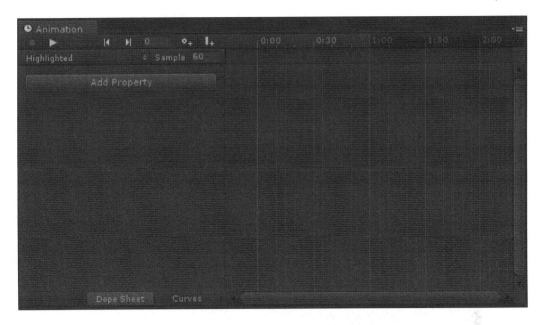

7. Now, navigate to **Add Property | Rect Transform | Size Delta**, and should appear on the windows with a couple of key frames, one at the zeroth frame and another one at the sixtieth frame.

8. We move the red line of the time to **60** frames, where we have the second key frame, and in the **Inspector**, we increase the width of **RectTranform** of **Animated Button** from **160** to **200**.

9. If we click on play and move the mouse arrow onto the button, it becomes larger, and then suddenly smaller, before it becomes larger again in a kind of pulsating motion. This happens because the animation is set as a loop. In order to set it properly, go through the **Project** panel to find the **AnimatedButton.controller** that you saved before, and then click on the small arrow at the beginning of its name. Now the four animations should appear. Let's click on **Highlighted**.

10. In the **Inspector,** just uncheck the **Loop Time** variable.

11. Click on the play button, and now everything should work as planned.

How it works...

Here, we used an **Animator** with a controller to handle the animation. In fact, when the mouse is over it, the controller triggers the **Highlighted** animation. As a result, the button is stretched. When the mouse moves away, it triggers the **Normal** animation, that is, just the button in its original state without a proper animation. However, since Unity handles the transition smoothly by default, the button is then stretched back to its original state.

There's more...

The following section teaches us how to slightly tweak the animation that we have created. By doing this, it helps to improve the quality of the animation.

Stretches back the button to the same speed of the Highlighted animation

When the mouse arrow is moved away, the button is stretched back very fast — 10 times the speed of the animation that we created. This is because **Transition Duration** is set to **0.1**, which means that the animation will be played 10 times faster. Let's see how to change this parameter.

Open the **Animator** window, and select the arrow that goes from **Any State** (the blue node) to the **Normal** node (the orange one). Now expand the **Settings** menu in the **Inspector** by clicking on the small triangle at the beginning of its name. Finally, change the **Transition Duration** variable to **1**. However, you are free to change this to any other value. If we want the animation faster, we just need to insert a number between **0** and **1**. If we want it slower, we insert a number larger than **1**.

Creating a pop-up menu

In this recipe, we are going to see how we can use the techniques learned in the *Creating a menu with an entrance transition* recipe to create a pop-up menu. Pop-up menus are useful when you want to give instant feedback or even instructions to the player. They can be an unobtrusive way of providing information to the user at specific points during the game.

How to do it...

1. In the first step, let's create a new menu — a panel called **Pop-up Menu** — and three buttons as its children.

2. After we have selected it, we then click on **Add Property** in the **Animation** window. Unity asks us to choose a folder and a name for our animation, and we can rename it to **MenuEntryPopUp**.

3. The next step is to create the animation, so click on the **Rec** button and move the vertical bar in the timeline to **1** second; this means the sixtieth key frame if the sample is set to **60**. Using **Rect tool**, reduce the dimensions of all the buttons to zero:

 The vertical bar is not shown by default. In order to make it show up, we can just click on the top section of the **Animation** window, where the time is displayed.

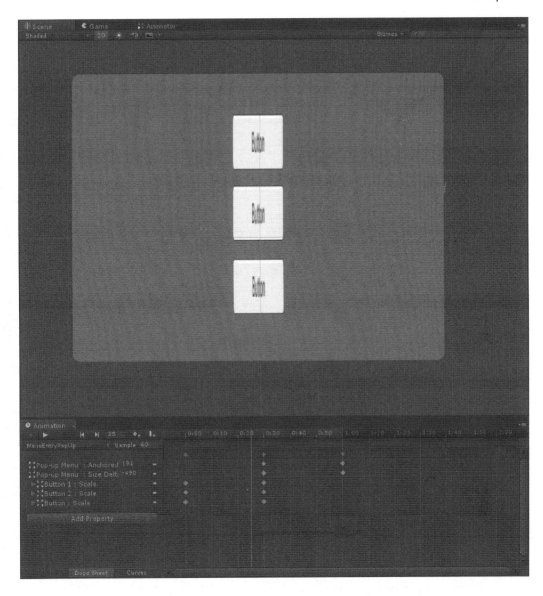

4. Then, move the vertical bar to the 120th key frame, at **2** seconds, and reduce the panel vertically as well, as shown in the following screenshot:

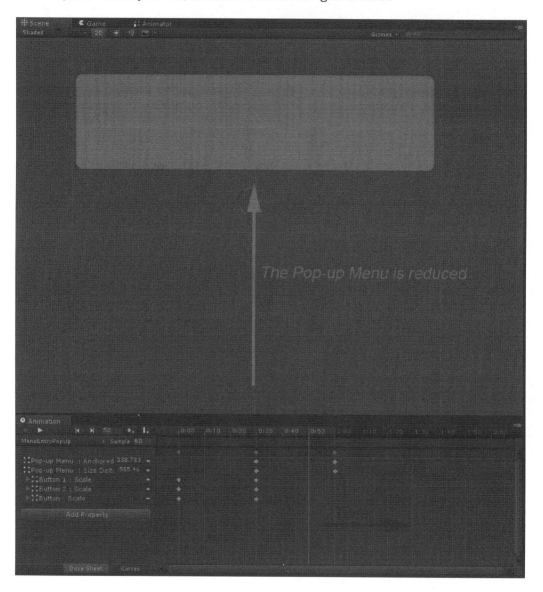

5. Click on the drop-down menu, find **MenuEntryPopUp**, and select **[Create new Clip]**.

6. Again, Unity will ask us to save the animation, so let's select the same folder as the previous one and rename it to **MenuExitPopUp**.

7. Now, it's time to make the same animation, but in reverse. At the zeroth key frame, we should have the same situation of the last frame as that of the other animation. Move the vertical bar in the timeline to **1** second, and using **Rect tool**, expand the panel to its original position. Lastly, move the bar to the 120th key frame, at **2** seconds, and expand all the buttons as well.

8. The next step is to get the animations that we have just created and put them into a controller. If we search in the same folder where we saved the animations, we can find a controller called **MenuEntryPopUp**. Double-click on it to open it in the **Animator** widow.

9. Since multi-editing of animations is not supported by Unity, we have to select the animations one at a time in the **Project** panel. In addition, we will also need to uncheck the **Loop Time** variable for both in the **Inspector**. By doing this, we are setting the animation as a single shot and not as a loop.

10. Now, we just need to create another button, above **MenuEntryPopUp**. By following the second recipe of this chapter, starting from step 11, we can trigger the animation accordingly. Just remember to change the animation names with the names of this recipe. After this, click on the play button to see your animated **Pop-up** menu.

How it works...

First, we created a couple of animations with the **Animation** window, and then we put them inside an **Animator** controller. Here, we used the controller just as a set of animation, since they are triggered by the **OnClick()** events from our buttons. When the trigger arrives, **Animator** plays the animation specified by us.

Animating hearts of the symbolic lives counter

In this recipe, we will discover how to animate the hearts of the symbolic lives counter made in the second chapter. In fact, we will use an **Animator** controller to handle the animation and use the **Animation** window to animate them. Also, we want to make all the hearts beat. As a result, the UI will be more dynamic and immersive.

How to do it...

1. You might remember that when we attached the script created in the *Creating a symbolic lives counter* recipe in *Chapter 2, Implementing Counters and Health Bars,* we needed to assign different images (in this case, hearts) in the **Inspector**. Now select one of them, for instance, **Heart1**, and then open the **Animation** window.

2. Click on **Add Property**, and Unity will ask you to choose a folder in which you want to save your animation and a name. Just choose one and click on **Save**.

3. Next, we should notice that Unity has added an **Animator** component to our image and filled the controller variable with a controller named **Heart1**. We can rename it to **HeartAnimationController**. If we open the controller by double-clicking on it, we should see in the **Animator** window that we have a node with the name that we gave to the animation.

4. Now, it should already be in record mode. Put the red bar at the zeroth key frame and set the scale of the image to **1** for both the **x** axis and the **y** axis. In this way, **Heart1** starts with the normal scale.

5. Next, move the red bar to half second, if the samples are **60**, this means the thirtieth key frame. Change the scale to **1.2**, on both the **x** and **y** axes. Therefore, in this case, we are going to enlarge the heart a little so that we can simulate a beat.

6. Finally, move the red bar to one second, again at **60** samples (which means at the sixtieth key frame). Now we have to conclude the heartbeat animation, so we set the scale back to **1**, on both the **x** and **y** axes.

7. After this, we need to interrupt the recording. To do this, just click on the red **Rec** button in the **Animation** window.

8. Finally, if we have already set up all the other images to interact with **SymbolicLivesCounterScript**, we select all of them except the first one, which we have already animated. In the **Inspector**, go to **Add Component | Miscellaneous | Animator**.

> If you haven't set the other images yet, please consider using the *Ctrl + D* shortcut to duplicate **Heart1**. By doing this, you will also duplicate the **Animator** component and its **Controller**, so you don't have to set them. As a result, you can skip this and the next step.

9. Now, we find the controller that we created indirectly when Unity asked us to save the animation file. It is in the same folder. Drag it into the **Controller** variable in the **Inspector**.

10. Finally, you can click on the play button and see all the hearts animated.

How it works...

We used an **Animator** with a controller to handle all the animations. In fact, when the game starts, the controller triggers the only animation available, and since it is set as a loop, Unity reproduces it consequently. Each heart has the same controller, so all of them are animated in the same way. When **SymbolicLivesCounterScript** handles the hearts in order to make them appear and disappear respectively if the player gains a life or loses it, it doesn't change the animation, and so our symbolic lives counter has an animation in our UI.

Changing animation of the hearts of the symbolic lives counter through the script

In this recipe, we will go even further than we went in the previous recipe. Here, we will see how we can control the **Animator** controller through a script. In this specific case, you will learn how to change the speed of the controller according to the number of lives that the player has left. In fact, we want to make the hearts beat at a normal speed when the player has all his lives intact and beat faster when the player has fewer lives.

Getting ready...

In order to get started, you should have completed the previous recipe, *Animating hearts of the symbolic lives counter*, because you need to have all the hearts animated through an **Animator** controller, called **HeartAnimationController**.

So first of all, we need to be sure that all the hearts have an **Animator** component attached along with the **Controller** variable filled by **HeartAnimationController**.

Since we need to change the **Animator** component through the script, we can do this directly inside **SymbolicLivesCounterScript**. We had written it in the second chapter in the *Creating a symbolic lives counter* recipe. You might remember that it handles all of the logic for the lives counter.

 If we don't want to override the script and keep the original one as well, we can rename it **SymbolicLivesCounterAnimatedScript**. Also remember to rename the class inside the script with the same name.

How to do it...

1. For the first step, double-click on **SymbolicLivesCounterAnimatedScript** to open it.

2. Next, go through it inside the `updateSymbolicLivesCounter()` function. Since this function in called every time a heart is lost or gained, it is the perfect object for making a general animation over all the hearts of the lives counter.

3. In particular, we need to go inside the `for` cycle, immediately after the `hearts[i].SetActive(true);` instruction. Since we are dealing with all the active hearts here, we need to change the animation to only these, and not to the other ones that are not on the screen anymore.

4. In this context, `hearts[i]` is an active heart, and we need to get its **Animator** component through the `GetComponent<Animator>()` function. Then we set the speed to `hearts.Length - lives`. So, let's add it to our code:

```
hearts [i].GetComponent<Animator> ().speed = hearts.Length - lives;
```

5. Finally, we just save our script, and click on play to test it.

How it works...

We start by getting the **Animator** of each active heart, and then we want to see them beating according to the number of lives the player has left. Therefore, the speed of the animation can be calculated as the difference between the maximum number of lives, which in this case is the length of the array, and the remaining lives. In fact, this difference gives us a bigger number with each life that is lost.

There's more...

In this recipe, we saw how to animate the lives counter differently through script, but maybe we need more control over these animations.

Adding a speed controller to customize speed in the Inspector and at runtime

Right now, our script uses just the difference to calculate the animation speed for each heart. If we want to tweak this speed in some way with a parameter but keep it dependent on the number of lives the player has left, we can add a new `public` variable to our script:

```
public float speedController = 1f;
```

As we can see, the default value is `1f`. This means that there is no difference in speed compared with before, since this variable will be multiplied.

Now, change the only line of code added in this recipe in this way:

```
hearts [i].GetComponent<Animator> ().speed = (hearts.Length - lives)*speedController;
```

By multiplying the difference of our parameters, we are able to control it through the **Inspector**, or even during runtime if we change this variable through another script, since it is a `public` variable. If `speedController` stores a number between `0` and `1`, the animation speed is reduced. Otherwise, if it is greater than `1`, the animation speed is increased.

Customizing each animation

On the other hand, if we want to customize each animation, we should change the code and write a long series of `if` statements. How to change the animation is entirely up to you. For instance, if we want to change only the first heart, we can put it inside the `updateSymbolicLivesCounter()` function outside the `for` cycle with these lines:

```
if (lives == 1) {
   hearts [0].GetComponent<Animator> ().speed = 2.5f;
} else {
   hearts [0].GetComponent<Animator> ().speed = 1.0f;
}
```

7

Applying Runtime Customizations

In this chapter, we will cover the following recipes:

- ▶ Creating a button that changes color
- ▶ Creating a slider that changes color gradually
- ▶ Creating a slide shower using a discrete slider
- ▶ Creating a slider that changes a single color channel
- ▶ Making an input field with personal text validation at runtime
- ▶ Making an input field for a password with a lower bound limit for characters
- ▶ Changing the cursor at runtime

Introduction

In this chapter, we will look at how to implement different levels of customization for the player, such as adjusting colors of objects using a slider. We will also see how to implement validation at runtime for input fields to ensure that the correct information is entered. Furthermore, we will set lower bound limits for characters so that the data input meets a minimum number of characters. Lastly, we will look at how we can change the cursor within a game.

Making a button that changes color

In this recipe, we will see the first basic customization that we can allow the player to do. This customization will allow him to change the color of a button by clicking on it, and then switch between two colors. In this way, you will learn how it is possible to use events to customize buttons when the player interacts with them.

How to do it...

1. In the first step, we have to create our UI button. Right-click on the **Hierarchy** panel, then go to **UI | Button**, and rename it to **ChangeColorButton**. Of course, it is possible to resize the button, change **Source Image**, the text, and place it as we wish in **Canvas**.

2. Now, it's already time to write our script to handle the whole process. Select **ChangeColorButton** and, in the **Inspector**, navigate to **Add Component | New Script**. Name it **ChangeColorButtonScript**, and then click on **Create and Add**.

3. Double-click on the script in order to edit it. Next, we have to add the `using UnityEngine.UI;` statement at the beginning of the script, since we are going to use the `Image` class. Before the beginning of the class, we can also add this line: `[RequireComponent(typeof(Image))]` (without the semicolon at the end). In this way, the script requires an **Image (Script)** component attached to the same game object of it.

4. We need two variables to store the two colors. The first variable is `public`, so it can be set in the **Inspector** with the new color, and the other one is `private`, in order to keep the original color of the **Image (Script)** component stored. Then, we also need a `private` variable to store the reference to the **Image (Script)** component that is attached to this script, and a third `private` variable - a `bool` variable, is needed to determine whether our script has to change the color or restore the original. So let's write this code:

```
public Color color;
private Color originalColor;
private Image img;
private bool b;
```

5. The next step is to write the `Start()` function, where we will store the initial values for our `private` variables. So, let's take the reference to the **Image (Script)** component using the `GetComponent<Image>()` function and use it to obtain the original color and store it in the other variable. Therefore, we can write the following:

```
void Start () {
  img = GetComponent<Image> ();
  originalColor = img.color;
}
```

6. Now, we don't need an `Update()` function but a function that can be triggered by some events instead, for instance, when our button is pressed. In order to do so, we need to make it public as well. Let's call it `onClick()` and, set the new or the original color, according to our bool variable, through an `if` statement to differentiate the two cases. Finally, update the `bool` value by inverting it. So, our function will look like this:

```
public void onClick(){
    if (b)
        img.color = color;
    else
        img.color = originalColor;
    b = !b;
}
```

7. Our script is now ready. We can save it and come back to Unity. The next step is to trigger our script through an event and - as we have done in a few other recipes from other chapters - we do the following: select **ChangeColorButton**, look inside the **Button (Script)** component, and click on the small **+** sign on the **On Click ()** event tab in the bottom-right corner.

8. Drag the script inside the **object** variable, and in the drop-down menu, navigate to **ChangeColorButtonScript | onClick()**. The final result should be like this:

9. As the final step, we ensure that the color variable in our script is changed to display another color. Finally, we can test whether what we have done works as we planned.

> When Unity creates a new color as the default, it has all the parameters set to zero, so it is black and the alpha channel is to zero. As a result, when we choose another color, we must also ensure that we set an appropriate alpha channel for what we want to get.

How it works...

Here, we created a function that switches between two colors. This system is created using a `bool` variable to determine whether we are going to change to the new color or restore the original one. In fact, every time we have an operation, we reverse the value of this variable. Then, we assigned our function to the **On Click ()** event on the **Button (Script)** component so that it is called every time the player clicks on the button.

There's more...

Maybe we want the button to change another image instead of itself. The next section will explain to us, how we can achieve this.

Changing another image instead of the one attached to the button

If we want the button to affect another image instead of itself, we can slightly modify our script. In fact, we have to make the `img` variable `public` so that it can be set in the **Inspector**:

```
private Image img;
```

Then, we can erase this line from the `Start()` function, since we set `img` on our own:

```
img = GetComponent<Image> ();
```

Finally, set the `img` variable from the **Inspector**, and we are done. Of course, if we want to test it, we can create, for instance, a panel and drag and drop it into the `img` variable.

Furthermore, it would be good to remove the `[RequireComponent(typeof(Image))]` statement so that we can place this script on other game objects as well.

See also

▶ If you need a gradual change between colors, you can refer to the next recipe, *Creating a slider that changes colors gradually*.

▶ However, in the last recipe of this chapter, there is another way to call events without touching the events in the **Inspector**. In fact, this could be achieved by using the handlers inside the script. More information is available in the *Changing the cursor at runtime* recipe.

Creating a slider that changes colors gradually

Here, you are going to learn another type of customization that the player can perform at runtime. With this, the player has more power on how he can customize his own UI to fit suit his needs. In fact, the player will be able to switch between two colors, as in the previous chapter, but gradually and through a slider. We will handle this with a script and, as usual, using the events that are inside the **Slider (Script)** component.

How to do it...

1. First of all, we need to create our slider. This can be done easily by right-clicking on the **Hierarchy** panel, then going to **UI | Slider**, and renaming it to **GraduallyColorSlider**. Of course, it is possible to resize the slider, change **Source Image**, or change the text inside. Finally, place it as you wish, in **Canvas**.

2. Next, we can write a script to handle the entire process. To do this, select **GraduallyColorSlider**. In the **Inspector**, navigate to **Add Component | New Script**, rename it **GraduallyColorSliderScript**, and then click on **Create and Add**.

3. Double-click on the script in order to edit it. As usual, when we deal with the UI, we have to add the `using UnityEngine.UI;` statement at the beginning of the script, since we are going to use the `Image` class.

4. We need three `public` variables. One is used to store the **Image (Script)** component that we want to change, and the other two store the two colors that we want our slider to lerp between. To do this, let's write the following code:

```
public Image img;
public Color firstColor;
public Color secondColor;
```

5. We don't need the `Update()` function or the `Start()` one. Instead, we need a function that can be triggered by some events, for instance, when our slider is changing. Therefore, it has to be `public`, and we can name it `change()`. It also takes a `float` parameter that will be passed by the event. Moreover, it will contain the value of the slider. Here is what we will write:

```
public void change(float value){
}
```

6. Then, we only need one line to change the color of the image. We can assign the new color in this way:

```
img.color = Color.Lerp(firstColor, secondColor, value);
```

7. Now our script is done. We save it and come back to Unity. As in the previous recipe, we have to trigger our script through an event, and so we select **GraduallyColorSlider**, look inside the **Slider (Script)** component, and click on the small **+** sign on the **On Change ()** event tab in the bottom-right corner.

8. Drag the script inside the **object** variable, and from the drop-down menu, navigate to **GraduallyColorSliderScript | change**. Also, be sure to select **change** in the first set of functions, labeled **Dynamic Float**, as shown in the following screenshot:

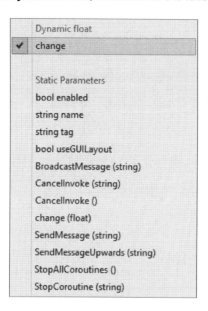

9. At the end, the event tab should be like this:

10. Next, we need to set our **Img** variable. In this recipe, let's create a panel to assign to it. To do this, right-click on the **Hierarchy** panel and navigate to **UI | Panel**. We can rename this to **GraduallyColorPanel**. Keep in mind that this can be any object in the scene, as long as it has an **Image (Script)** component attached to itself. Thus, we can drag and drop it into the **Img** variable.

11. As a final step, we can ensure that both the color variables in our script have been set. Finally, click on play and use the slider to see how the panel changes color gradually.

As in the previous recipe, Unity creates new colors with their alpha channels set to zero. Therefore, when we choose the colors for both our variables, we must also ensure that we set an appropriate alpha channel to suit what we want to achieve.

How it works...

Unlike the previous recipe, where we had to switch between two colors, here we had to make this transition occur gradually. So, as we have done previously, we used the **On Change()** event of the slider in a dynamic way to give its value to our script. In it, we simply used the **Color.Lerp()** function to interpolate the two colors set in the **Inspector** along `value`.

See also

▶ If you don't require a gradual change, you can look at the previous recipe, *Creating a button that changes color*.

▶ In addition, more information about the **Color.Lerp()** function can be found in the official documentation, which is located at `http://docs.unity3d.com/ScriptReference/Color.Lerp.html`.

▶ Finally, in the last recipe of this chapter, there is another way to call events without touching the events in the **Inspector**. In fact, this can be achieved using the handlers inside the script. More information is available in the *Changing the cursor at runtime* recipe.

Creating a slide shower using a discrete slider

Here, we can go further in providing additional customization for the player. In this case, we are going to implement a slide shower. The player will be able to scroll between pictures using a slider. To achieve this, we will see how to write a script to run this system. Again, we will use the events from the **Slider (Script)** component.

How to do it...

1. To begin, we need to create our slider, which will be the controller of the player, so let's right-click on the **Hierarchy** panel and then go to **UI | Slider**. Finally, rename it to **SlideShowerSlider**.

2. Then, select the slider and, in the **Inspector**, navigate to **Add Component | New Script**. Name it to **SlideShowerScript** and then click on **Create and Add**.

3. Now, double-click on the script in order to edit it. Like every other time when we deal with the UI, we have to add the `using UnityEngine.UI;` statement at the beginning of the script, since we are going to use some UI classes.

4. We need two `public` variables, one to store all the pictures that we want to show, and another to store the **Image (Script)** component to show all the pictures, so let's write this code:

```
public Sprite[] pictures;
public Image img;
```

5. The next step is to create a function that will be called by an event so that when the slider changes its value, it takes its value as a parameter. Since the slider value is a `float` variable, we need to make `value` a `float` variable. Here is the structure of our function:

```
public void changePicture(float value){
    }
```

6. In the body of our function, the first thing that we have to do is transform `value`, which is a `float` variable, into an `int`, since array indexes are `int`. We can achieve this through a cast in this way:

```
int index = (int)value;
```

7. Next, we can simply assign the correct picture as the sprite of the **Image (Script)** component stored in `img` using `index`, which is found in the previous line:

```
img.sprite = pictures [index];
```

8. Save the script and come back to Unity. Then select **SlideShowerSlider**. As usual, we have to call our function using an event, so we click on the **+** sign in the **On Value Changed (Single)** event tab. Finally, we drag our script into the **object** variable, and our event tab should be like this:

9. Now, in the drop-down menu, select **SlideShowerScript.changePicture**. Also, be sure that you have selected **changePicture** in the first set of functions, labeled **Dynamic Float**, as demonstrated in the following screenshot:

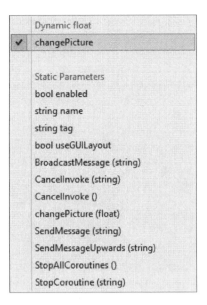

10. The next step requires us to assign a value to the `img` variable in the **Inspector**. So let's create a new UI image by right-clicking on the **Hierarchy** panel and then going to **UI | Image**. Lastly, rename it **SlideShower**. Again, it is possible to resize it and place it wherever we want in the **Canvas**. Modifying **Source Image** is futile, since it will be replaced by our script. Once we are done, we should have something similar to this:

11. We can drag **SlideShower** into the `img` variable on our **SlideShowerScript**.

12. We should add all the pictures that we want onto the `pictures` variable in the **Inspector**. We can expand the variable by clicking on the little triangle to the left of the name of the variable, and in **Size**, we enter the number of the pictures that we want. It should appear as a row for each picture, and we can set them with whatever pictures we want. Here is an example of this concept; it uses image elements from previous chapters:

13. We cannot use our slide shower yet, since we have to finish setting up **SlideShowerSlider**. In fact, in the **Slider (Script)** component, we have to tweak the **Min Value** and **Max Value** variables according to the number of pictures we selected in the previous step. So, let's set **Min Value** to **0** and **Max Value** to the number of pictures minus one (for instance, if there are four pictures, the number we set will be **3**).

14. Furthermore, we have to check the **Whole numbers** variable and set the value of the variable to **0** (this can also be done by dragging the variable slider completely to the left).

15. Finally, save the scene. Now, we are ready to click on the play button to see our slide shower in action, like this:

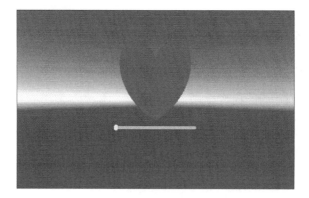

How it works...

In this recipe, we created a slide shower that is controlled by a slider. We also wrote a script to handle this. Every time the slider changes its value, an event is triggered and it calls the function inside our script. This function just changes the image inside the slide shower accordingly.

There's more...

The following sections will give us some useful suggestions on how to improve our discrete SlideShower.

Adding a text label to show the number of pictures

Sometimes, we might want to show the player how many pictures are contained within the slider and which picture is currently being viewed. We can do this by adding a text label next to **SlideShower** and controlling it through our script.

As the first step, right-click on the **Hierarchy** panel and go to **UI | Text**. Rename it **SlideShowerLabel**. Of course, we can resize it and change the font or size of the text as we wish. Finally, place it next to **SlideShower**.

Now we open our script again and add a new variable to keep track of **SlideShowerLabel**:

```
public Text label;
```

At the bottom of the body of the `changePicture()` function, we have to update the text of our label in this way:

```
label.text = (index + 1) + "/" + pictures.Length;
```

In order to obtain the current number of pictures that are being displayed, we added 1 to `index`. We did this because it is the current picture, but it starts from zero. Then we obtained the length of the array in order to find out the total number of pictures.

Save the script and then drag **SlideShowerLabel** in the `label` variable in the **Inspector** inside your script. And the trick is done!

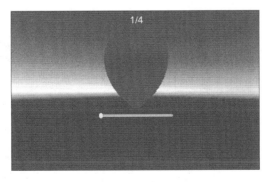

Making the slider continuous

Right now, the slider moves in a discrete way, since we have constructed it to be like that. But if, for some reason, it has to be continuous, we can achieve this very easily by simply unchecking the **Whole Numbers** variable. In fact, we used in our script a `float` as a parameter and converted it into `int` in the first line of the **changePicture()** function. Therefore, we don't have to worry about float conversions.

Automating the slider setup

Each time we have to change the number of pictures of our **SlideShower**, we also need to update the **SlideShowerSlider** settings in the **Slider (Script)** component. We can automatize this process in the script. Therefore, we don't have to worry about this anymore.

To do this, let's add a new function called `updateSliderSettings()`. This is its body:

```
private void updateSliderSettings(){
}
```

First of all, we have to retrieve the `Slider`, like this:

```
Slider slider = GetComponent<Slider> ();
```

Then we can start setting its values. The first values are the `minValue` and `maxValue` variables. We have to set the former to zero, and the latter equals the number of pictures, which we know through the length of the array:

```
slider.minValue = 0;
slider.maxValue = pictures.Length - 1;
```

The next values are the `WholeNumbers` Boolean, for making our `slider` discrete, and `value`, for initializing `slider` at the beginning:

```
slider.wholeNumbers = true;
slider.value = 0;
```

 If we want to make the slider continuous, as done in the *Making the slider continuous* section, we will have to change the line in `slider.wholeNumbers = false;`.

Next, we have to reset our **SlideShower** at the beginning as well, by calling the `changePicture()` function. We do this by passing `0` as the parameter:

```
changePicture (0);
```

Finally, in the `Start ()` function, we have to call the `updateSliderSettings ()` function, as follows:

```
void Start () {
  updateSliderSettings ();
}
```

Now, we don't have to take care of changing the slider settings in the steps starting from step 14 anymore because we have automatized the process inside our script.

Adding pictures at runtime

We may want to change the number of pictures at runtime. We can do this by creating another `public` function. Therefore, it can be called by other scripts that create a new array. The `public` variable copies all the values in the new one plus the new picture, and at the end, it calls the `updateSliderSettings ()` function again, so it is updated as well.

Keep in mind that by calling the `updateSliderSettings ()` function, we are going to reset **SlideShower** to zero, which means it will begin from the first picture. If you don't want this, we can create another function (or directly in this one) to preserve that number when new pictures are added.

See also

▶   In the last recipe of this chapter, there is another way to perform call events without touching the events in the **Inspector**. In fact, this can be achieved by using the handlers inside the script. More information is available in the *Changing the cursor at runtime* recipe.

Creating a slider that changes a single color channel

In this recipe, we are going to see how to provide the player with the ability to completely customize the color of something. In this case, we will allow the player to customize an **Image (Script)** component. It is important to keep in mind that we are not limited to customizing just the **Image (Script)** component. In fact, we can change everything that has a color, including lights. Changing lights is useful if you want to create ambience and immersive UIs. This is associated with what you learned in *Chapter 4, Creating Panels for Menus*, in the *Making UI Elements affected by different lights* recipe. Compared to the *Creating a button that changes color* and *Creating a slider that changes colors gradually* recipes, here the player will be able to change colors in a better way. He will be able to tweak every color channel.

In order to implement all of this, we need to create a slider that controls, through a script, the single color channel, and modify the **Image (Script)** component accordingly.

How to do it...

1. To create the slider, right-click on the **Hierarchy** panel and then go to **UI | Slider** and rename it **RedChannelColorSlider**. Of course, it is possible to resize it, change the **Source Image**, change the text inside, and finally place it as we wish in **Canvas**.

2. Select the slider. Then, in the **Inspector**, navigate to **Add Component | New Script**, name it **ChangeColorChannelSliderScript**, and click on **Create and Add**.

3. Double-click on the script in order to edit it. Since we are going to use the **Image** class, we have to add the `using UnityEngine.UI;` statement at the beginning of the script.

4. For this script, we only need one `public` variable. Here, we are going to store the **Image (Script)** component whose color we want to modify through our slider by a single channel. So, we can write this:

   ```
   public Image img;
   ```

5. The next step is to write a function that changes one color channel of the **Image (Script)** component, stored in the `img` variable. In this step, we are going to change only the red channel, but in the *There's more...* section, you will see that it is possible to change other channels as well. In order to get it, our function takes `value`, a `float`, as a parameter and assigns a `new Color` to `img`. Here, all the parameters of the color channels are the same, except the red one; it is assigned with `value`. This is our function:

   ```
   public void changeRed(float value){
       img.color = new Color (value, img.color.g, img.color.b, img.
   color.a);
   }
   ```

6. Now, we can save the script and come back to Unity. As usual, we have to call our function using an event, and in this case, we can use the one in the **Slider (Script)** component. Select **RedChannelColorSlider** and click on the **+** sign in the **On Value Changed (Single)** event tab. Finally, we drag our script into the **object** variable, and we should have the event tab looking as follows:

7. Next, in the drop-down menu, select **ChangeColorChannelSliderScript.changeRed**. Be sure to select **changeRed** in the first set of functions, labeled **Dynamic float**, as displayed in the following screenshot:

8. The last thing that we have to do is assign a value to the img variable in the **Inspector**. To do this, let's create a new panel and right-click on the **Hierarchy** panel. Then go to **UI | Panel** and rename it **ChangeColorPanel**. Again, keep in mind that it is possible to resize it, modify the **Source Image**, and finally place it wherever we want in the **Canvas.**

9. We drag **ChangeColorPanel** in the img variable onto our **ChangeColorChannelSliderScript**. If we want, we can also add a text label next to the slider so that we can show to the player what color channel the slider changes.

10. Finally, save the scene and click on play to check whether everything works as expected:

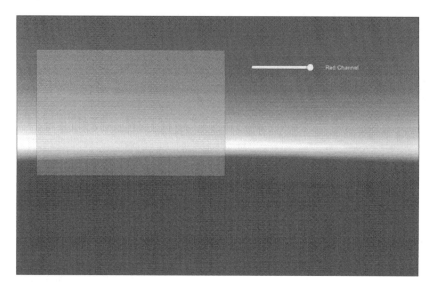

How it works...

We started by creating a script that takes a `float` as a parameter and uses it to change the red color channel. In fact, it creates a new color that has all the channels, including alpha, with the same value of the previous color. After all, we have acquired them from it. We assigned the value that was received as a parameter in the red channel.

Lastly, in order to call our function, we set the `On Value Change ()` event so that it is triggered every time the value of the slider changes. Instead of selecting the `Static` parameter, we chose the same function in the **Dynamic float** set. By doing this, we can automatically pass the value of the slider itself as a parameter to the function. Finally, this function assigns a new color after it has tweaked its color channels.

There's more...

We can definitely extend the concepts that have been learnt in this recipe to the other channels, including the alpha channel, or applying this to lights.

Changing all other color channels

If we give a player the ability to change the color of something, which in this case was the **Image (Script)** component, it would be ideal if we could also provide the player with the ability to change the other two color channels.

In order to do so, we need to add two other functions, one for each channel. We can call them changeGreen() and changeBlue(). Similar to changeRed(), which we have written before, they take value as a float parameter and change the color to the **Image (Script)** component stored in img. They work exactly in the same way, but instead of assigning a value to the red channel, they assign a value to their channel and keep the red one unaltered.

So here are our new functions:

```
public void changeGreen(float value){
    img.color = new Color (img.color.r, value, img.color.b, img.
color.a);
}

public void changeBlue(float value){
    img.color = new Color (img.color.r, img.color.g, value, img.
color.a);
}
```

Of course, the next step is to create two other sliders (if we want, we can also create text labels), and rename them GreenChannelColorSlider and BlueChannelColorSlider respectively. Then we have to follow the steps starting from step 6, and instead of selecting the changeRed function, we select the function pertaining to what we want the player to change:

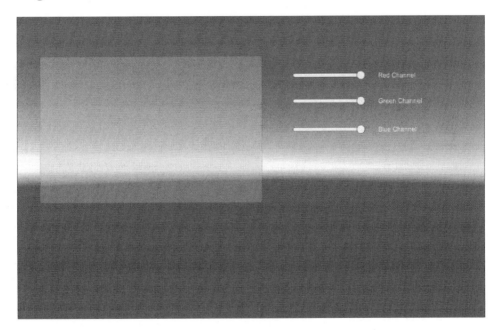

Changing the alpha channel

If we want to provide the player with an additional level of customization, we can allow him to adjust the alpha channel. Again, we can achieve this in the same way — by leaving all the color channels untouched and changing only the alpha channel.

Let's create another function:

```
public void changeAlpha(float value){
    img.color = new Color (img.color.r, img.color.g, img.color.b,
value);
}
```

Like the previous section, we need to create a new slider. Once we have done this, we can call it **AlphaChannelColorSlider** and again follow all the steps from step 6 onwards:

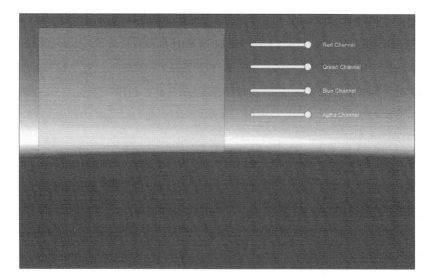

Sometimes, we don't want to allow the player to make the object completely disappear while he is tweaking the alpha channel by setting it to 0, or make the object completely appear on the screen by setting it to 1. So, to ensure that this will not happen, we can select **AlphaChannelColorSlider**. Then, in the **Inspector**, we set a bigger value for **Min Value** or a smaller one for **Max Value**.

Of course, this can also be applied to the other sliders if we wish.

If we really want to provide the player with the idea that something is blocked in the slider — something that he will be able to unlock later — we can do this using what we covered in the *Adding upper and lower bounds to the slider* recipe in *Chapter 4, Creating Panels for Menus*.

Integrating with lights instead of image components

Since these sliders are very powerful tools, and they provide the player with options for real-time customizations, they can also be used to change other components, such as lights. This is especially true if these lights affect our UI, as we explored in the *Making UI Elements affect by variable lights* recipe in *Chapter 4, Creating Panels for menus*.

 Here, we are going to change the script, but if we want to keep the old one, we just change the name of its class, along with the filename, which has to be the same.

First of all, we cannot use the `img` variable anymore, since it cannot store a light. So, we can erase it. Having done this, we can also delete the `using UnityEngine.UI;` statement at the beginning of the script, since we won't use UI classes anymore. Therefore, let's replace the old variable with the new one, that is, `Light`:

```
public Light light;
```

Now we have to replace every occurrence of `img` with `light`. So, the `changeRed()` function will be as follows:

```
public void changeRed(float value){
   light.color = new Color (value, light.color.g, light.color.b, light.color.a);
}
```

Here is what the `changeGreen()` function looks like:

```
public void changeGreen(float value){
   light.color = new Color (light.color.r, value, light.color.b, light.color.a);
}
```

The `changeBlue()` function becomes like this:

```
public void changeBlue(float value){
   light.color = new Color (light.color.r, light.color.g, value, light.color.a);
}
```

And finally, we have the `changeAlpha()` function:

```
public void changeAlpha(float value){
   light.color = new Color (light.color.r, light.color.g, light.color.b, value);
}
```

For the final step, we need to set the `light` variable in the **Inspector** by dragging a light from the **Hierarchy** panel. We might also use the one that we created in *Chapter 4, Creating Menus and Panels*, and if needed, we can set the events on the sliders again.

See also

> ▶ In order to integrate this recipe in amazing ways inside your game, you can refer to the *Making UI elements affected by variable lights* and *Adding upper and lower bounds to the slider* recipes in *Chapter 4, Creating Panels for Menus*.

> ▶ Furthermore, we should also refer to the official documentation about lights at `http://docs.unity3d.com/Manual/class-Light.html`.

Making an input field with personal text validation at runtime

Here, we are going to create another kind of customization, different from the previous recipes. In this case, we have an input field that we want to perform checks on, thus not allowing the player (instead of allowing, as in the previous recipes) to do something. Unity already has some of these controls in the **Input Field (Script)** component, but in this recipe, you will learn how you can create your personal filters. In this example, we will develop a simple filter in order for you to understand the concept of how filters work. For instance, we want the player to insert an identifier, maybe for the score database, and we don't want his name to start with a number — because in many programming languages, identifiers cannot start with a number. We can perform this check at runtime by developing a script.

This filter is a basic filter, since it is static and it doesn't check the input in a dynamic way. "Dynamic" in this context means having some parametric constrains in the middle that depend on the sentence itself (for example, every number has to be followed by the letter "a"). In this case, we need to use loops and `for` cycles to perform the check, but how this interacts with our UI is the same for the basic filter. Therefore, you can learn here how to implement personal text validation at runtime inside your UI. However, in the *There's more...* section of this recipe, you will see that it is possible to find a way to implement the preceding example of dynamic filtering.

Furthermore, the same section describes how we can modify the script to give feedback to the player. This is very important since we need to communicate what the constraints are to the player, if we don't want to frustrate him.

How to do it...

1. First of all, we need to create our input field by right-clicking on the **Hierarchy** panel and then going to **UI | Input Field**. Rename it to **myInputField**. Of course, we can place it wherever we want.

2. Select the input field. Then in the **Inspector**, navigate to **Add Component | New Script**, name it **PersonalTextValidation**, and then click on **Create and Add**.

3. Now, double-click on the script in order to edit it. Just like every other occasion when we have dealt with the UI, we have to add the `using UnityEngine.UI;` statement at the beginning of the script, since we are going to use the `InputField` class. Before the beginning of the class, we can add this line: `[RequireComponent(type of(InputField))]` (without the semicolon at the end). Thus, the script requires an **InputField** component that is attached to the same game object of it.

4. We need two `private` variables: one to keep track of the **Input Field (Script)** component attached to **myInputField**, and the other to store the old text of the input field, since it could be needed to reverse the player's changes if he violates our validation format. So let's write these lines:

```
private InputField inputField;
private string oldText;
```

5. As usual, in the `Start()` function, we are going to store the initial values for our `private` variables. First is a reference in `inputField`, by calling `GetComponent<InputField>()` function, which takes the **Input Field (Script)** component attached to the same game object in which this script is placed. Then comes `oldText`, with the starting text of our input field. So, we have this code:

```
inputField = GetComponent<InputField> ();
oldText = inputField.text;
```

6. The next step is to create a new function that will be called every time we want a check in the text. This function only takes one parameter, which is the text that needs to be checked. Therefore, we can add this:

```
public void Check (string newText) {
}
```

7. We have created the `Check()` function; now we have to fill in it. So, let's add the first control through an `if` statement. We check whether `newText` is an empty string, and if so, we just assign this new value to `oldText` and return, since there is nothing to check:

```
if(newText == ""){
  oldText = newText;
  return;
}
```

8. The next `if` statement is the one that really performs our check: no numbers at the beginning of our string. So, as a condition, we verify that the first character is not a number using a chain of OR operators. We retrieve the first character of `newText` by accessing it as an array, and we are sure that here it contains at least one character; this is because in the previous check, we would have returned if the string was empty. So, we can write the following:

```
if (newText[0] == '1' ||
    newText[0] == '2' ||
    newText[0] == '3' ||
    newText[0] == '4' ||
    newText[0] == '5' ||
    newText[0] == '6' ||
    newText[0] == '7' ||
    newText[0] == '8' ||
    newText[0] == '9' ||
    newText[0] == '0') {
```

9. Now, if the condition is verified, we have to restore `oldText` inside the text of `inputField`, since this `newText` didn't pass our checks. Otherwise, if the condition is not verified, it means that our string has passed the checks. We have to update `oldText` with `newText` in an `else` statement, so let's continue the code of the previous step with this:

```
    inputField.text = oldText;
}else{
    oldText = newText;
}
```

10. Save your script and come back to `Unity`. The next step is to pass the `string` that the player is writing to our script, so we need an event that sends it every time the text inside the input field is changed. If we select and then look inside the **Input Field (Script)** component, we can notice that there are two events. Let's click on the small **+** sign on the **On Value Change (String)** event tab in the bottom-right corner.

11. Drag the script inside the **object** variable and in the drop-down menu, go to **PersonalTextValidation | Check**. We also have to ensure that we have selected **Check** in the first set of functions, called **Dynamic string**, as shown in the following screenshot (and not **Check (string)** in the second set, called **Static Parameters**):

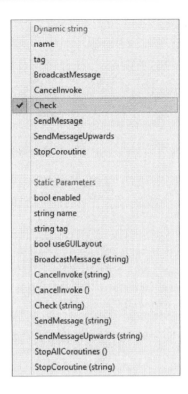

12. The final result should look like this:

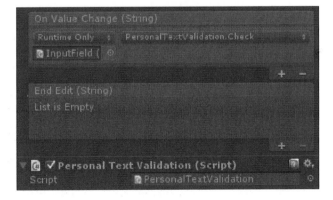

13. Now everything is ready, so we can click on the play button to check whether everything works. Thus, when the player types something in our input field, it cannot start with a number.

How it works...

We started by creating a script in which there is a function that takes the parameter as a string and it checks whether the string starts with a number. If so, it restores the string that was there before to insert the number at the beginning. Otherwise, it doesn't affect the input field. Then, we had to create an event that, every time the string inside the input field changes, it triggers our function by passing to it the `string` that the player is typing.

There's more...

The following sections help us to improve the text filtering and to understand how the dynamic filtering works so that we can implement our own ones.

Checking the string when the player finished to type

Sometimes, the design of the game requires that the string checking should happen after the player has finished typing it. In such cases, we don't have to perform the check every time that the string changes, but only when the player completes edit that input field. The easiest way to do this is by changing the event in order to trigger our function, only at the end. We need to change what we did in step 11 Instead of adding an event to the **On Value Change (String)** tab, we have to create a new one on the **End Edit (String)** event tab by clicking on the **+** sign in the bottom-right corner. So finally, we should have something that looks like this:

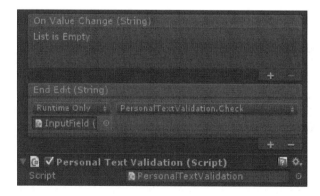

Our function is called only when the player finishes editing the input field. However, keep in mind that in this way, if the string typed is invalid, the last valid string will be restored — the one that was present before, at the beginning of the last edit session. Giving feedback to the player on why the string he is writing is not acceptable for this input field is important.

It may be confusing for the player when he cannot insert some characters at certain points, for example, inserting numbers at the beginning. Thus, in some way, we should give feedback to the player to make him understand why he cannot use some strings or to indicate what has gone wrong.

To do this, we have to use another **Text (Script)** component and handle it inside our script. Thus, let's change our script.

First, we need three `public` variables. The first one is for storing the reference to the **Text (Script)** component, and the other two are for customizing it. The second is for the error string to place on it, and the third is for changing its color. We can write the following lines:

```
public Text feedbackText;
public string errorString;
public Color newColor;
```

However, we also need two private variables to store the original values of `feedbackText`, like this:

```
private string originalFeedbackText;
private Color originalFeedbackColor;
```

These variables need to be assigned in the `Start()` function by adding the following two lines at the bottom of the function:

```
originalFeedbackText = feedbackText.text;
originalFeedbackColor = feedbackText.color;
```

Now, we should go through the `Check()` function inside the `then` branch, which is inside the `if` statement. Then we can assign the new parameters, the text and the color, to `feedbackText` in this way:

```
feedbackText.text = errorString;
feedbackText.color = newColor;
```

Next, restore the originals in the `else` branch by adding these lines:

```
feedbackText.text = originalFeedbackText;
feedbackText.color = originalFeedbackColor;
```

After saving the script, we are able to assign a **Text (Script)** to the **Feedback Text** component, along with the text (which can be **The string cannot start with a number**) and a color (which can be red).

We can create another UI text to assign to **Feedback Text**. In this case, we may create an interesting variation, since this checking is at the beginning of our script. We can assign to it **Placeholder**, which is one of the children of **myInputField**. It is the text that there is inside the input field when it is empty.

So, if the player tries to insert a number at the beginning, we should get something like this:

Using for cycles for dynamic filtering

In this section, we will present some basic notions on how a dynamic filter can be executed using `for` cycles. We will see that the concept is the same as that which we've used so far. In the introduction, we made the following example: every number has to be followed by the letter "a." In this case, what we need is looping over the string, and every time we find a number, it must be followed by the letter "a." Otherwise, the filter will restore the old string that the player was writing.

The first part of the `check()` function is the same:

```
if (newText == "") {
    oldText = newText;
    return;
}
```

In fact, we always want to check whether the new string is empty. If it is, we return so that we don't waste time in performing a check on an empty string.

> In some cases, the input field may require at least a single character. In this case, we can check whether the string is empty, and if so, we reverse the modifications that are done to the string.

Now we will create a `bool` variable to determine whether we have a number, from one cycle to the next. To do this, we need to write the following:

```
bool mustFollowA = false;
```

Finally, the `for` cycle will go through all the characters of the `string`. If we find a number, we set our `mustFollowA` variable to `true`. By doing this, we know that before the next cycle, there was a number. Of course, if we find another number, we can still keep iterating, since the new digit is part of the same number. For example, suppose we have a string `bc12a`. When the cycle reaches the number 2, it knows that before 2 there was a number, 1 in this case. However, the letter a must follow any number, and 12 is a number. Then, if we find an a, in lowercase or uppercase, we don't need to be concerned with what was there before. So, we can just deactivate the constraint by setting the `mustFollowA` variable to `false`. Otherwise, if the character is neither a number nor a, we check whether the `mustFollowA` variable is `true`. If so, it means that our test has failed. Hence, we restore the old string and return. Then, if the `for` cycle terminates, the test doesn't fail. Thus, we can assign the new string to our `oldText` variable:

```
for(int i=0; i < newText.Length; i++){
    if(newText[i] == '1'||
        newText[i] == '2'||
        newText[i] == '3'||
        newText[i] == '4'||
        newText[i] == '5'||
        newText[i] == '6'||
        newText[i] == '7'||
        newText[i] == '8'||
        newText[i] == '9'||
        newText[i] == '0'){
        mustFollowA = true;
        continue;
    }else if(newText[i] == 'a'||
            newText[i] == 'A'){
        mustFollowA = false;
        continue;
    }
    if(mustFollowA = true){ //FAIL: There is a number followed by
another letter
        inputField.text = oldText;
        return;
    }
}
oldText = newText;
```

See also

> ▸ If you want to put a lower bound limit for characters, it is worthwhile taking a look at the next recipe, *Making an input field for password with a lower bound limit for characters*.

Making an input field for a password with a lower bound limit for characters

Sometimes, a password cannot be shorter than a lower bound character limit. This happens for a lot of reasons, including security. In Unity, we can easily set an upper bound limit for characters by specifying it in the **Input Field (Script)** component inside the **Character Limit** variable. In this recipe, what we are going to achieve is the checking of lower bound limits for characters in input fields. So, you will learn how to write a short script to handle this, and as a consequence, the input field will also be reset. This means an empty string is assigned to the text variable.

How to do it...

1. To begin, we need to create our input field, right-click on the **Hierarchy** panel, then go to **UI | Input Field**, and rename it **myInputField**. Finally, place it wherever you want.

2. As we discussed in the introduction to this recipe, we are going to create a password input field. We should also select **Password** in the drop-down menu of the **Content Type** variable, as shown in this screenshot:

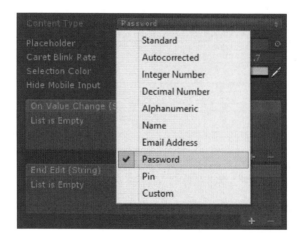

3. In this way, only asterisks are shown on the screen, as shown in the following screenshot:

4. Select it and, in the **Inspector**, navigate to **Add Component | New Script**. Name it **LowerBoundLimitForCharactersScript**, and then click on **Create and Add**.

5. In order to edit the script, double-click on it. Again, because we are dealing with the UI, we have to add the `using UnityEngine.UI;` statement at the beginning of the script. This is also because we are going to use the `InputField` class. As we did in the previous recipe, we can add this line before the beginning of the class: `[Requir eComponent(typeof(InputField))]` (without the semicolon at the end). Thus, the script requires an **InputField** component attached to the same game object of it.

6. We need just one `private` variable to store the reference to our **Input Field (Script)** component. And we need a `public` variable so that we can decide in the **Inspector** which is the lower bound limit. Therefore, let's write the following:

```
private InputField inputField;
public int characterLimit;
```

7. In the `Start ()` function, we are going to assign the **Input Field (Script)** component to our `private` variable. We can get the reference by calling the `GetComponent<InputField> ()` function. Thus, we can write the function in this way:

```
void Start () {
   inputField = GetComponent<InputField> ();
}
```

8. Now, we need to create a function that performs the check at the end of editing. So, it takes a string as a parameter and checks whether its length — the number of its characters — is less than `characterLimit`. If so, it empties the input field. Here is the function:

```
public void Check (string newText) {
    if(newText.Length < characterLimit){
        inputField.text = "";
    }
}
```

9. After saving the script, the next step is to give the `string` that the player has written to our script. Thus, we need an event to achieve this. In particular, if we look inside the **Input Field (Script)** component, we can see that there are two event tabs. Let's click on the small **+** sign on the **End Edit (String)** event tab in the bottom-right corner.

10. Drag the script inside the **object** variable, and in the drop-down menu, navigate to **LowerBoundLimitForCharactersScript | Check**. Ensure that the **Check** in the first set of functions is selected in **Dynamic String**, as shown in the following screenshot, and not the **Check (string)** in the second set, called **Static Parameters**:

11. Don't forget to set the **Character Limit** value in the **Inspector**. In this example, we will set it to **3**. As a result, we should get something that looks like what is shown below:

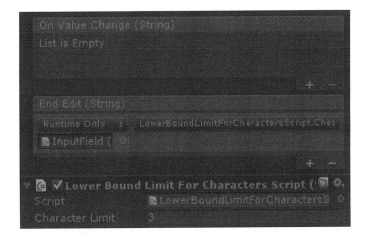

12. Now, everything is ready to be tested. Click on the play button to test. When the player finishes typing something in our input field, it should reset if the number of characters is less than `characterLimit`.

How it works...

Like in the previous recipe, we have written a function that takes a string as a parameter. In fact, its role is to check whether the string length is less than `characterLimit`, a variable that we can set in the **Inspector**. Then, in order to trigger this function, we created an event in the **Input Field (Script)** component. So, every time the player finishes typing, the check is performed, and if it fails, it means that the string is invalid. Then, the text of the input field is restored to an empty string. In fact, the event passes the string typed in the **Input Field (Script)** component to our function. It is possible to change the action that our function takes after the check (by changing our script), and we can also adapt it to our needs.

There's more...

Giving feedback to the player is very important to let the player know what is happening and also to provide a response to his interaction within the game, albeit good or bad.

Giving feedback to the player on why the string is not acceptable for the input field

Even though there is a clear statement that reads **this input field has a lower bound limit for the amount of characters that can be entered**, which is well indicated to the player, it could still be confusing for the player if the text that he has just written disappears after he presses *Enter*.

One of the options that we have is giving an error message to the player. Since this recipe is similar to the previous one, you can refer to the *There's more...* section of the *Making an input field with personal text validation at runtime* recipe.

See also

▶ If you want to perform some other checking on the input field, you can refer to the previous recipe, *Making an input field with personal text validation at runtime*.

Changing the cursor at runtime

The cursor is another important UI element that is not directly controlled by UI classes. This is the case since they are new in Unity, while the cursor was already implemented earlier. However, changing the cursor at runtime could be very useful for the player to distinguish different actions, and it can also be graphically nicer. For instance, in a **Real-Time Strategy** (**RTS**) game, the cursor can change when the player decides to move units or orders them to attack enemies.

At this stage, you are also ready to learn other techniques to deal with UI events, directly inside your scripts, instead of setting them through the **Inspector**, maybe also using the **Event Trigger** component. In fact, here you will learn how to use event handlers to triggers events in your script.

In this example, we will see how to change the cursor when it enters or overlaps another UI element. This is the most common case of cursor changing, and you will come across different games that have this mechanism.

How to do it...

1. To begin, we have to create a UI element that will allow us to change our cursor. In this example, we can create a panel by right-clicking on the **Hierarchy** panel and then navigating to **UI | Panel**. Finally, rename it to **CursorChangingPanel**. Of course, as usual, it is possible to resize it, change the **Source Image**, change the text inside, and finally place it as we wish on the **Canvas**.

2. Since our script will be ready to use and it contains handlers, we don't need to set anything. In order to create it, select **CursorChangingPanel** and, in the **Inspector**, navigate to **Add Component | New Script**. Name it **ChangingCursorScript** and then click on **Create and Add**.

3. Double-click on the script to edit it. Now, we are going to use event handlers, and in order to do this, we need a new `using` statement that we haven't used so far. This is because the script needs to import all the functions relative to the event system. So, let's write at the beginning of our script `using UnityEngine.EventSystems;`.

4. The next step is to declare the handlers. In some way, our script depends on them and extends itself with pre-designated functions. So, after `MonoBehaviour` add these two interfaces: `IPointerEnterHandler` and `IPointerExitHandler`, all of them separated by commas. Thus, the entire class line should be as follows:

```
public class ChangingCursorScript : MonoBehaviour,
IPointerEnterHandler, IPointerExitHandler {
```

5. We need three `public` variables to store all the parameters that we need for a new cursor. The first one is, of course, its texture. The second one is a vector for storing the hotspot (that is, the distance from the top-left corner of the texture) to place the real pointer of the cursor (the place where we can actually click). Finally, we have the mode of the cursor. Furthermore, we can initialize both the vector and the mode with default values, but in general, they have to be set from the **Inspector**. So let's write this code:

```
public Texture2D cursorTexture;
public CursorMode cursorMode = CursorMode.Auto;
public Vector2 hotSpot = Vector2.zero;
```

6. Now, it's time to implement the pre-designated functions that we have quoted before. Here, the first functions, that it is called when in the pointer enters the UI element, where this script is attached. We change the cursor to the new one, but calling `SetCursor()`, here it is:

```
public void OnPointerEnter(PointerEventData eventData){
    Cursor.SetCursor(cursorTexture, hotSpot, cursorMode);
}
```

7. The next one is the opposite to the previous one, and it resets the cursor when the pointer exits from the UI element:

```
public void OnPointerExit(PointerEventData eventData){
    Cursor.SetCursor(null, Vector2.zero, cursorMode);
}
```

 The preceding two functions cannot have a different signature — names plus parameters. This is because they are all called, since we are using handlers.

8. Save the script. Since the script is ready to work, we only have to set the `texture` cursor in the script, and nothing else. The last thing to do is click on play and see whether it works as it should.

How it works...

Here, we created a script that changes the cursor when it enters a UI element.

When we implement handlers, we have to write specific functions with a specific signature so that they can be called when the event that they are "listening" for occurs. In this case, when the pointer enters our panel, the `OnPointerEnter()` function is called, because this script is attached to it. A similar thing happens to the `OnPointerExit()` function.

Of course, we can implement this mechanism for the previous recipe in its entirety, where it was needed to trigger a specific function when it occurs. Furthermore, for this specific function, there is also a parameter called `eventData`. This is a `PointerEventData`, and it contains useful information that we may want to use in order to achieve the goal of the function.

There's more...

By changing the cursor at runtime, it is possible to create animated cursors.

Animating the cursor

Besides determining how the change of cursor is performed, in some games, we can also have animated cursors. Unluckily, there isn't a way to do this natively. As a result, we need coroutines to keep changing the cursor in order to animate it.

First, we need to change the `cursorTexture` variable to an array of textures so that we can have a different texture, one for each frame. Therefore, we should have the following line:

```
public Texture2D[] cursorTexture;
```

Then, we also need another variable to be set in the **Inspector** that represents how many seconds should elapse before the change to the next frame, like this:

```
public float secondsBetweenFrames;
```

Now, in `OnPointerEnter()`, we need to make the `animateCursor()` coroutine start. We will write this later, so this is what the function becomes:

```
public void OnPointerEnter(PointerEventData eventData){
  StartCoroutine (animateCursor());
}
```

Alternatively, in `OnPointerExit()`, we need to stop the coroutine and restore the cursor to its original state. Therefore, we can write it in this way:

```
public void OnPointerExit(PointerEventData eventData){
  StopCoroutine (animateCursor());
  Cursor.SetCursor(null, Vector2.zero, cursorMode);
}
```

Now let's create the coroutine. We need to create an infinite loop using a `while(true)` cycle so that our cursor keeps changing until we stop the coroutine. Then we need to scan the array of textures. As a result, we can create a `for` cycle for it. Finally, we can assign the current texture, the one that our code is scanning, and wait for the amount of time that is specified in the `secondsBetweenFrames` variable using a `yield` statement. Here is the code:

```
IEnumerator animateCursor(){
  while (true) {
    for(int i = 0; i<cursorTexture.Length; i++){
      Cursor.SetCursor(cursorTexture[i], hotSpot, cursorMode);
      yield return new WaitForSeconds(secondsBetweenFrames);
    }
  }
}
```

See also

For more information, you can refer to all of the official documentation related to these topics:

- **Cursor**: `http://docs.unity3d.com/ScriptReference/Cursor.html`
- **SetCursor()**: `http://docs.unity3d.com/ScriptReference/Cursor.SetCursor.html`
- **List of event handlers**: `http://docs.unity3d.com/Manual/SupportedEvents.html`
- **Coroutines**: `http://docs.unity3d.com/Manual/Coroutines.html`

8
Implementing Advance HUDs

In this chapter, we will cover the following recipes:

- ▶ Creating a distance displayer
- ▶ Creating a directional radar
- ▶ Developing a subtitle shower

Introduction

In this chapter, you will learn how to implement some advanced HUD elements. Such elements may include displaying the distance of an object, creating a radar to detect objects, as well as incorporating an inventory system and developing a subtitle shower. In this chapter, we will develop the skills required to obtain information from the 3D world and implement it as UI elements. Furthermore, through the development of a subtitle shower, you will learn how to control it from other parts of the game. Finally, as the UI reacts from input that relates to other parts of the game, we will be able to coordinate sounds related to the UI.

Creating a distance displayer

In this recipe, you will learn how to create a distance displayer, which can be a very useful feature. For instance, when we want to display the proximity of an object or a character, a visual displayer or even an auditory distance displayer can give us a better indication of how far or close we are from a particular thing. This is done in order to assist us during gameplay, for example, to avoid a particular enemy, or not enter a dangerous region of a game.

How to do it...

1. To begin, we have to create a UI image that will be our distance displayer. Right-click on the **Hierarchy** panel, then go to **UI | Image**, and rename it **DistanceDisplayer**. Of course, it is possible to resize the image, change **Source Image**, and then place it as we wish in **Canvas**.

> We are going to change the color of the **Image (Script)** component. However, in order to avoid color distortion on our **HUD** component, we should make **Source Image** completely white, with the form of the part we want to change color. In other images, we construct all the decorations around the component. In this recipe, for the sake of simplicity, we will keep the square image as default.

2. Now, we need to create the UI text that will display the distance as a number to the player. Again, right-click on the **Hierarchy** panel, then go to **UI | Text**, and rename it **DistanceDisplayerText**. Resize to fit the image, tweak all the parameters that deal with the font as you like, change **Color** to **white**, and finally place it in the middle of **DistanceDisplayer**. It doesn't matter if the text cannot be seen, since the background has the same color. This is because it will change at runtime.

3. Select **DistanceDisplayer**. In the **Inspector**, navigate to **Add Component | New Script** and name it **DistanceDisplayerScript**. Finally, click on **Create and Add**.

4. Double-click on the script in order to edit it. Every time that we deal with the UI, because we are going to use the **Image** class, we have to add the `using UnityEngine.UI;` statement at the beginning of the script. Before the beginning of the class, we can also add this line: `[RequireComponent(typeof(Image))]` (without the semicolon at the end). As a result, this script requires an **Image (Script)** component that is attached to the same game object of the script.

5. The first variables that we need are used to store both **DistanceDisplayer** and **DistanceDisplayerScript**. Since we can easily assign them through the script, we can make them private:

```
private Image img;
private Text txt;
```

6. Then, we need a couple of variables to store the **Transform** component of the player and the target of this distance displayer. They have to be `public` in order to be set in the **Inspector**:

```
public Transform player;
public Transform target;
```

7. Furthermore, we want to have the possibility of setting two colors. As such, **DistanceDisplayer** lerps between them in the **Inspector**. So again, the variables have to be `public`:

```
public Color firstColor;
public Color secondColor;
```

8. We need one more `public` variable. Hence, we can set it from the **Inspector**, which is used to calculate the color lerp that will be implemented later on. Therefore, let's add this line:

```
public float farthestDistance;
```

9. The next step is to write the `Start()` function in which we will store the initial values for our `private` variables. So let's take the reference to the **Image (Script)** component using the `GetComponent<Image>()` function. Then, we will also use the `GetComponentInChildren<Text>()` function to get the **Text (Script)** component that is attached to **DistanceDisplayerText** in the child of **DistanceDisplayer**. Thus, we can write the following:

```
void Start () {
    img = GetComponent<Image> ();
    txt = GetComponentInChildren<Text>();
}
```

10. Since **DistanceDisplayer** has to be updated often, we can do it in every frame by implementing the logic inside the `Update()` function. Here is its structure:

```
void Update () {
}
```

11. The first operation that we need to do is calculate the distance between the player and the target. This can be done easily using the default `Distance()` function in the `Vector3` class. Add this line in the `Update()` function:

```
float distance = Vector3.Distance (player.position,
target.position);
```

12. Next, we can update the text of **DistanceDisplayerText** by assigning to it the distance transformed into a string. We will also need to shorten the value of the float. To do this, we will need to pass the `F2` string as a parameter:

```
txt.text = distance.ToString ("F2");
```

13. The last thing that we need to do in the `Update()` function is assign a color to `img` using the `Lerp`:

```
img.color = Color.Lerp (firstColor, secondColor, 1 -
(distance / farestDistance));
```

14. After we have completed all the previous steps, our script will be ready to run. Save it and then come back to Unity.

15. Then, we need to assign the `public` variables. Depending on how our game is structured, the way in which we assign them will change. However, in the *There's more...* section, you can find out how to test the script that we have just written.

16. Now we can run the game. Once the game is running, the **Distance Displayer** should look like this:

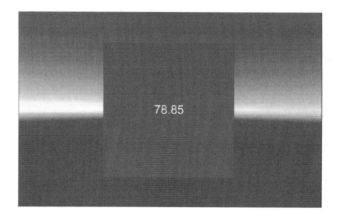

How it works...

Here, we created a distance displayer that shows the distance from the player and the target, and it also changes color according to the linear interpolation between the two colors.

Since the distance could be between zero and infinity, we need to set a scale to perform the lerping of the color. In this case, the `farthestDistance` variable will specify the farthest distance when the lerp is complete. Therefore, we divide the distance by `farthestDistance` so that we can obtain the percentage of the distance normalized between zero and `farthestDistance`. In fact, if the distance is greater than `farthestDistance`, the lerp is considered to be completed. If so, since there is a -1 that makes the value of the lerp smaller than zero, `firstColor` is shown. Otherwise, the resulting value controls the lerp.

There's more...

We can improve our distance displayer by integrating some new features. These will be explained by the following sections.

Testing the script

Since this script is intended to work when it is integrated inside a game, we need to ensure that it works the way it is supposed to, given this context. To do this, we need to construct a test scene. A simple way of doing this is by creating an entire scene inside the canvas using 2D UI elements. However, we must keep in mind that this script also works for a 3D environment.

Let's begin to create our test scene by creating a couple of images inside the canvas. To do this, right-click on **Canvas** and then go to **UI | Image**. So that we don't get confused, we can name them **TargetObject** and **PlayerObject** respectively. Once we have done this, the next step is to allow the player to move inside the scene. We can easily do this by attaching the drag script that we created in the *Making a draggable panel* recipe in *Chapter 4, Creating Panels for Menus*, to the player. Remember that we also need to attach the **Event Trigger (Script)** component as specified in that recipe to make it work. Once we have completed these steps, we should have something like this:

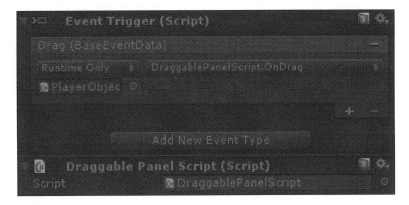

An interesting alternative is to modify the script by adding handlers. We did this in the *Changing the cursor at runtime* recipe in the previous chapter. By adding handlers to the script, we can achieve the same result in a more user-friendly way, since it avoids the need to add the **Event Trigger (Script)** component. After we have done this, we are able to move the **PlayerObject** by dragging it on the screen.

Now it's time to set the parameters of **DistanceDisplayerScript** in the **Inspector**. Drag **PlayerObject** inside the **Player** variable and **TargetObject** inside the **Target** variable. Next, we need to set the colors so that we can identify the proximity of an object. For instance, if it is not ideal for the player to be close to an object, we should assign a *positive* color, such as green, to firstColor when the player is significantly distant from the object. In contrast, if the player is too close to the object, we can assign a more *negative* color, such as red, to secondColor. Otherwise, we can reverse them, or adapt them for our game.

> When Unity creates a new color as the default, it has all the parameters set to zero, so it is black. But the alpha channel is also set to zero, so when you choose another color, ensure that you also set an appropriate alpha channel for what you want to achieve.

The last parameter that we want to set is **Farthest Distance**. This depends on the spatial scale of our game. However, the meaning of this parameter is as follows: it is the farthest distance at which the player must be from the target object for the color of the displayer to not change anymore. To set it properly, we should experiment with different values in our game in order to achieve the desired results. In this example scene, just try setting it to **400**.

In the end, we should see something like this in the **Inspector**, which reflects the parameters and colors that we identified within our script:

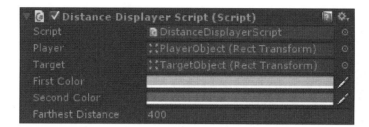

Next, we can click on play and drag **PlayerObject** around to see how the distance displayer changes its color based on the location of **PlayerObject** with respect to the target. We can also get an idea of the distance by seeing it expressed as a number in **DistanceDisplayerText**. Furthermore, if it is required, we can tweak the `farthestDistance` variable using this information.

Here is a screenshot of the scene:

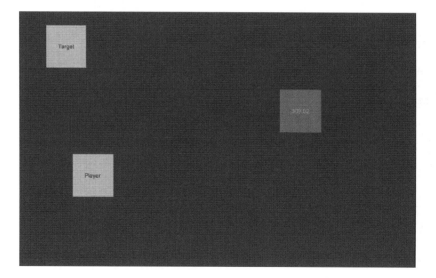

Optimizing the code by using a delayed update through coroutines

It could be computationally expensive to update **DistanceDisplayer** for every frame. As a result, we can use coroutines to optimize our code.

To do this, let's create a new `public` variable to set the amount of time that we want to wait for before the UI element is updated. As the default, we can choose `0.8f` as its value. Hence, we use this line:

```
public float updateTime = 0.8f;
```

Moreover, we need to create a new function that returns an `IEnumerator` type, and we can call it `updateDistanceDisplayer()`, as follows:

```
IEnumerator updateDistanceDisplayer(){
}
```

Since this is a coroutine and it has a behavior similar that of to the `Update()` function, we need to place an infinite cycle in it by adding the following code:

```
while (true) {
}
```

Before you erase the `Update()` function, cut its body by pressing *Ctrl + X*, and paste the code in the `while` statement by pressing *Ctrl + V*.

Finally, we have to wait until a certain amount of time has elapsed before the cycle repeats. It should be noted that in general, this amount is greater than the time that Unity takes to render a frame. As a result, this is a more efficient solution than the previous one. It works because we don't need to constantly change **Distance Displayer**. Furthermore, it can simulate more realistic **Distance Detector** that has a delay. Also, the coroutine structure allows us to implement other types of functionality, such as sound. Therefore, we need a `yield` statement along with calling the `WaitForSeconds()` function to wait as many seconds we want. After incorporating this into the script, we should have the following:

```
    float distance = Vector3.Distance (player.position, target.
position);
    txt.text = distance.ToString ("F2");
    img.color = Color.Lerp (firstColor, secondColor, 1 - (distance /
farthestDistance));
    yield return new WaitForSeconds(updateTime);
```

Even if we cannot notice any difference, the code is more optimized and is ready to incorporate new functionality (for example, multitarget detecting or sound), as described in the following sections.

Multi target detecting

In some games, it could be useful if our **Distance Displayer** could detect more than one target. For example, consider a shooter game in which we want to show the location of the closest enemy, or a platform game in which we want to show where the closest treasure is located. In these examples, we have to change our **Distance Displayer** to detect multiple targets. In order to do this, we have to convert the **target** variable into an array so that we can override its definition with this one:

```
public Transform[] targets;
```

It is worth noting that we have also changed the name of the variable from **target** to **targets**. This has been done to maintain consistency and indicate that we are now detecting more than one target. If you have followed the previous section, you will notice that we cannot calculate the distance within our coroutine with just one line of code anymore. In fact, we have to iterate over all the targets that we have set in the **Inspector** and then pick the closest one. So let's fix this issue by replacing the distance calculation with these lines:

```
float distance = float.MaxValue; //Or Vector3.Distance (player.
position, targets[0].position);
foreach(Transform t in targets){
  if (distance > Vector3.Distance (player.position, t.position)){
    distance = Vector3.Distance (player.position, t.position);
  }
}
```

In the first line, we set the distance to the maximum `float`. This is because every time the `foreach` cycle selects a target in our array, it checks whether the distance with this one is less than the lowest distance it has found so far. We can also change this value, the initial distance, to the distance between the player and the first target of the array.

> Since the `targets` variable is `public`, we have to be sure that the array contains at least one element. So, if we are not sure of this, we should add a control to check whether the array contains at least one element. Furthermore, this control should go in the coroutine and not in the `Start()` function. This is because its value could change over time.

Then, we actually use the `foreach` statement to cycle over the array. Next, using an `if` statement, we can check whether the new element picked from the array is closer to the player or not.

We can take advantage of the fact that the `targets` array is public. What this means is that we can add and remove elements dynamically. For instance, we can remove dead enemies or add new ones when they are spawned. Lastly, we should also convert the array into `List<T>` to handle the dynamic nature of a set of objects more easily.

Something to keep in mind regarding performance is that until we make the element count in the array relatively small, this script should not have any problem running from a computational standpoint. However, if the array becomes very large, it could take a while to render a frame, especially if our game is already full of heavy scripts. In this case, we have the option of handling the dimension of the array dynamically to remove futile objects (such as enemies that we already know are too far, maybe because they are in another room of the level). It could solve the problem and add them back in a second moment.

Beep sound

If we want to add a beep sound to **Distance Displayer** to make the player aware when it has been updated (using a sound), we can achieve this by adding another `public` variable. We do this so that we can set the sound from the **Inspector**:

```
public AudioClip beep;
```

Finally, to reproduce the sound through each cycle of our coroutine, let's add this line before the `yield` statement:

```
AudioSource.PlayClipAtPoint (beep, Input.mousePosition);
```

Since the sound comes from the user interface, we have chosen to play it to `Input.mousePosition`. As a result, we do not need to instantiate an `AudioSource`.

Increasing the ratio of the beep sound according to the distance

There are many ways by which we can indicate distances of objects or characters during gameplay. In this recipe, we used color as a way to indicate the proximity of the player to an object. However, what can also be a nice way to indicate distance to a player is through the use of audio. For example, a player may be trying to avoid being seen by an enemy, which encourages the player to use a great degree of stealth as he navigates throughout the level. So, in order to indicate to the player that he is coming in the view of an enemy, we may use a beep sound. It can be heard once the player begins to get closer to the enemy. This may start with quite a large amount of time between each beep, and as the player gets closer, the time between two beeps is reduced. This can create a more dramatic atmosphere, which a change in color may not be able to achieve. So, let's see how to do it.

Every time the `updateTime` changes, we don't need this variable anymore. So, we can remove it and change the argument of the `WaitForSeconds()` function to this:

```
Mathf.Clamp01(distance/farthestDistance)
```

By doing this, we calculate the ratio between the distance from the target and `farthestDistance`, and clamp its value between 0 and 1. In this way, we can obtain a percentage of how far the target is, where 0% means the same point as that of the player (distance is zero) and 100% means that the target is farther than `farthestDistance`. Then we use this percentage, converted into a decimal, for the time to wait until the next update of **Distance Displayer**.

We can also decide to keep the `updateTime` variable in order to still control how much time to wait, by multiplying it with our new argument in this way:

```
Mathf.Clamp01(distance/farthestDistance)*updateTime
```

If we do, the percentage will be on `updateTime`. For example, if the distance is half of `farthestDistance`, the next update will be in half of `updateTime`.

See also

▸ If you want to get a better understanding of how to change colors gradually, you can refer to the previous chapter in the *Creating a slider that changes colors gradually* recipe, or consult the official documentation about the `Lerp` function at `http://docs.unity3d.com/ScriptReference/Color.Lerp.html`.

▸ Furthermore, in order to test the script as described in the *There's more...* section, we can refer to the *Making a draggable panel* and *Changing the cursor at runtime* recipes contained in chapters 4, 5, and 7 respectively. In *Chapter 4, Creating Panels for Menus*, we have taken the drag script; whereas, in *Chapter 7, Applying Runtime Customizations*, you can refer to use handlers and therefore also have another point of view to solving problems.

▸ Finally, if you want to better understand how you can shorten the float number with the `ToString()` function, you can refer to the *Implementing a numeric timer* recipe from *Chapter 3, Implementing Timers*.

▸ In addition, if we want more control over the number of digits, we can implement the structure that is explained in the *Change the number of decimal digits shown* section contained in the same chapter, inside the *There's more...* section of the *Creating a mixed timer* recipe.

Creating a directional radar

Sometimes when we play games, we want to know the direction of objects that may be out of view or not visible. A radar is a UI element that makes it possible for this to happen. There are many ways in which a radar can appear, but in this recipe, we will make a directional radar that will take the form of an arrow and show the player the direction of the target.

How to do it...

1. Let's start by creating a new UI image that will be our arrow. Right-click on the **Hierarchy** panel, navigate to **UI | Image**, and rename it **RadarArrow**. Of course, we can place it wherever we want on the screen and then change the **Source Image** to an arrow like this one:

   If you are using Photoshop, you can easily create this by using the custom shape tool. You can select it by pressing *U* in the toolbox and *Shift + U* to cycle through the different shapes. Once the custom shape tool is selected, right-click to bring forth the shape selection panel. Select the arrow that you like. In this example, we selected the second arrow that was listed. Next, drag the arrow out onto the canvas while holding down the *Shift* key in order to constrain the proportions. Now we have a basic arrow icon.

    Of course, it is possible to construct all the graphic components of the radar around this arrow, but remember that the arrow should still be visible on the top.

2. Our script will control the rotation of the arrow according to the position of the target. Therefore, select **RadarArrow**. In the **Inspector**, go to **Add Component | New Script**, name it **SubtitleShowerScript**, and then click on **Create and Add**.

3. Double-click on the script in order to edit it. Since we are going to use the `Image` class every time we deal with the UI, we have to add the `using UnityEngine.UI;` statement at the beginning of the script.

4. Similar to what has been done in previous recipes, we need to store our UI element in a variable. In this case, we will need to store the **Image (Script)** component. We can make this private, since we can set it in the **Start()** function:

```
private Image arrow;
```

5. Next, we need to create a couple of variables so that we can store the transforms of `player` and `target`. Let's make these variables `public`, since we should set them in the **Inspector**. So, let's add the following lines of code:

```
public Transform player;
public Transform target;
```

6. In the `Start()` function, we have to get the value of our `arrow` variable, like this:

```
void Start () {
   arrow = GetComponent<Image>();
}
```

7. Going further, in the `Update()` function we have to first calculate the projection of the position of the player on the floor, which is the `xz` plane. In fact, most 3D games use this plan as the floor, and we want our radar to detect as if it is looking at the scene from the top view. We can do this very easily just by changing the `y` component of the vector to zero (refer to the *There's more...* section to see how to project it on different planes). Therefore, we use this code:

```
Vector3 playerProjection = new Vector3 (player.position.x, 0,
player.position.z);
```

8. The same has to be done for the target position. Since considerations similar to the previous step are valid, we can write the following:

```
Vector3 targetProjection = new Vector3 (target.position.x, 0,
target.position.z);
```

9. We also need to calculate the direction that the player is facing, because it will change the orientation of the radar, and again we have to project this on the floor. This time, we also have to normalize since it is a direction:

```
Vector3 playerDir = (new Vector3 (player.forward.x, 0,
player.forward.z) .normalized);
```

10. With the two positions projected, we can also calculate the direction of the target relative to the player. So, we have to subtract the two position vectors and again normalize, because this is also a direction:

```
Vector3 targetDir = (targetProjection -
playerProjection) .normalized;
```

11. Now, the problem becomes a two-dimensional problem, but we still work with 3D vectors so that we do not lose generality just in case we change the projection plan (check out the *There's more...* section).

12. The next thing to calculate is the angle between the two directions, and this can be achieved by calculating the arccosine of the dot product between the two direction vectors. Finally, we multiply everything with a constant to convert the angle from radians to degrees:

```
float angle = Mathf.Acos(Vector3.Dot (playerDir,
targetDir))*Mathf.Rad2Deg
```

13. Since the calculated angle returns a value between 0 and 180 degrees, we still don't have enough information to know whether our radar has to turn clockwise or not. So, we have to distinguish two cases: whether the target is to the *left* or to the *right* of the player. If we perform the cross product between the two direction vectors and take the y coordinate to check whether it is negative, we can distinguish the two cases. Finally, we assign a rotation along the z axis to our arrow accordingly:

```
if (Vector3.Cross (playerDir, targetDir).y < 0){
    arrow.rectTransform.rotation = Quaternion.Euler (new
Vector3 (0, 0, angle));
    } else {
    arrow.rectTransform.rotation = Quaternion.Euler (new
Vector3 (0, 0, -angle));
    }
```

14. We save the script and our work is done. We are yet to assign the target and player public variables. However, this will depend on how the game is structured. You can refer to the *There's more...* section, in which a way of testing the radar is described. If you follow that example, the radar should appear like this:

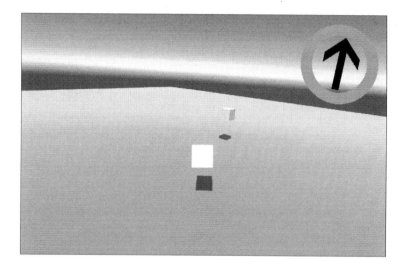

How it works...

If you do not understand the concept of 3D geometry with vectors, this recipe may be a bit difficult to follow. However, the concepts covered in this section are not too difficult to work through, especially if we pay attention to the pictures.

We started by projecting both the player's position and the target's position, on the floor, like this:

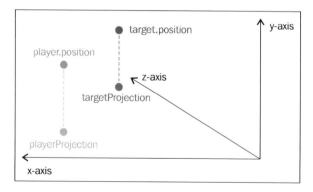

Next, we projected the direction that the player is facing. We then called this projection vector `playerDir`. Calculating the direction of the target respective to the player is simple, since we can just take the difference between the two vectors and normalize. We called this vector `targetDir`.

Thus, we reduced the problem to just two dimensions. As a result, we only had to calculate the acute angle, theta, between `playerDir` and `targetDir`. It can be calculated as the arccosine of the dot product between the two vectors. Here is a diagram that shows the geometry of the player and the target:

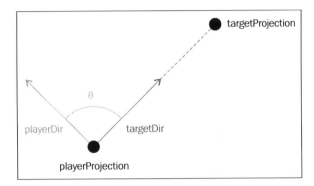

Finally, we rotated the arrow of the radar accordingly, using theta.

There's more...

As for the distance displayer, the following sections will teach us how to extend the directional radar to suit different situations that may happen in the design of the game, such as changing the projection plane.

Testing the script

Even after we have followed all the steps in this recipe, we are still not able to make it run, since this script works when it is integrated into a game. Hence, in order to test it, we need to construct a test scene. The one that is used in this example can be found in the resource bundle of this book. Otherwise, this can be done by placing a plane and then increasing the scale so that we can see it as the floor within the scene. Next, we can add a cube that represents our player and another cube that represents the target. Set the public variables by dragging both the cubes that you have created, and then click on play. If we move the two cubes in the scene in the **Scene** view, we can see the radar reacting in the **Game** view.

 We have projected all the vectors onto the *xz* plane. So, if the target or the player changes position along the *y* component, the radar isn't affected.

If we want to see the angles projected on the plane more clearly, just for debugging or learning purposes, we can use the `Gizmos` function to better observe this process. We can do this by moving the plane down a little and then adding this function to our script:

```
void OnDrawGizmos() {
  Gizmos.color = Color.red;
  Gizmos.DrawLine(new Vector3 (player.position.x, 0,
player.position.z), new Vector3 (target.position.x, 0,
target.position.z));
  Gizmos.color = Color.green;
  Gizmos.DrawRay (new Ray(new Vector3 (player.position.x, 0,
player.position.z),(new Vector3 (player.forward.x, 0,
player.forward.z).normalized)));
  }
```

It draws the two directions `playerDir` and `targetDir` in the **Scene** view.

Changing the projection plane

Our game may have another floor that isn't the classical one that is found on the `xz` plane. For example, if it is a 2D game, the entire game is on another plane, or if the gravity of the game changes at runtime, we should be able to change the projection plane accordingly.

If we only need to project onto the other two orthogonal planes, we just have to set the missing component to 0 (for example, in the `xz` plane, the missing component is `y`; in the `xy` plane, it is `z`). So, the two position projections along with the facing direction in the `xy` plane are as follows:

```
Vector3 playerProjection = new Vector3 (player.position.x,
player.position.y, 0);
Vector3 targetProjection = new Vector3 (target.position.x,
target.position.y, 0);
Vector3 playerDir = (new Vector3 (player.forward.x,
player.forward.y, 0).normalized);
```

And these are for the `yz` plane:

```
Vector3 playerProjection = new Vector3 (0, player.position.y,
player.position.z);
Vector3 targetProjection = new Vector3 (0, target.position.y,
target.position.z);
Vector3 playerDir = (new Vector3 (0, player.forward.y,
player.forward.z).normalized);
```

In general, as long as we have the normal of the plane where we want to project, we can use the following static function to project:

```
Vector3.ProjectOnPlane(vectorToProject, planeNormal)
```

Of course, in all of these cases, we also have to change the check inside the `if` statement so that the arrow can rotate in the right direction.

Closest target detection

Since the part of the script that detects the closest target in a set is very similar to the script used in the previous recipe, inside the *There's More...* section, we can just refer to it. This time, however, we don't have to store the distance but the target itself, so we use the following code:

```
float distance = float.MaxValue;
Transform target;
foreach(Transform t in targets){
  if (distance > Vector3.Distance (player.position, t.position)){
    distance = Vector3.Distance (player.position, t.position);
    target = t;
  }
}
```

Adding a delay in the radar through a coroutine

Again, the modification for adding a delay in the radar is very similar to one in the previous chapter, so just revisit that section to learn how to implement the coroutine.

More ideas on how to use the radar

The directional radar can be used in a number of different ways, such as detecting enemies in shooter games or assisting the player in locating treasure in platform games, especially if we integrate it with a **Distance Displayer**. Since this radar shows only the direction and not the distance, we can provide the player with an option to choose a **Distance Displayer** or a **Directional Radar**. Furthermore, we can incorporate both of them together in order to provide the player with more powerful equipment.

Lastly, we can consider implementing a 3D directional radar. In it, the arrow can rotate in all directions to point towards the target. In this case, we don't need to project the vectors, but we should be careful while calculating all the angles in order to rotate the arrow properly.

Developing a subtitle shower

There are many ways of narrating different parts of a game. We may use audio and sometimes visuals, such as text, in order to explain what characters are trying to communicate to us. However, one of the easiest ways to explain to a player what a character is saying is through subtitles. Subtitles not only allow players to read what is sometimes also narrated by voice, but can also improve the accessibility of a game for people who may not be able to hear or may have difficulties hearing. Subtitles are always a useful addition to any game when there are things that need to be communicated to the player properly.

How to do it...

1. As we have done previously, the first thing to do is create an UI element. In this example, we will create a panel. To do this, right-click on the **Hierarchy** panel, then go to **UI | Panel**, and rename it **SubtitleShowerPanel**. We should resize it and place it in the bottom part of the screen. It is also possible to change the **Source Image** in order to personalize the UI.

2. The next step is to create the real UI text element that will allow us to show subtitles to the player. To do this, we right-click on **SubtitleShowerPanel** so that we can nest it in our panel. Then we go to **UI | Text** and rename it **SubtitleShowerText**. Again, we can tweak all its properties to fit our needs, such as **Font**, **Font Size**, **Alignment**, or **Color**.

 While setting **Font Size**, keep in mind how much text will be on the subtitle shower. At the same time, this depends on what kind of game we are developing.

3. Now it's time to start writing our script. Select **SubtitleShowerPanel**, and in the **Inspector**, navigate to **Add Component | New Script**. Name it **SubtitleShowerScript**, and then click on **Create and Add**.

4. Double-click on **SubtitleShowerScript** in order to edit the script. Again, since we are dealing with the UI and we will be using the `Text` class, we have to add the `using UnityEngine.UI;` statement at the beginning of the script.

5. We need a variable to store **SubtitleShowerText**. It's also possible to assign its value in **SubtitleShowerScript** itself. So, we set it to `private` and also `static`:

```
private static Text uiText;
```

6. In fact, we can set it in the `Start()` function. By doing this, we can automatize the setting of the variable by searching in the children of **SubtitleShowerPanel**. We also have make sure that we have just one text between all the children:

```
void Start () {
   uiText = GetComponentInChildren<Text> ();
}
```

7. Before we can continue, we also require a constant. Feel free to change its value according to the kind of game that you are intending to develop. If you don't want to specify it when the coroutine is called, it will store the default duration, that is, the duration of that specific line of the subtitle:

```
const float defaultDuration = 5f;
```

8. Next, we have to create our coroutine, and it has to be public. This is because we want to call it from other scripts. We will also make it static so that we can get access to it without the reference to **SubtitleShowerPanel**. Furthermore, it should take three parameters. The first is the text that our subtitle shower has to show, the second one is how long the duration of the subtitle should be, and finally the third is `AudioClip`, in order to play a sound. The `subtitle` parameter is not an optional parameter, whereas `duration` and `clip` have default values. The `defaultDuration` constant we have declared before `null`. So, the structure of the function is as follows:

```
public static IEnumerator show (string subtitle, float
duration = defaultDuration, AudioClip clip = null){
   }
```

9. As the first step inside the function, we will set the `text` to `uiText` so that it is immediately displayed to the player:

```
uiText.text = subtitle;
```

10. The next step is to check whether `clip` is null or not. If it isn't, we have to play the clip and wait until the audio stops. This means that we wait for a specified amount of time, which is equal to the length of clip. Otherwise, we just wait for the `duration` amount of time:

```
if (clip) {
    AudioSource.PlayClipAtPoint (clip,
Input.mousePosition);
    yield return new WaitForSeconds (clip.length);
} else {
    yield return new WaitForSeconds (duration);
}
```

11. Finally, after we have waited for the specified time, we want the subtitle to disappear. To do this, set `uiText.text` to an empty string:

```
uiText.text = "";
```

12. Save the code, and now everything is ready to be used.

How it works...

In this recipe, we created a static coroutine so that it can be called from anywhere in the game with the following function:

```
StartCoroutine(SubtitleShowerScript.show(subtitle,duration, clip);
```

But in order to keep it static, we had to set the variable as `static`. This is fine, as long as there is only one **Subtitle Shower** in the scene that it is supposed to be in. As a result, when the coroutine begins, it will handle everything. This includes setting the text and removing it after the right amount of time.

We need to pay attention when we call this coroutine. For instance, we shouldn't create more than one instance at a time, or else the two instances will overlap in controlling the components, especially because all the variables are static. Refer to the first part of the *There's more...* section of this recipe; it demonstrates that every time the coroutine is called, we need to wait until it is finished before it is called again.

This waiting can be done by yielding on the `show()` coroutine with the following instruction:

```
yield return StartCoroutine(SubtitleShowerScript.
show(subtitle,duration, clip);
```

There's more...

The subtitle shower created in this recipe does the job, but it could be improved by displaying more information to the player, such as the name of character who is talking along with the avatar picture. Hence, the following sections will guide us through implementing these features.

Testing the script

In order to test the script, we need another function that calls our subtitle shower. So, let's create another script and add these variables:

```
public string line1, line2, line3;
public AudioClip clip;
public duration;
```

Then this line in the `Start()` function:

```
StartCoroutine (test ());
```

So, we call the following coroutine:

```
IEnumerator test () {
   yield return StartCoroutine(SubtitleShowerScript.show(line1));
   yield return StartCoroutine(SubtitleShowerScript.
show(line2,duration));
   yield return StartCoroutine(SubtitleShowerScript.show(line3, 0f,
clip));
}
```

Here, we have triggered our subtitle shower three times. However, before we trigger the next one, we have to wait until the previous one has finished. Furthermore, we used the `public` variables just to show something on the screen. Finally, we attached the script somewhere in the scene and filled the `public` variables. By doing this, it is possible to see our subtitle shower in action.

 If we look at the last line of the script, we can see that we are passing the audio clip as a parameter. Therefore, the value of the duration doesn't matter. So every value that we pass doesn't affect **Subtitle Shower**.

Adding a picture of the character who is talking

When we play games, we have what is known as an avatar. It represents our character within a game. There are many different ways in which our character can be represented during a game, such as the actual itself that we control, or as an image within the HUD. During moments in the game when two characters are interacting or even conversing, having a picture of our avatar and the characters that we are engaging with can often make it easier to understand what is happening. This is especially true in moments when there is a lot of text, such as in a conversation. In such moments, a picture of our avatar next to the text that we are saying helps to distinguish between who is saying what.

If we want to implement this in our subtitle shower, we can do so by adding an **Image (Script)** component to **SubtitleShowerPanel**. Let's rename it **SubtitleShowerCharacterIcon**.

It is also important to place **SubtitleShowerCharacterIcon** inside **SubtitleShowerPanel** such that it is coherent with the game we are developing.

Now, we have to add a new variable to store it in our script:

```
private static Image uiImage;
```

Then we set the reference in the Start() function:

```
uiImage = GetComponentInChildren<Image> ();
```

Furthermore, the coroutine has to be changed to take a new parameter in this way:

```
public static IEnumerator show(string subtitle, float duration =
defaultDuration, AudioClip clip = null, Sprite icon = null)
```

Finally, we have to set the picture at the beginning of the coroutine:

```
uiImage.sprite = icon;
```

As the last instruction, take it off:

```
uiImage.sprite = null;
```

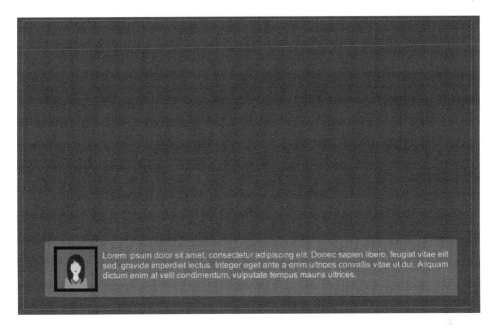

Adding the name of the character who is talking

Much like our avatars, which visually represent who we are in a game, names also add another layer of personalization to our experience. Furthermore, in some games, the quality of the graphics may not be very detailed because of either their resolution or their size, as is the case with a number of mobile games. As a result, it may be hard to distinguish between different avatars, especially when they are able to be customized. Including the names of our character as well as other characters within the game can make it easier to distinguish between different characters, as opposed to visual representations alone.

We can add this feature into our **Subtitle Shower**. First, we need to create another **Text (Script)** component inside **SubtitleShowerPanel** and rename it **SubtitleShowerCharactername**.

Again, it is important to place it inside **SubtitleShowerPanel** so that it suits the game that we are developing.

Next, we have to add a new variable to store it in our script:

```
private static Image uiName;
```

Set the reference in the `Start()` function. This time, however, we need to change the way in which we refer to the two `Text` variables, `uiName` and `uiText`, since they both are children of **SubtitleShowerPanel**. We need to call the `Find()` function to find the game object to which they are attached before we get the actual components:

```
uiName = GameObject.Find("SubtitleShowerCharactername").
GetComponent<Text>
();
uiText = GameObject.Find("SubtitleShowerText").GetComponent<Text>
();
```

Furthermore, the coroutine has to be changed to take a new parameter:

```
public static IEnumerator show(string subtitle, float duration =
defaultDuration, AudioClip clip = null, Sprite icon = null, string
name = "")
```

Finally, we have to show the name at the beginning of the coroutine:

```
uiName.text = name;
```

At the end, as the last instruction, take it off:

```
uiName.text = "";
```

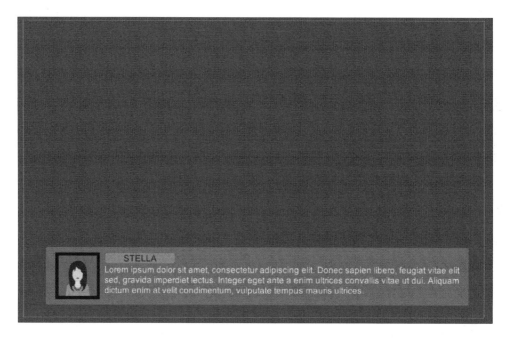

9
Diving into 3D UIs

In this chapter, we will cover these recipes:

- ▸ Creating a 3D menu
- ▸ Adding a smooth tilt effect
- ▸ Creating and placing a 3D UI
- ▸ Creating an animated 3D UI warning

Introduction

In this chapter, you will learn how to implement some 3D effects as part of the UI. Often in modern games, menus are in 3D. This is done for many reasons, sometimes to make them more visually pleasant and interesting. In some cases, UI elements are placed in the 3D world along with other game objects. For example, when a player goes to collect a pickup, some information may be displayed to him about that object. This chapter will teach you how to do this effectively in Unity. Some of the skills that will be covered in this chapter will be advanced features for placing UI elements within a 3D space and taking advantage of the z axis. In order to do this, we will also cover various scripts that enable our UI to interact with the 3D world to exchange input/output with the UI.

Creating a 3D menu

In this recipe, you will learn how to create a 3D menu in Unity. 3D menus can provide an array of options that traditional menus cannot. For instance, 3D menus offer opportunities for UI elements to enter the game space in ways that 2D menus are unable to support. These techniques go beyond the classical UI and allow more levels of customization and player immersion within a game. In fact, a 3D UI has the potential to become very effective when animated, since we can see elements from different perspectives.

How to do it...

1. Let's start by creating an UI panel that will be the root of our menu. As we are developing our menu, it is important to keep in mind that all additional elements that we create will become children of the root element. Right-click on the **Hierarchy** panel, then go to **UI | Panel** and rename it to **MenuRoot**. Of course, it is possible to resize the image and change its other settings, such as color. In the **Inspector**, we can make it fit the design of our game, and we can even place it wherever we want on **Canvas**.

2. Now, we need to add some more contents to our menu. But first, we need to have a clear idea about what our design will be. In this recipe, we are going to create a menu by following this design:

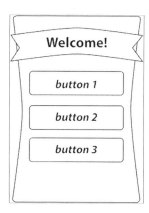

3. Therefore, we need to create some other panels, as we did before, and rename them to **TitlePanel**, **ButtonPanel1**, **ButtonPanel2**, and **ButtonPanel3**.

 Here, we are using panels instead of the **Button** component, since we are interested in understanding how to project our menu in the 3D world rather than implementing a functional menu.

4. Right-click on each panel and navigate to **UI | Text** to create a **Text (Script)** component. To keep our components' names consistent, we should rename them to **TextTitle**, **TextButton1**, **TextButton2**, and **TextButton3**. Finally, the structure of our menu should look something like this:

5. Now, it's time to take advantage of the third dimension using the *z* axis. In order to see this better, we can switch to 3D view (by clicking on the **2D** button in the upper part of the scene view). Otherwise, we can just keep the 2D image and tweak the *z* axis through the **Inspector**. Let's slide the **z** axis of **TitlePanel** to **-45**. Then, we can set **TextTitle** to **-40** on the **z** axis. Next, we can set the buttons a little closer to the observer. Let's set them to **-80** and their text to **-45**. If you have already switched to 3D view, you can now see something like this:

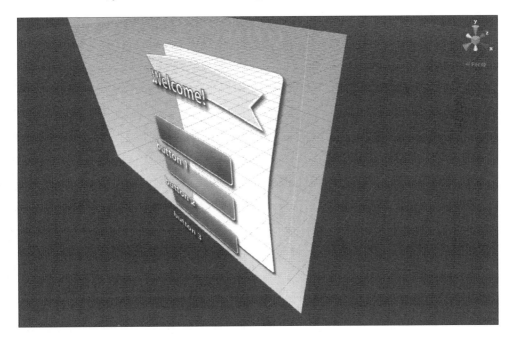

6. Thus, our menu is ready. But if we click on the play button, we don't notice any difference. This because it is still rendering as a static menu that is projected onto **Canvas**. This recipe is just an introduction, and it provides us with a foundation for the proceeding sections.

How it works...

Usually, we are bound by the x axis and the y axis. However, with the use of 3D, it is possible to have various UI elements projected in the third dimension, by providing values for their respective z axes. We have chosen negative values because we want to project them towards the user, and by doing this, it brings them closer to the user. If we were to choose positive values, the UI elements would appear farther away from the user within the Unity scene. In fact, this will be useful in the next recipe, where the tilt effect will emphasize this effect.

There's more...

Adding shadows to our menu is a great aesthetic improvement. Thus, the following section will remind us about a component that we used in *Chapter 5, Decorating the UI*, to quickly add shadows to improve the appearance of our menu.

Quick shadows

We will see in the following recipes how it is possible to move UI elements and consequently the entire menu within the scene space. Furthermore, we will look at how shadows can be incorporated as a nice addition to the aesthetics of our menu, as well as emphasize the depths of certain elements. While we can draw shadows directly on our graphics (before we export them from our graphics program), we can also add shadows quickly in Unity. To do this, we will simply use the **Shadow** component that we covered in *Chapter 5, Decorating the UI*, in the *Adding shadows to text* recipe.

See also

▶ If you want to bring this menu to life, you will have to go on with the *Adding a smooth tilt effect* recipe or the *Creating and placing a 3D UI* recipe.

▶ For further information about the **Shadow UI Effect** component, you can refer to the *Adding shadows to text* recipe in *Chapter 5, Decorating the UI*.

Adding a smooth tilt effect

There are many effects that can be applied to both 2D and 3D menus. Some of them can be small and subtle, such as a glow effect when the player moves the mouse cursor on a menu item. But while these effects are typically a nice touch for creating more dynamic interactions, they are usually complementary to 2D menus. 3D menus provide us with the ability to add another layer of movement along another dimension. As such, we can have the entire menu perform a range of different movements, such as rotation and tilting, both on its own and via user interaction. Since we are able to utilize the z axis, we are able to have elements projected in a different way. For instance, we are able to have the elements placed at various locations along the z axis. When we rotate items that are farther away, they rotate at a slower rate than those that are closer (to the camera). This is known as the parallax effect. This recipe will touch on some basic movements, such as moving and rotating the 3D UI element. These movements could be for the entire menu, by making it rotate according to the mouse's position.

How to do it...

1. If we apply this effect to a menu that doesn't use the third dimension (all the elements have the z axis set to zero), it will just deform the menu and ultimately ruin the user experience. Therefore, it's important to use an adequate menu to apply this effect to - one that takes the z axis into consideration. Let's take the menu that we created in the previous recipe, or if you prefer, you can create another menu by keeping in mind to use the third dimension.

2. Select the root of your menu. This is the element that has all the others as children. In the **Inspector**, go to **Add Component | New Script** and name it **TiltEffectScript**. Finally, click on **Create and Add**.

 If your menu does not have a root, it is good practice to always have one. This is for keeping the contents of your menu in an ordered structure and applying modifications to all the elements in an easier way within your scripts. In order to create it on an existing menu, right-click on the **Hierarchy** Panel and then select **Create Empty**. Finally, rename it to **MenuRoot**. Use **Rect Tool** to modify the size of **MenuRoot** until it includes all the UI elements that belong to the menu. Now, select all the elements and drag them onto **MenuRoot**. We do this because it allows us to parent them to our root.

3. Double-click on the script in order to edit it. Since we are not going to directly use the UI components, but just their transforms, in order to manipulate their rotation, we don't have to add the `using UnityEngine.UI;` statement at the beginning of the script.

4. We need a `public` variable to set in the **Inspector** that stores the range of degrees to which the UI element can turn on the *x* axis and the *y* axis. Therefore, we can use `Vector2` and set some arbitrary starting values:

```
public Vector2 range = new Vector2(10f, 6f);
```

5. Since we also want to give the possibility to decide the velocity of rotation, we need to create a `public` variable for it. Again, set its starting value arbitrarily:

```
public float speed = 5f;
```

6. Next, we need a vector variable to set at the beginning to zero. This variable will store the value by which the UI element has been rotated from the starting position in the previous frame. Again, since we need one value for each axis of rotation, we can use `Vector2`:

```
private Vector2 tiltRotation = Vector2.zero;
```

7. Since the rotation of the UI elements has to be calculated and updated for every frame, the implementation of the tilt effect will be in the `Update()` function. Since the mouse can move all over the screen, we have to, in some way, clamp its value between -1 and 1 so that we can also distinguish which side of the screen it is on. This is done in order to represent a percentage of how far the mouse is from the center of the screen. Let's start by calculating the two coordinate halves of the screen:

```
float halfWidth = Screen.width / 2f;
float halfHeight = Screen.height / 2f;
```

8. After we have identified the position of the mouse in terms of how far it is from the center of the screen, we have to clamp its value along both the axes in order to get a kind of percentage of this distance from the center:

```
float x = Mathf.Clamp((Input.mousePosition.x - halfWidth) /
halfWidth, -1f, 1f);
float y = Mathf.Clamp((Input.mousePosition.y - halfHeight)
/ halfHeight, -1f, 1f);
```

9. At this point, we could calculate the value of the tilt rotation and assign it to our UI element. However, if we do this, it wouldn't be smooth. Therefore, we have to introduce a delay in the movement. By giving the `x` and `y` that we have calculated in the previous step, we have to start from the rotation that the UI element had in the last frame and make it rotate a little towards the rotation that it should have at the end. Therefore, to achieve this, we need to linearly interpolate. While doing this, we can pass the time from the last frame as the control parameter. In fact, if we assign this value to `tiltRotation`, we can start from this frame and move on to the next one. Furthermore, if we multiply `deltaTime` with our speed stored in `speed`, we can control how smooth the rotation will be:

```
tiltRotation = Vector2.Lerp(tiltRotation, new Vector2(x,
y), Time.deltaTime * speed);
```

10. Finally, we have to assign the new rotation to the UI element, so by converting the `Euler` angles in `Quaternion`, we can make the assignment:

```
transform.localRotation = originalRotation *
Quaternion.Euler(-tiltRotation.y * range.y, tiltRotation.x
* range.x, 0f);
```

11. Save the script and your work is done. The result at runtime is better when it is moving because it provides more dynamic visuals, as opposed to a static image. However, as shown in the following screenshot, we are still able to gain some information about what we will see in the final outcome:

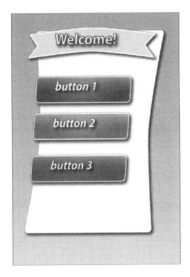

There's more...

It is possible to slightly change the script to make it more customizable by designers. This is the aim of the following sections that will teach us how to do this.

Starting from the original rotation

Some menus can have an initial rotation that determines where they start with the tilt effect. In order to do this, we need to store the initial rotation in a `private` variable, like this:

```
private Quaternion originalRotation;
```

Then, we have to initialize it in the `Start()` function with this line:

```
originalRotation = transform.localRotation;
```

Finally, in the last line of our `Update()` function, we just multiply the new rotation with the original one:

```
transform.localRotation = originalRotation * Quaternion.Euler(-
tiltRotation.y * range.y, tiltRotation.x * range.x, 0f);
```

Now, every time the tilt effect is applied, it will start from the initial rotation of the UI element that we have set.

Converting the speed in the smoothness factor

In some instances, we might want to provide an easier way for designers to tweak the smoothness of the rotation instead of the velocity. In this case, we can replace the `speed` variable with this one:

```
public float smoothnessFactor = 0.2f;
```

Then, we use `smoothnessFactor` in the code in this way:

```
tiltRotation = Vector2.Lerp(tiltRotation, new Vector2(x, y),
Time.deltaTime * (1f/ smoothnessFactor);
```

Inverting the axis

In some games, both the axes are inverted, and in others, only one axis is. Since we have scripted our tilt effect to include a range vector that can have negative values, we can achieve inversion by changing the sign to the components of the range vector. Of course, it is possible to have only one negative value to invert a specific axis. Furthermore, to simplify designers' lives, we can keep the values for the vector positive. Thus, we just need to change the signs of the vector components when they are utilized in the script. This means negative to positive and vice versa. In particular, we have to change the following line in this way:

```
transform.localRotation = originalRotation * Quaternion.Euler(-
tiltRotation.y * -range.y, tiltRotation.x * -range.x, 0f);
```

Asymmetric range for the rotation

If we want to rotate our UI element using an asymmetric tilt effect, it could be a bit tricky, because it is a little more complicated than other concepts that we have previously covered. An asymmetric tilt effect means that when the mouse goes from one side of the screen to another, the range of rotation changes. Therefore, we need another range vector for the symmetric part:

```
public Vector2 symmetricRange = new Vector2(7f, 4f);
```

Now, when the script is running, we have to use one vector or the other depending on where the mouse is. Hence, we have to use an `if` statement by checking this and applying one range vector or the other when we rotate the UI element:

```
if(tiltRotation.y > 0 && tiltRotation.x > 0)
   transform.localRotation = originalRotation * Quaternion.Euler(-
tiltRotation.y * range.y, tiltRotation.x * range.x, 0f);
if(tiltRotation.y < 0 && tiltRotation.x > 0)
   transform.localRotation = originalRotation * Quaternion.Euler(-
tiltRotation.y * symmetricRange.y, tiltRotation.x * range.x, 0f);
if(tiltRotation.y > 0 && tiltRotation.x < 0)
   transform.localRotation = originalRotation * Quaternion.Euler(-
tiltRotation.y * range.y, tiltRotation.x * symmetricRange.x, 0f);
if(tiltRotation.y < 0 && tiltRotation.x < 0)
   transform.localRotation = originalRotation * Quaternion.Euler(-
tiltRotation.y * symmetricRange.y, tiltRotation.x * symmetricRange.x,
0f);
```

Changing the reference of the mouse from the screen to an arbitrary rect

In some cases, we don't want the area in which the tilt effect takes place to be extended along all of the screen size. In such cases, we should replace it with an arbitrary `Rect`. In this case, when we calculate the x and y values, we have to use the size of `Rect`, as follows:

```
float x = Mathf.Clamp((Input.mousePosition.x - halfRectWidth) /
halfRectWidth, -1f, 1f);
float y = Mathf.Clamp((Input.mousePosition.y - halfRectHeight) /
halfRectHeight, -1f, 1f);
```

If `Rect` is not centered in the middle of the screen, remember to add the offset of the position of `Rect`.

 We can also notice that if some part of the `Rect` is outside the screen, the clamp will never be 1 or -1. Therefore, the rotation will not be complete. While we may want to do this, it is better practice to tweak the range vector in order to achieve the same effect.

Creating and placing a 3D UI

Traditionally, UIs are static and are bound to the x and y axes. However, 3D UIs are more dynamic. As such, it is necessary to consider the placement of 3D UIs. In this recipe, you will learn how to place a 3D UI.

How to do it...

1. To begin, we need to create **Canvas**. We can do this by adding any UI element to the scene, as we have done many times during this book so far, or we can add it directly by right-clicking on the **Hierarchy** panel and then going to **UI | Canvas**.

2. Next, select **Canvas** in the **Hierarchy** panel, and in the **Inspector**, change **Render Mode** to **World Space**. Setting the **Canvas** to the **World Space** mode means that it is positioned in the space and it can be viewed from all the cameras within the world, provided they are pointed towards it.

3. Now that we are working in 3D, we need to keep the scale of our project in mind. As such, we need to make sure that we change the project settings from **2D** to **3D**. We do this in order to have adequate reference points (keeping in mind the added dimension). To change from **2D** to the **3D** mode, we have to click on the **2D** button in the upper part of the **Scene** panel in order to uncheck it, as shown here:

4. As with any game, when creating UIs, we need to consider the resolution and size of our canvas within the world. This is because the resolution will differ from one project to the next, depending on the intended device that our game is likely to be experienced on.

5. After we have chosen a resolution for our UI, we are ready to scale our canvas down using **Scale tool**.

6. At this point, we need to consider the scale of the current UI elements. Depending on the locations of their anchor points, they may or may not be displayed on the **Canvas** (for example, located off-screen). Therefore, it is important to take this into consideration as we place each UI element on the canvas. Thus, especially for an already implemented interface, it's important to have all the anchor points correctly placed for all the UI elements.

7. Next, we can rotate and place the UI where we like it on the scene. As in the previous recipes, we can do this by clicking on the rotation icon or using the keyboard shortcut *E*.

There's more...

The next section will give us a better idea about how to take advantage of the 3D world for our UIs.

Using the 3D world

As we have seen in all the recipes so far in this book, it is possible to use scripts to manipulate various UI elements. For instance, it is possible to hide and unhide certain elements or even change them. Considering what you have learned in this recipe about 3D UIs, it could be useful to create scripts that instantiate new elements. For example, some 3D elements can be better represented as part of a 3D UI than a 2D UI. In addition, a 3D message can appear when the player gets close to dangerous areas, valuable items, or a health bar attached above the player or a timer on a door.

They can be instantiated using the `Instantiate()` function, as with all other game objects in Unity. However, this function requires the original object to clone, which for UIs is often a prefab.

There are many other possibilities for creating and modifying UI elements from the script, such as those covered within this chapter (and even in previous chapters). These include having individual buttons behave differently depending on the types of interactions with the player (for example, clicking, hovering, and so on), and also depending on how a UI element is intended to respond to an input from the player. For instance, a UI element changes shape, color, or even text if a player interacts with it in a particular way. These kinds of dynamic customizations occur by getting various components and changing their properties. This is the essence of user interfaces, and it plays a fundamental role in 3D UIs, whereby they also need to react to the world around them.

Making an animated 3D UI warning

Warnings in games can be provided in many ways, for doing both the right and wrong things. However, having the option of 3D capabilities allows us to create more interesting and dynamic warning messages.

How to do it...

1. To begin, let's create our warning in the UI. We can start by adding a panel. Right-click on the **Hierarchy** panel, then go to **UI | Panel** and rename it as **3DWarning**. We can continue to add other UI elements, so we want a title inside another panel to evidence it and maybe add some text. As best practice, every time you add a component, tweak its anchor points as well so that everything can scale properly. At the end, we should have something that looks like this:

2. Now, we should take advantage of the third dimension and adjust the value of the *z* axis for the components in the foreground. We can adjust it incrementally, similar to what we did in the first recipe of this chapter - *Creating a 3D menu*. At the end, we should see something like what is shown here:

3. The next step is to animate it. We can animate it as we have previously done in the *Creating a pop-up menu* recipe in *Chapter 6, Animating the UI*. However, instead of having buttons, we have a title along with the warning text. This text needs to be reduced first and then the panel (or vice versa if it has to pop up), keeping in mind how they will be animated. After we have followed these steps, we should attach our **Animator** component to **3DWarning**.

4. If we have set all the anchor points properly, we shouldn't have any problems in scaling the UI. Therefore, we are ready to change the **Render Mode** of **Canvas** to **World Space**. Then, we can just follow the previous recipe in order to place it in the space.

5. Now, we have to create a script that triggers the **3DWarning** and when it disappears. Furthermore, the **3DWarning** could be nicer if it always faces the player when it comes up. Therefore, select **3DWarning**. In the **Inspector**, go to **Add Component | New Script** and name it **WarningScript**. Finally, click on **Create and Add**.

6. Double-click on the script in order to edit it. Since we want to control the animation, we need to create a `private` variable that will store the **Animator** component. To do this, let's write the following line:

```
private Animator animator;
```

7. Now, in order to get the player's position, we need a variable to store it in. Also, we need another variable to indicate the distance at which the warning should be triggered. These are both `public` variables, since they are supposed to be set in the **Inspector**:

```
public Transform player;
public float activationDistance;
```

8. Furthermore, we need two more `public` variables to set the name of the animation that we created before:

```
public string appearingAnimation;
public string disappearingAnimation;
```

9. Finally, we also need a `bool` variable; it is used to trigger the animation. However, this is done only once and is used to distinguish between whether the warning is enabled or not:

```
private bool isEnable;
```

10. In the `Start()` function, we need to assign the value to the `animator` variable. We can do this by getting the component:

```
void Start () {
animator = GetComponent<Animator> ();
}
```

11. Next, in the `Update()` function, we have to check whether the distance between the warning and the player is less than `activationDistance`. If so, it means that the player is close enough to trigger the warning. Then, we need to see the value of the `isEnable` variable to check whether the warning is already activated. In fact, if it is not, then we set the `isEnable` variable to `true` and trigger `appearingAnimation`. Otherwise, we do the opposite of this process. Thus, if the player is far enough, the warning is deactivated. In fact, we can set the `isEnable` variable to `false` and trigger `disappearingAnimation`. Therefore, we can write this code:

```
void Update () {
    if (Vector3.Distance (player.position, transform.position) <
activationDistance) {
        if(!isEnable){
            isEnable = true;
            animator.Play(appearingAnimation);
        }
    } else {
        if(isEnable){
            isEnable = false;
            animator.Play(disappearingAnimation);
        }
    }
}
```

12. Now the script is ready and we can save it.

13. We create a test scene, as we have done in the previous chapter. Alternatively, we can directly use our game. Assign all the public variables and check whether everything works as it should.

How it works...

After we have created our 3D warning along with its two animations and placed it in the environment, we have to create a script that makes it pop up when the player gets close to it. We need to trigger the animation once, using the `bool` variable `isEnable`.

There's more...

The focus of the next sections is to show us how it is possible to improve our 3D warning message.

Transforming the update function into a coroutine

If we want to improve computational performance, we can consider transforming the `Update()` function into a coroutine. We have discussed coroutines in greater detail in the previous chapter, so you can revisit it again, especially in the *There's more...* section of the first recipe.

Always orienting the warning towards the player

Imagine that we are using the 3D warning to trigger a pop-up message for a pickup item on the floor. Since the player can reach it from different directions, it's not nice that when it comes up, it has a different orientation. So, until the warning for instance on the wall, the player can see it from only one direction and it doesn't need to face the player. But in other cases, this is necessary. In order to do so, we have to change our script a little.

Let's add the following line at the end of the `Update()` function of our script:

```
transform.LookAt (player.position);
```

In this way, we force the warning to always face the player.

Adding a floating effect

This UI element is supposed to be in the environment. An example of its use may be to indicate to a player an item to pick up. In this example, it is possible to have the UI element floating rather than static in the air. So, we can follow the steps in the *Making a floating UI element* recipe in *Chapter 5, Decorating the UI*. Contrary to what we did in the *Adding a smooth tilt effect* section, where the floating logic could still be set in just two dimensions, here we might want to extend the floating effect to the third dimension. This should be used with the *Rotating along its axis* section rather than the *Always orienting the warning towards the player* section.

Therefore, if we decide to implement this extension, we have to change `FloatingUIScript` a bit by adding two variables:

```
public float zspeed, zAmplitude;
```

Also, change the `Update()` function like this:

```
void Update () {
   rectTransform.localPosition = new Vector3 (xAmplitude*Mathf.
Sin(Time.time*xspeed), yAmplitude*Mathf.Sin(Time.time*yspeed),
zAmplitude*Mathf.Sin(Time.time*zspeed));
   }
```

In this way, we can change the position and value of the *z* axis as well. As a result, we are utilizing the third dimension.

See also

▶ Throughout this chapter, we discussed how to animate UIs and how various elements such as the warning message can be helpful to a player during the game. In particular, we can see that an ideal way to animate a 3D warning message is as a popup during gameplay. In fact, this kind of animation is very similar to the one that is described in the *Creating a pop-up menu* recipe in *Chapter 6, Animating the UI*.

▶ Additionally, we deal with not only the animation of various UI elements, but also how to trigger them. This was covered in the *Creating a menu with an entrance transition* recipe, also in *Chapter 6, Animating the UI*. That recipe demonstrated how we can use the OnClick() event to trigger the animation. This is done by calling the Play() function on the **Animator** component. In contrast, we called the function directly inside our script, but the way it works is the same. So, refer to these two recipes to handle the animation of the 3D warning.

▶ As we saw in the *There's more...* section, we are able to implement the 3D warning message with a coroutine. This example refers to the *Optimizing the code using a delayed update through coroutines* section contained in the *Creating a distance displayer* recipe in *Chapter 8, Implementing Advanced HUDs*.

▶ Finally, the last subsection in *There's more...* explained how we can extend FloatingUIScript. A good place to refresh our memories about how to do this is the *Making a floating UI element* recipe in *Chapter 5, Decorating the UI*.

10
Creating Minimaps

In this chapter, we will cover the following recipes:

- ▶ Creating a minimap
- ▶ Implementing advanced features for minimaps

Introduction

In previous chapters, we looked at various HUD and UI elements. In this final chapter, you will learn how to implement one more HUD/UI element — minimaps. Minimaps can serve a number of purposes, such as identifying locations of interest, objects, and even characters (such as the locations of enemies and other players, which can be shown as icons on the minimap). Please keep in mind that you will need to have Unity Pro installed in order to create both the minimaps in this chapter, as Unity Pro provides certain features we will be using in this chapter, such as render textures, that are not available in the free version.

Getting ready

There are two ways that we can activate an installation of Unity Pro: through online and manual activation.

Once you have downloaded, installed, and run the Unity editor, you will be asked to choose which version of Unity you want. Select **Unity Professional** (as this is required for this chapter).

Online activation requires that you have an existing serial number, which you have previously purchased, the Unity editor, downloaded and installed, and an Internet connection. During the process, you will be asked to input these details along with some other demographic data, such as your reasons for using Unity. Once you have worked your way through these, you will be able to start using Unity, ready to create your minimaps!

If, for some reason, you cannot activate your Unity license online, you will need to do it manually. Furthermore, manual activation is the fallback when online activation fails. To manually activate Unity, you will need to ensure that you have the Unity editor installed. Manual activation is a slightly more complicated process than online activation, so more details regarding the steps involved can be found at `https://unity3d.com/unity/activation`.

Creating a minimap

In this recipe, we will create a minimap. An ordinary minimap features the basic points of navigation, typically in the shape of a circle or a square. In some instances, a minimap features a scaled-down real-time version of a map. In others, it may be a simplified version of the terrain. Whatever the case may be, minimaps prove to be a useful feature when traversing large landscapes, and they are also a way of indicating to the player the locations of various items. In this recipe, you will start learning how to use render textures and raw images. You will also learn how to set the position of the camera according to the player's position.

How to do it...

1. First of all, we need to create the scene in which we can test the minimap.

2. To quickly generate a 3D environment, we can use the **Terrain** object, which we can create by right-clicking on the **Hierarchy** panel and then going to **3D Object | Terrain**.

3. Now, in the **Inspector**, we can choose different tools to model it. Feel free to consult the official Unity documentation on how to use them. We can find the link in the *See also* section of this recipe. However, what we want to achieve is something like this:

4. Therefore, we need to create some mountains, and maybe mold a valley. Also, to give the terrain some colors, we can use the **Brush** tool to paint the world with some nice textures. Even though this part doesn't directly relate to how we create a minimap, it is worthwhile to spend some time on creating a nice 3D environment if we don't have any. In this way, we will have a better scene to test the minimap and ultimately understand how it works. In fact, as we will see in the *There's more...* section of the next recipe, a lot of improvements make sense in real game environments only. For instance, we cannot improve shadows if our terrain is completely flat, because we don't have any shadows. Furthermore, we should also add a player object to the scene and attach a script to it to make it move. Now that we have an environment, we can implement the minimap system.

5. To display the minimap, we will use another camera, which is different from **MainCamera**. This camera will display the scene from a top-down view and will be the background that our minimap is based on. Right-click on the **Hierarchy** panel and select **Camera**. Finally, rename it to **MinimapCamera**.

6. By default, a **Camera** comes with **Audio Listener** attached to it. Since we should keep only one **Audio Listener** in the scene at any single point in time, we have to remove this component from **MinimapCamera**. To do this, right-click on **Audio Listener** and select **Remove Component**.

7. Next, we need to create a **Render Texture**. Keep in mind that this feature is available in Unity Pro only. It is a very powerful component because it updates its texture at runtime. This could be useful to create reflections, monitors, and even mirrors in our games. However, here we will use them to render the minimap. In order to create a **Render Texture**, right-click on the **Project** panel and select **Create | Render Texture**. Let's rename it **MinimapRenderTexture**.

8. Then, we need to link the **RenderTexture** to **MinimapCamera**. By doing this, we ensure that everything that is in view of the **Camera** will be shown on **Render Texture**. Select the camera and drag the **MiniMapRenderTexture** into **Target Texture**. Once we have done this, we should have something that looks like this:

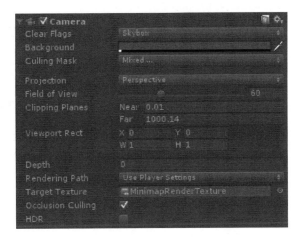

9. Now, we are ready to create our UI. We are going to use a UI component that we haven't used previously. This component is called **Raw Image**. The main reason for using a raw image, and not the ones that we have used in all other chapters of this book, is that this one can handle every kind of texture type in Unity, and not only sprite textures. Since **Render Texture** isn't a **Sprite**, we have to use **Raw Image**. The way of creating it is similar to other UI elements. First, right-click on the **Hierarchy** panel, and then go to **UI | Raw Image**.

    Finally, rename it **Minimap**.

10. Place it in the **Canvas** in the top-right corner, or whichever position best suits your game.

11. Now, we have linked **MinimapRenderTexture** to the camera so that we can receive data from it. However, we also have to link **Render Texture** to the **Raw Image** that we created in the previous step. In this way, **Minimap** can show the frame rendered by the camera on-screen. Let's do it by dragging **MinimapRenderTexture** into the **Texture** of **Minimap**. After we have done this, we should see the following:

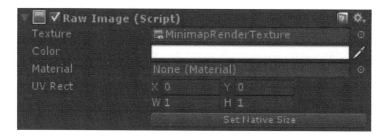

12. The next step is to make **MinimapCamera** follow the player from a top-down view. This means that **MinimapCamera** should move only along the x and z axes, because we don't want it to get closer or further away from the map. To do this, let's create a script on the **MinimapCamera**.

13. Select **MinimapCamera** in the **Inspector**.

14. Navigate to **Add Component | New Script** and name it **MinimapScript**.

15. Next, click on **Create and Add**.

16. Now, double click on the script in order to edit it. To keep the script as general as possible, let's create a new `public` variable that stores the player's `Transform`, since we will access to the position of this component every frame. In fact, in some games, the player can switch between characters, and this value can change at runtime without us having to modify this script. Keeping this in mind, we will need to add the following to our script:

```
public Transform playerTransform;
```

> If the player object doesn't change over time, we can automatically set this variable in the `Start()` function, by calling the `GameObject.Find("Player").transform` function. Of course, if it is necessary, replace `"Player"` with the name of the player object in your scene.

17. Now, in the `Update()` function, we have to assign a new position to our camera. Therefore, we will need to assign a new vector to it, where the `x` and `z` components, are the same as those of the player, while `y` is constant, for the reason explained in step 9. By doing this, we ensure that it will not only follow the player but also be centered on him:

```
void Update () {
   transform.position = new Vector3
(playerTransform.position.x, transform.position.y,
playerTransform.position.z);
}
```

18. Save the script and come back to Unity. Finally, we drag the **Player** into the `public` variable of our script, and now everything is ready. Let's click on play and test what we have done so far.

How it works...

In this recipe, we saw how to use render textures and raw images to create a minimap.

In fact, we linked the render texture to the camera by setting its target `texture` variable. By doing this, the camera has lost its ability to render on-screen. Thus the output of the camera is then stored in **Render Texture**. When we assign this render texture to **Image Raw**, it takes the data from the render texture. Finally, it is rendered as a UI element on the screen, which displays what is seen through the camera.

The process is shown in the following diagram:

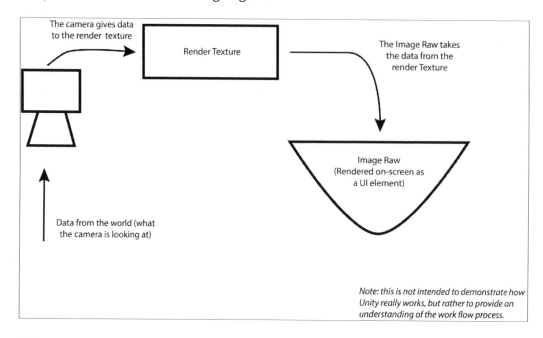

The camera gives data to the render texture

Render Texture

The Image Raw takes the data from the render Texture

Image Raw
(Rendered on-screen as a UI element)

Data from the world (what the camera is looking at)

Note: this is not intended to demonstrate how Unity really works, but rather to provide an understanding of the work flow process.

There's more...

Now that we have seen how to create a minimap, the following section will teach us how to improve it by setting the camera to work orthographically.

Setting an orthographic camera

Often, the design of a game requires that the minimap is flat. As far as we have a perspective camera, it will never be as perfectly flat as we would like it to be. Therefore, in this case, we have to change **MinimapCamera** in such a way that it renders in an orthographic mode rather than a perspective one.

To do this, we need to select **MinimapCamera** and then change **Projection** to **Orthographic** in the **Inspector**. Now, since **Field of View** is a parameter that is only for perspective cameras, it disappears. As a result, **Size** takes its place.

At this moment, the rendering of the camera may appear very close to the terrain. We can try to solve this issue by changing the position value of the y axis. Since it is a top-down view (rotation along the x axis equals 90 degrees, and it is zero otherwise), this doesn't affect the view. This is because all the view rays that are projected are parallel between them. So, we have to change the **Size** value in order to see more inside our minimap.

Now, we render orthographically and the camera component should look like this:

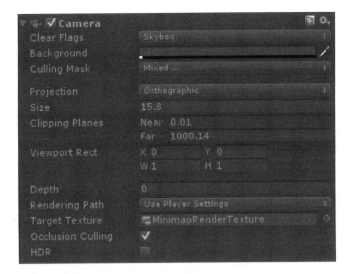

See also

▶ We have used some not-so-common features of Unity. As such, it could be helpful to check out the following resources from the official documentation:

  ❑ http://docs.unity3d.com/Manual/script-RawImage.html

  ❑ http://docs.unity3d.com/Manual/class-RenderTexture.html

▶ If you want to refresh your understanding of how to use the terrain tool in Unity, you can refer to the official manual by visiting http://docs.unity3d.com/Manual/script-Terrain.html

Implementing advanced features for minimaps

In comparison to the simple minimap that we created in the last recipe, a more complex minimap features more detailed attributes, such as the shape of a minimap. In this recipe, we will make the minimap circular using masks. Also, you will learn how to add layers to hide various objects so that they don't feature inside of the minimap. This may be particularly useful if you want to hide specific objects and characters and even some locations throughout your game. Finally, we will look at how to add icons to the minimap, also through the use of layers.

Furthermore, in the *There's more...* section of this recipe, you can find other advanced features to implement in your minimap.

How to do it...

1. Since this recipe will teach you how to implement some advanced features in a minimap, it is assumed that the previous recipe for creating a minimap has been completed. However, you don't have to follow the entire recipe. You can also take ideas on how to improve your minimap with these advanced features. So, let's start by shaping it.

2. In order to transform the minimap's shape into a circle, we have to use masks. You learned about them in *Chapter 1, UI Essentials* in the *Adding a circular mask to an image* recipe. We can take the mask that we created in that recipe and use it again here. Thus, we can create a new image, rename it **MinimapMask**, and set the white circle to its **Source Image**.

 It is possible to use any other shape that we want. Just keep in mind that if you create any shape, the white sections of the mask texture will be the parts that are visible.

3. We place **MinimapMask** over our **Minimap** and parent the latter with the first one.

4. The next step is to add the **Mask** component to **MinimapMask**. To do this, go to **Add Component | UI | Mask**. Since we don't want to see the original graphic of our mask, we need to make sure that we uncheck **Show Mask Graphic**.

5. Now, our minimap should have a circular shape, as shown in the following screenshot:

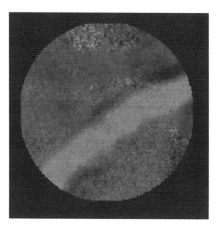

6. Another interesting feature that we can add to the interface of the minimap is a compass. To do this, create another image element and rename it **Compass**. Finally, attach a sprite to it, like this:

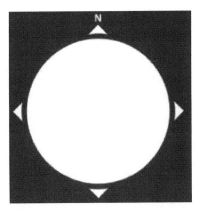

7. Now, we have only to place it behind the minimap, and ensure that the part of the interface we want is visible. We should end up with something similar to the following:

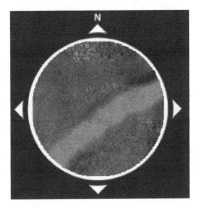

 In the _There's more..._ section of this recipe, you can find out more about the compass.

8. Furthermore, minimaps often use icons or symbols within themselves as a way of indicating to the player various objects and even characters. For instance, the player could be represented as a little white arrow and the enemies as red dots. To implement this feature on the minimap, we have to use layers. To edit layers, go to the top-right corner of Unity, click on **Layer**, and then click on **Edit Layers...**, as shown here:

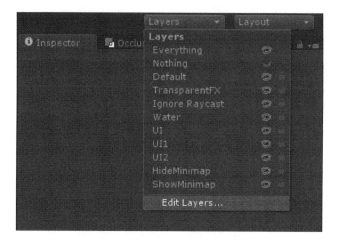

9. As we can see, a menu now appears in the **Inspector**, showing all the layers. Some of the layers, from **0** to **7**, are built-in layers and cannot be modified. In contrast, all other layers are user layers, which we are going to modify. If you have followed the *Making UI elements affected by different lights* recipe contained in *Chapter 4, Creating Panels for Menus* you should see that some of the user layers have already been set. If they are, we can just use the other ones:

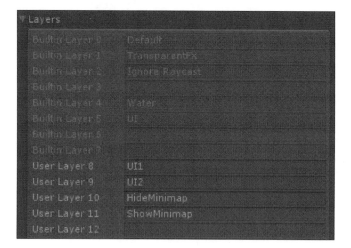

10. Now, let's add another couple of layers and call them **HideMinimap** and **ShowMinimap**. We do this so that all the objects that belong to the first layer are not displayed on the map but in the main camera. Thus, all the objects that belong to the second layer are shown in the minimap but not in the main camera. Ultimately, all the objects that belong to another layer, including nothing/default, are shown in both the cameras (such as the terrain).

According to the design of our game, different objects in the world could already have a layer assigned to them. This may have been done in order to implement other functions of the game. Therefore, we have to extend the concepts that we are covering in this recipe to multiply layers, since we cannot change the layer of an object that is used by other scripts in the game.

Therefore, instead of creating these two layers, we have to imagine them as a set of other layers that are already implemented — the ones we want to show on the minimap and the ones we don't want to. So in the next steps, every time we perform an operation with one of the two layers, we have to perform that action on all the layers that belong to the set of layers that we want to show in the minimap.

11. Next, we have to assign these layers to our objects in the scene. Let's start assigning the **HideMinimap** layer to the **Player** and to all other objects that we don't want to show in the minimap. This can be because they may be replaced by an icon, or simply because we don't want them to be displayed at all in the minimap (for example, other characters in a scene, treasure to find, and coins to collect). To assign a layer, select the object and change the layer from **Default** to **HideMinimap**. This option can be found just under the name of the object in the **Inspector**, as shown in this screenshot:

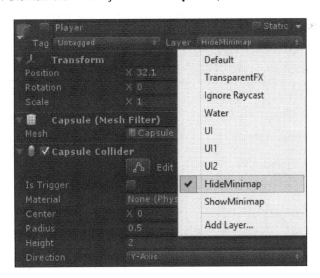

12. We have to hide this entire set of objects from **MinimapCamera**. We can do this by selecting it and, then in the **Inspector**, changing **Culling Mask** in order to uncheck the **HideMinimap** layer. In fact, the camera will not render these objects anymore, and as a result, they will not appear on the **Render Texture** that is attached to our **Minimap**:

13. Now, we have to create the icons that will be displayed in the minimap. In this recipe, for the sake of simplicity, we will use only spheres, which will be rendered as dots from the top-down view of the camera. But feel free to attach your own icon as a texture on a quad. However, keep in mind that you should rotate it along the *y* axis only, because it is supposed to rotate like an icon. This means that it can only rotate left or right and not in all directions like a 3D object.

 By using monochromatic spheres, we don't have to consider rotation, since it will always be rendered as a circle of their color, independent of the rotation they have.

14. So, let's create a new sphere and a new material for it. We can change the **Albedo** value of **Texture** to a color that we want to give to the dot in the minimap that will be our player (for example, cyan). Rename the sphere **PlayerMinimapIcon**. Put it under the **MinimapCamera**. If needed, depending on the **Size** you have set previously, increase or decrease the scale of the sphere so that it appears bigger or smaller in the minimap. Next, place the sphere at the same position of the player and then attach it to the player object.

15. The main camera is still able to render **PlayerMinimapIcon**. However, we don't want this. In order to stop the camera from rendering this, we change the **PlayerMinimapIcon** layer to **ShowMinimap**, as we did in step 12. Next, cut this layer from the rendering of the main camera by unchecking the **Showminimap** layer from its **Culling Mask**.

16. Repeat these three last steps for all the objects that you want to represent as icons. Also, we don't have to change the cameras this time, since their **Culling Masks** are already set properly.

17. Finally, we have created a nice minimap that is ready to be used. Especially if we have already built our 3D world, it will be a pleasure to navigate through it with the minimap. Furthermore, take a look at the *There's more...* section to implement some even more advanced features.

How it works...

In this recipe, we added new features to the minimap that we had developed in the first recipe of this chapter.

First, we gave our minimap a shape using the mask component. In fact, as you learned in *Chapter 1, UI Essentials*, we can use another picture to shape our UI elements.

Then we added a new **Image** element to our minimap so that we can use a compass in the interface. This works as both a decorative element and also a way to indicate north to the player.

Finally, we used layers. By using them, it is possible for us to tell elements that are rendered by our cameras from elements that are not. This is useful for both hiding elements on the minimap and showing something only in the minimap, such as icons.

There's more...

If we have implemented all the features so far, we already came up with a very good minimap. However, if you want to push your skills and learn more about how to improve your minimap, the following sections will give you the right tools to achieve this.

Limiting the boundaries of the minimap camera

It is good practice to design well-structured boundaries for our level, ideally so that when the player gets closer to the boundaries, the minimap shouldn't display areas of the game environment that the player cannot access. However, in spite of our best efforts, a player may still go close to the boundaries, and since the minimap is centered on the player, it could display these areas, which are outside the bounds. Therefore, we want to make the minimap stop being centered on the player when he is close to the boundaries, and return to tracking the player when he goes back inside the area where the minimap could follow him without showing inaccessible parts of the world.

In general, the shape of the map could be anything, and in this case, we have to set the script to properly distinguish between whether or not the player is close to the edge of this area. Here, for the sake of simplicity, we will implement rectangular edges.

Let's set two variables for our edge. The first variable is a `Vector2`, where the first value is for the `min` and `max` movement along the x axis that the minimap can reach. The second one is also a `Vector2`, but this time for `min` and `max` along the z axis:

```
public Vector2 xBoundaries;
public Vector2 zBoundaries;
```

In the `Update()` function, we want to find out whether the player is inside this area or not. If so, we can just set the position as we usually do. Otherwise, we have to set the minimap to the closest position that it can reach to best track the player when he is outside the area. If the player still manages to view past the boundaries of the map, it is likely that there are issues with the way in which the map is designed, or that there is a bad setting of the boundaries' vectors. Thus, during the design of the map, designers need to ensure that its boundaries are kept adequately constrained to the dimensions of the minimap. Therefore, we can replace the line of code that updates the position with these lines:

```
float newXPosition = playerTransform.position.x;
float newZPosition = playerTransform.position.z;

if (newXPosition < xBoundaries.x)
  newXPosition = xBoundaries.x;
```

```
if (newXPosition > xBoundaries.y)
  newXPosition = xBoundaries.y;

if (newZPosition < zBoundaries.x)
  newZPosition = zBoundaries.x;
if (newZPosition > zBoundaries.y)
  newZPosition = zBoundaries.y;

transform.position = new Vector3 (newXPosition, transform.position.y,
newZPosition);
```

Now let's set the vectors in the **Inspector** and test it.

Rotating the minimap according to where the player is facing

In the same game, the minimap doesn't always face the same direction, but changes according to where the player is facing. This is so that everything that is displayed is done in a way that is relative to the player's perspective. This is often used in first-person games. In order to implement it, we have to change the rotation of the minimap time after time.

So, at the end of the Update () function, we not only have to move the camera but also have to rotate the minimap according to the player's direction. Therefore, we want to rotate the y axis of **MinimapCamera** so that it matches the rotation along the y axis of the player. The other two axes are not touched, so set them equal as before. To do this, we can add the following to our script:

```
transform.rotation = Quaternion.Euler(new
Vector3(transform.rotation.eulerAngles.x,playerTransform.rotation.
eulerAngles.y,transform.rotation.eulerAngles.z));
```

As the camera rotates, the view is reflected inside the minimap, which also assumes the same rotation as the player.

Smoothly rotating the minimap compass to point towards the relative north of the game environment

A compass in the minimap is a nice element that complements it, not only as an additional aesthetical element, but also for actually indicating the location of north within our game to the player. Especially if our minimap rotates according to the direction that the player is facing, we cannot use a static compass, and thus we have to move it. However, just as in reality, the compass should not be instantaneous. Therefore, we need to add a slight delay in rotating the compass so that it feels realistic.

We have to store the transform value of the compass. To do this, we need to create a variable for it:

```
public Transform compass;
```

Since it is a public variable, we can assign it in the **Inspector**. It is also worth keeping in mind that we should provide designers with the ability to tweak the velocity of rotation of the compass according to the design of the game. To do this, we again need to add a variable:

```
public float compassRotationSpeed = 1f;
```

Because the north of our game could be located anywhere, we need to provide designers with the option of changing the direction of the compass through an offset from the standard north, which can often be the immediate direction that the player is facing when the scene is loaded. Therefore, we should create a variable for this as well:

```
public float compassOrientationOffset = 0f;
```

At the end of the `Update()` function, we have to set the rotation of the compass. This is so that it can accurately point toward north relative to the game environment. Now, in order to make this rotation smooth, we have to perform a `Lerp` from the current rotation of the compass to the desired one, which assumes the same direction that the player is facing. Furthermore, at this rotation, we can add `compassOrientationOffset` in order to reposition the location of north so that it reflects the in-game bearing of north. As a final parameter to control the lerp, we take the time from the last frame and multiply it by `compassRotationSpeed`:

```
compass.rotation = Quaternion.Lerp (compass.rotation,
Quaternion.Euler (0, 0,
playerTransform.rotation.eulerAngles.y+compassOrientationOffset),
Time.deltaTime * compassRotationSpeed);
```

We have used the `Quaternion.Lerp()` function because it works very well with rotations. In fact, when the player changes rotation from +160 degrees to -160 degrees, we would want the compass to traverse the shortest path of rotation possible to reach the final orientation. As a result, in this example, we would want the rotation path to be only 40 degrees, and not 320 degrees, as it would have happened if we had used the normal lerp between angles. By using Quaternions, we can avoid this problem and thus find the shortest path to rotate our compass.

Improving the lighting within the minimap

Sometimes, within the game world, lighting can add to the game experience. However, the minimap does not require the same amount of detailed lighting. In fact, it should be clear and easy for the player to follow while he is traversing the game's environment. As such, we need to take into consideration the fact that the lighting that we have for the minimap allows it to be viewed easily.

If we try to modify the lighting by setting a layer to some lights and then excluding that layer from the **Culling Mask** of the minimap camera, we won't see any change. This is because the light, along with the shadows that it casts, is independent from the layer and from the **Culling Mask** of the camera. Therefore, we have to use some advanced features of Unity.

Similar to `Start()` and `Update()`, there are other special functions that Unity itself calls at certain moments during all the processes to render the final frame on the screen. In particular, we will implement the `OnPreCull()` function, which is called before a frame is rendered with a specific camera, and also the `OnPostRender()` function, which is called when the frame for that specific camera is already rendered.

 Keep in mind that these two functions are called by Unity only if they are implemented in a script attached to an active camera.

These two functions allow us to change the world's state before the camera renders a frame, and then put the world back to its original state after the frame has been rendered. We will see how to use these functions at the end of this section.

In order to avoid having shadows, we can turn the shadow casting of the lights off in our world and then turn it on again after the rendering. Keep in mind that even if we turn off the shadows, there might be some parts of the game that are not illuminated and thus appear like soft shadows. This is because it also depends on which shader the object has, and this affects how it is seen in the 3D world.

Since we have used the **Terrain** object in Unity to build this test scene, we can change its shader. We can achieve this by going to its settings (select it in the **Hierarchy** panel and then click on the **cog** in the **Inspector**). Then we go to **Material** and change to **Built in Legacy Diffuse**. Using a directional light with **Shadow Type** set to **No Shadow** and a rotation of 90 degrees on the x axis and zero on the other two axes, it is possible to render a **Terrain** that appears to have no shadows of any kind.

Shadows are not the only issue that we have to face. For instance, some lights may feel right within the 3D world but not in the minimap. An example of this would be if we have a fire in the game. While a fire may look appealing and contribute to the atmosphere, it is probably not ideal to have it in a minimap. So, we may want to remove it. Furthermore, including something such as a fire inside the minimap as well could be computationally expensive. This is because it needs to be rendered twice, once with the main camera and also for **MinimapCamera**. However, even if we remove the fire from the minimap through layers, the light of the fire will still be present when the minimap is rendered. Therefore, we have to remove this light as well when we render the minimap.

Additionally, imagine that our game implements a day-night cycle. Ideally, we would like our minimap to always appear the same and not reflect the changes throughout the cycle. Therefore, we have to maintain the same lighting for our minimap. This means that we have to render different settings for the lighting on each of the two cameras.

We can deal with all of this by using the two aforementioned functions. In order to do this, let's create some variables. The first is an array for all the lights that we want to disable when the minimap is rendered. By setting it as `public`, we can just drag all the lights that we don't want on the minimap in this variable, within the **Inspector**. So, let's add this to our script:

```
public Light[] minimapLightsVisible;
```

 If we have a lot of lights that are useful for the game but not for the minimap, we should put all of them here. Furthermore, by doing this, we can also improve performance.

Now, we need another array for all the lights whose shadows we don't want to cast in our minimap. Even this time, we make it `public` so that we can set it in the **Inspector**:

```
public Light[] minimapLightsNoShadows;
```

Finally, an array with all the lights we want to render only in the minimap. We can keep these `public` for the same reason:

```
public Light[] minimapLightsNotVisible;
```

Now we can write the special functions that we mentioned earlier. Let's start with `OnPreCull()`. Here, we have to disable all the lights in `minimapLightsNotVisible`, make all the lights in `minimapLightsNoShadows` stop casting shadows, and turn all the lights in `minimapLightsVisible` on. Therefore, we use these lines:

```
void OnPreCull (){
  foreach(Light l in minimapLightsNotVisible)
    l.enabled = false;

  foreach(Light l in minimapLightsNoShadows)
    l.shadows = LightShadows.None;

  foreach(Light l in minimapLightsVisible)
    l.enabled = true;
}
```

Finally, we have to do the opposite process in the `OnPostRender()` function, as follows:

```
void OnPostRender(){
  foreach(Light l in minimapLightsNotVisible)
    l.enabled = true;

  foreach(Light l in minimapLightsNoShadows)
    l.shadows = LightShadows.Soft;

  foreach(Light l in minimapLightsVisible)
    l.enabled = false;
}
```

However, there is still more about lighting for us to know. In this example, every time we put a light in one of the three arrays, it will be enabled and disabled — every time in the same way. For instance, suppose that we have a light that is turned on or off during runtime in the game environment. If we don't want to render it on the minimap, we include it in the `minimapLightsNotVisible` array. However, when `OnPostRender()` is called, it is turned on irrespective of what its state was before the rendering of the minimap. Therefore, a more sophisticated implementation of this technique would include to store the original lighting of the scene in the `PreCull()` function, and then to restore it back into the `PostRender()` function.

Ideas for implementing the minimap in closed environments

In a closed environment, this minimap might not work. For instance, there is a multi-storeyed building, and ideally we wish to render on the minimap the floor where the player currently is. Otherwise, our icon could also be hidden by other elements. Therefore, we have to use layers to hide different parts of the building and change the **Culling Mask** of **MinimapCamera** at runtime. Another solution is to use different cameras and then switch between them every time the player goes to a new floor. In this case, it's preferable to keep all the other cameras that are not in use disabled, for performance reasons.

Other techniques for minimaps

Of course, the techniques that are explained here are not the only ways to implement a minimap. This section is aimed at giving you an idea about other ways to implement minimaps.

If our graphics team has drawn the levels' schematics, we can use them to implement a minimap. Here, instead of using another camera, we can use these level schematics along with a mask, as we did before in this recipe by shaping the map as a circle. The main issue here is to move and rotate the picture according to where the player is. However, the limitation here is that this is hard when the map keeps changing over time. For instance, if we want to display moving platforms, we have to link them with other pictures or icons in the minimap and move them with respect to the main map schematics. The advantage in this case is performance, since we don't have to render what appears in the minimap frame by frame. Furthermore, the aesthetic aspect of the level schematics as a minimap could have a nicer result than the realistic look of a map with a top view. In addition, if we implement this system in Unity, we don't need **Render Textures**, and therefore we don't necessarily require Unity Pro.

Another technique is a mix of the following two: one technique that you learned in this chapter, using another camera for a minimap; and the previous one, using level schematics. The basic idea here is to render the top view of the map only once, in order to keep the top view of the map and make gains in performance. So, we can take pictures of the map from the top view by setting all the layers, merge them into a unique picture, and use that one as level schematics with the previous technique.

In both of these implementations, we have to consider how to properly include icons on the minimap. This is because their positions depend on the locations of objects or characters in the real world that they are representing. Again, if we use UI elements as icons, we have to properly position and rotate them on the minimap.

This helps us understand that there isn't a single technique that is best; all of them have their own advantages and disadvantages, which have to been taken into consideration when we design our game. Thus, at this stage, we need to carefully choose the technique that better suits our needs.

Index

U

W

About Packt Publishing

Packt, pronounced 'packed', published its first book, *Mastering phpMyAdmin for Effective MySQL Management*, in April 2004, and subsequently continued to specialize in publishing highly focused books on specific technologies and solutions.

Our books and publications share the experiences of your fellow IT professionals in adapting and customizing today's systems, applications, and frameworks. Our solution-based books give you the knowledge and power to customize the software and technologies you're using to get the job done. Packt books are more specific and less general than the IT books you have seen in the past. Our unique business model allows us to bring you more focused information, giving you more of what you need to know, and less of what you don't.

Packt is a modern yet unique publishing company that focuses on producing quality, cutting-edge books for communities of developers, administrators, and newbies alike. For more information, please visit our website at www.packtpub.com.

About Packt Open Source

In 2010, Packt launched two new brands, Packt Open Source and Packt Enterprise, in order to continue its focus on specialization. This book is part of the Packt open source brand, home to books published on software built around open source licenses, and offering information to anybody from advanced developers to budding web designers. The Open Source brand also runs Packt's open source Royalty Scheme, by which Packt gives a royalty to each open source project about whose software a book is sold.

Writing for Packt

We welcome all inquiries from people who are interested in authoring. Book proposals should be sent to author@packtpub.com. If your book idea is still at an early stage and you would like to discuss it first before writing a formal book proposal, then please contact us; one of our commissioning editors will get in touch with you.

We're not just looking for published authors; if you have strong technical skills but no writing experience, our experienced editors can help you develop a writing career, or simply get some additional reward for your expertise.

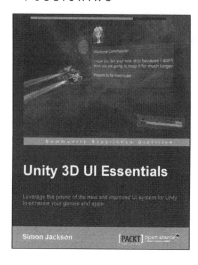

Unity 3D UI Essentials

Leverage the power of the new and improved UI system for Unity to enhance your games and apps

Simon Jackson

Unity3D UI Essentials

ISBN: 978-1-78355-361-7   Paperback: 280 pages

Leverage the power of the new and improved UI system for Unity to enhance your games and apps

1. Discover how to build efficient UI layouts coping with multiple resolutions and screen sizes.

2. In-depth overview of all the new UI features that give you creative freedom to drive your game development to new heights.

3. Walk through many different examples of UI layout from simple 2D overlays to in-game 3D implementations.

Unity Game Development
Blueprints

Explore the various enticing features of Unity and learn how to develop awesome games

John P. Doran

Unity Game Development Blueprints

ISBN: 978-1-78355-365-5   Paperback: 318 pages

Explore the various enticing features of Unity and learn how to develop awesome games

1. Create a wide variety of projects with Unity in multiple genres and formats.

2. Complete art assets with clear step-by-step examples and instructions to complete all tasks using Unity, C#, and MonoDevelop.

3. Develop advanced internal and external environments for games in 2D and 3D.

Please check **www.PacktPub.com** for information on our titles

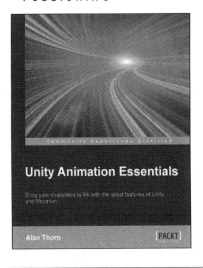

Unity Animation Essentials

ISBN: 978-1-78217-481-3   Paperback: 200 pages

Bring your characters to life with the latest features of Unity and Mecanim

1. Learn the latest features of Unity 5 to develop the most amazing animations for all types of games.

2. Refine your character animations by applying more advanced workflows and techniques with Mecanim.

3. A comprehensive book that explores core animation concepts and demonstrates their practical application in games.

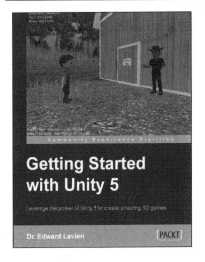

Getting Started with Unity 5

ISBN: 978-1-78439-831-6   Paperback: 184 pages

Leverage the power of Unity 5 to create amazing 3D games

1. Learn to create interactive games with the Unity 5 game engine.

2. Explore advanced features of Unity 5 to help make your games more appealing and successful.

3. A step-by-step guide giving you the perfect start to developing games with Unity 5.

Please check **www.PacktPub.com** for information on our titles

75053166R00160

Made in the USA
San Bernardino, CA
24 April 2018